INSIDE THE MONKEY HOUSE

MY TIME AS AN IRISH PRISON OFFICER

JOHN CUFFE

The Collins Press

365·92

FIRST PUBLISHED IN 2017 BY
The Collins Press
West Link Park
Doughcloyne
Wilton
Cork
T12 N5EF
Ireland

A CIP record for this book is available from the British Library.

Paperback ISBN: 978-1-84889-299-6
PDF eBook ISBN: 978-1-84889-626-0
EPUB eBook ISBN: 978-1-84889-627-7
Kindle ISBN: 978-1-84889-628-4

Typesetting by Patricia Hope
Typeset in AGaramond
Printed in Dublin by PrintDynamics

Contents

Prologue

*It is said that no one truly knows a nation until one
has been inside its jails. A nation should not be judged
by how it treats its highest citizens, but its lowest ones.*

NELSON MANDELA (1918–2013)

A perception exists of the Irish criminal justice system
as an unbroken chain, where all the participants work
together to ensure its strength and safety. That is risible.
The fact is that the Irish criminal justice system is the
perfect example of a hierarchy. Sitting atop are bewigged
and black-gowned judges and their retinue of tipstaffs,
snuff and brandy, and old-world etiquette. Each layer
beneath them tries to replicate their status: barristers,
solicitors, experts of all hues, including Gardaí and court
clerks. At the bottom, vying for air, wrestle the accused
and their keepers.

I was one of those keepers for thirty years and this is
my story. It is intended neither to slant nor to skew. I tell
it as the cards fell: I favour neither prisoner nor employer,
workmate nor inmate.

This is the story of John F. Cuffe 02318C.

Introduction

Stone walls do not a prison make, nor iron bars a cage.

RICHARD LOVELACE (1618–58)

No one grows up wanting to be a prison officer. As a kid I wanted to be a fireman, train driver, marine, sailor, submariner or cowboy. Indeed, my years in national school were lived out *Moone Boy* style: I pretended I was in the US cavalry. In first class I was a private, second class a corporal, third class a sergeant, fourth class a lieutenant, fifth a captain and sixth a general. Then reality and a grey boarding school knocked me for six as the real world intruded.

My exposure to prisons was non-existent. Coming from a west-of-Ireland seaside village, my habitat was lighthouses and fishing boats, sand, sea and rocks. That and emigration. Scenery and beautiful wilderness do not fill the belly or sate the soul. The bit I saw of prisons was via the American cowboy genre shown on RTÉ television, jails with sheriffs, deputies and bad hombres. Occasionally, black-and-white Jimmy Cagney movies showed mean-street stubble and talk from the side of the mouth. All framed within steel bars and sombre wardens.

Even the lightweight Elvis film *Jailhouse Rock* depicted the warder as cold and uncaring as Elvis at his meanest uttered, 'Hey, Screw . . . fill me a can of water,' proffering his tin mug in the hot jail. I knew a score from my village who joined the lighthouse service, myself included. I knew nobody who joined the prison service. Around 1970 I saw an advertisement in the *Irish Press* looking for twelve prison warders for Mountjoy. I was neither interested nor motivated.

Note I have used the words prison officer, warder, warden, guard and 'screw' to title the job. Prison staff are described by one or other of those titles in the media. Indeed, I have seen articles that used three of those names within the one story. The *Evening Herald* in March 1988 ran the headline 'Prison Wardens Threaten Strike', with the piece continuing, 'Prison Officers today decided blah-de-blah' and ending 'Warders will, however, meet the minister . . .' The place of work is itself called everything from prison, jail, nick, slammer, can and gaol to place of detention.

As you travel on my journey you will see me use all those descriptions as the need and context arise. You won't see me use 'screw' because I find it repulsive, and in my thirty years' service very few prisoners referred to us directly using that title. However, those in the outside world who should have known better have. It's akin to describing a Garda as a 'pig'. You wouldn't do it.

Around 1994 staff from Arbour Hill did a cycle around Ireland to raise funds for a charity. They sought some publicity and sponsorship. The *Evening Herald* duly obliged with a banner headline 'Arbour Hill Screws Cycle for Charity'. I rang the editor; he seemed perplexed. 'Would you describe a guard as a pig?' I asked. 'No,' he replied, and then silence . . . until finally the penny dropped . . . oops. You see, people know very little about prisons.

Perceptions are formed often by hearsay or knowledge of a criminal, warder or film. Perceptions are confirmed by the media. A one-time lifer released from Arbour Hill after serving around eight years once surfaced on a number of radio shows. Describing himself as a former armed robber – sexy title and Jesse James connotations – cleverly he left out that he had, in fact, been locked up for murder, as they botched an armed robbery, killing the owner of the would-be robbed store. He then started going around the schools lecturing secondary kids. He regaled them with tales of how he 'ran the gauntlet' in Arbour Hill. A younger brother of a colleague of mine arrived home and asked my workmate about the 'gauntlet' that the Hill had. Perplexed, my colleague asked the younger brother more.

Apparently the 'guest armed robber' told them that the officers in the Hill formed two lines, batons drawn, and the prisoners had to run through the lines as the blows rained down. I did see this once, in an American film where Apaches ran captured US cavalrymen in such a fashion. No officers carried batons in Arbour Hill; there was never a 'gauntlet'. In the main, the inmates were just compliant sex offenders, many too old and unfit to take two stair steps at a time. What he didn't tell those kids was that he was involved in the murder of a hard-working storekeeper and that the man was killed in cold blood. Why ruin a good story?

My own kids came home from school in early 2007 with a more fanciful spin from another ex-prisoner doing the school circuit. This ex-prisoner filled them full of multi-channel American Super Max jail rubbish; my son gave me a knowing look, a grin along with a 'you kept that a secret for a long time, Dad' kinda thing. I elicited from him a fairy tale of fairly damaging and libellous rubbish, full of fanciful imagery. Yes, you've guessed it: another Jesse James.

Where I live there are many prison staff who contribute greatly to the local institutions, be they sporting, housing or charitable committees. Their children attended the same school as mine. I rang the Vice Principal and pointed out the danger of allowing someone into a class like that where those being tarred have neither opportunity nor recourse to defend their good name. After I explained where I was coming from, the Vice Principal agreed with my point of view.

So how does one wind up working in a jail (or gaol) or prison? It's mostly via a circuitous route. I envy the youth of today in many ways – their style, clothes, modern technology – but I don't envy the rat race for the jobs, the treadmill that chews them up and spews them out. When I left school around 1970, those that had a moderate education could aspire to a job with the old Posts and Telegraphs as either a clerk or postman; some got jobs in the civil service, where those with brains became Higher Executive Officers (HEOs). The ESB was an outlet especially if you were a good footballer; the Gardaí, the army and the banks took many more.

For those less educationally gifted there were the county council, factories, CIÉ and, of course, the prison service. I myself trained to be a chef and did a City & Guilds catering course in London. A single summer toiling in a sweaty kitchen with a manic chef exorcised the Jamie Oliver in me. A clout across the cheek from the fraught cook belittled and ironically emboldened me to ensure nobody would ever do that to me again. That kitchen literally became too hot to stand. I hated the kitchens, a good cook yes, but a chef, no. My past as a chef would catch up with me in the prison service but more of that anon.

After my cuisine career I applied for many jobs. Despite having honours in English, Irish, History and Geography, failure to pass Maths meant I didn't have a Leaving Certificate (nor, for the same reason, an Inter Cert). Boldly, I entered mainstream life with the old Primary Certificate. As door after door closed, a clear sense of entrapment entered my life. Blacksod, my home village and the fountain of my youth, became my prison. I started to hate it, with no money, no prospects and no escape.

I had applied for the lighthouse service but got no reply. My mother, in that gentle but steely way of hers, told me that it was time to move on . . . anywhere. Some lads home from England for Christmas kindly took me back to the English Midlands with them in early January 1973. I still recall getting on the ferry in Dublin port and the dark bay as the ship headed across the channel on that freezing January night. I still remember Liverpool as dawn broke across that city. On the motorway towards the Birmingham area I recall Paddy John Sibby's Ford Escort from home with its IZ Mayo registration number passing us. It was at that point that I got homesick.

My first job was for a small building firm. I nearly died. In freezing-cold weather, a canal bank too narrow for a digger needed a trench cut in it. We had to light fires to soften the ground. My uncle's old boots cut the feet off me and I was perpetually hungry and homesick. This was not how it was supposed to be. I ditched the labouring but quickly ran out of money. My mother, my old reliable, wired £20 to me. I applied for a job in a pie factory. The manager, a Northern Irish man, was more interested in my religion. When I said Catholic, a sinking feeling told me I wouldn't be making pies.

Eventually I got good work. Lockheed AP in Leamington Spa were hiring. I got a job on a line making high-class engine parts. This was a three-man team and the work, though tough, was financially rewarding. Losing an empty wallet with, of all things, just an old grey Irish Provisional Drivers' licence in it brought me to a police station to enquire whether it had been handed in. It had, and the constable and I got talking. I decided after that I would apply to the various forces in the UK.

Eventually I was accepted by the Heathrow Airport Police, then run by the Hounslow and Middlesex Authority. Later it was subsumed into the London Met. Having signed up and been measured up, I came home for a two-week break before heading to Ryton-on-Dunsmore Police Academy to train. It was the one nearest to me in the Warwick area. Back at home in Blacksod was a letter requesting me to appear in Pembroke Street in Dublin for an interview for the lighthouse service. Initially I had no interest: returning to England was the only show in town. But the weather at home that summer was glorious and it was easy to love the old village again. As the time for returning drew closer, my resolve was tested.

Finally and with great misgiving, I wrote asking the police to defer my training. I was interviewed for the lighthouses and was successful. After training in the Baily Lighthouse, I was unleashed around Ireland's coast for about four years. With a month on the lighthouse and a month off on leave, rotating across the year, and travel by helicopter, my life with my two fellow keepers was a cross between being a hermit and a member of The Eagles. The extremes were too much. Solitary and wind-lashed but beautiful coastal scenes intermingled with wads of money to squander in the downtime. I burned the candle at both ends, returning to the lighthouse to recuperate and top up the tan in summer. The nightly music from the then Red Island Holiday Village in Skerries, across from Rockabill Lighthouse in County Dublin, my station and home of the tern, tipped me over the edge. I had to get out.

Salvation sailed across the sea on a small yacht. May 1977 was a scorcher. John Boland, a future Government minister, owned a small yacht and was of the habit of calling to the lighthouse during the summers, tying up his small yacht and showing his guests around the rock. We permitted him to climb the cold stairs of the lighthouse where the view stretched across the Irish Sea to the mountains of north Wales and south beyond the Wicklow Hills.

Boland was a gentleman and always brought out three fresh loaves for us, sliced ham, three bottles of beer and the best of all, the Sunday newspapers. I devoured the papers as well as the beer and chunky sandwiches. On the appointments page was an advertisement for 400 prison officers. This was my escape from the rocky lighthouse! Once ashore I applied for the job, was called for an exam – an easy one, I have to say – and then an interview. To ensure that I didn't miss the boat, metaphorically this time, I resigned from my permanent, pensionable forty-year career as a lighthouse keeper. Whilst I was happy to go, it would be remiss of me not to acknowledge them as excellent employers.

Ahead lay thirty years of a career as a warder. In this book I will refer to various actors and players: 'the Department' refers to the Department of Justice; the 'POA' is the Prison Officers Association, our union; the 'IPS' refers to the Irish Prison Service, domiciled nowhere near a prison and situated in Longford. 'ACO' refers to the first senior rank of supervisor in the prison service, called Assistant Chief Officer, a rank I held for about twenty-three years. 'CO' refers to the Chief Officer, the fulcrum of the jail: a good one ensured the oil was poured smoothly on the jail gears, a poor one crashed them.

'The governor' was nominally in charge of the prison. 'The Welfare' was the Welfare and Probation Service. Very few prison staff referred to prisoners as 'lags', a few did, guys that were best avoided and generally useless. The more extreme body of prison officers, thankfully counted on a single hand, might refer to prisoners as 'dirt birds'. Their language tells you what you need to know about them. 'Time' referred to the length of the sentence. We all did time, staff and prisoners. Each of us had a number, each wanted the finality of getting out that gate. The 'Gate' was just that, but with connotations: coming in could be deflating, leaving was always welcome.

The following chapters tell the story of the young man who left a sedentary village in Ireland's west, and chart his progress as life and the prison service see him emerge thirty years later – wiser or damaged?

1

Off to Dublin for the Blue

'Anyone who has been to an English Public School will always feel comparatively at home in prison.'

EVELYN WAUGH (1903–1966)

Despite finishing inside the top eighty out of 3,000 plus in the entrance exam for the Prison Service and completing my medical successfully, it was almost a year before I was called to training. I had given up on the call and was actually about to go to Saudi Arabia with my mother's cousin who was a roustabout on the oilfields. The proposition was attractive: good money, sun guaranteed and, of course, hard work. I loved the first two and the third held no fear for me.

Then, in early May 1978, a brown envelope arrived for me confirming my call-up and giving me a starting date to report to Mountjoy Jail. I was by then working in Killala, County Mayo, in Asahi, a Japanese company which manufactured, amongst other things, synthetic wool. Asahi was a massive plant, possibly running about a mile and a half in length. The 'wool' started life at one end as a highly inflammable and toxic liquid and came out as slightly sweet-smelling warm white wool at the other end. My job, along with three others, was to tamp and seal the boxes at the final stage.

As coincidence would have it, the four of us were hoping to join the prison service. Asahi, though good employers, had a Japanese work ethic where everybody wore the same garb consisting of a two-piece grey canvas uniform with a flat cloth cap. In time the process started to numb us and many of our colleagues. It was pitched at a deceptive speed that looked slow but was in fact relentless, on and on, eternal hell on earth. Today you read of something similar afflicting electronics workers in China. That brown envelope saved me from the ultimate institutional machine, the conveyor-belt factory.

The night before leaving the village, this time for real and for good, we packed my suitcase. My mother was so proud of me: a permanent, pensionable government job. I was excited too. Blacksod, combined with Asahi, had ironically become a prison for me: sleep, work, sleep, work, travel, sleep. Not a life for anyone. I now regretted leaving the lighthouse service and envied them the security of their money and conditions. All my life's possessions went into that suitcase. I always travelled light but this time the case was bulging. I made a quick trip down to the shore and fish tanks where I lopped off a length of the fishermen's thin blue rope and fastened it around my case to ensure it didn't burst open en route. My mother gave a disapproving 'hmnnn' as the blue rope was tied but she finally smiled.

Next morning we had breakfast. From the age of twelve to twenty-four, I had been coming and going: boarding school, England and the lighthouses. But that morning was different. The air in the kitchen was heavy, the scent from the teapot on the range was strong, the two slices of toast lay uneaten, and my heart was heavy. I suppose we both knew that this time the departure was for real. There was a lump in my throat, and in my mother's too, I assume.

'You've got somewhere to stay in Dublin?' she asked, knowing full well that my friend, a schoolteacher from our village, was collecting and keeping me.

We hugged and clung to each other at the door and my dog Monty sidled away, tail down and sad. I silently cursed him for that show. I would miss him as much. My mother then shoved something into my pocket, drowned me in holy water and muttered a quick Gweedore prayer for me *as Gaeilge* before patting my forehead and telling me not to look back. Other memories returned, of my dad who had passed away at sixty a few years earlier, as I carried the suitcase to the bus. This was not just a CIÉ bus: to us it was always Tom Cuffe's bus. He drove the damned thing through hail, rain and storm for thirty years, right up to his demise. The driver welcomed me on board and when I went to pay he told me to keep the cash in my pocket but to sit near him . . . just in case an inspector came aboard on the journey.

As the bus pulled away I ignored my mother's advice and had a quick peek back towards the house. Monty, the fecker, was sitting at the doorstep, head down and weight of the world on his shoulders. My mam let slip the net curtain as the bus went past Kavanagh's bridge. There was to be no more looking back.

The train from Ballina to Dublin was eventful in the sense that I babysat seven-year-old twins for their mam as she tended her younger child. Nearing Dublin I rummaged through my suit pocket and fetched out the envelope my mother had put in there earlier. Two £20 notes reared their heads. My eyes blinded with tears.

At Heuston Station, my friend, the teacher from home, was there to meet me. He had a new car, a Ford Escort with a black vinyl roof, and was accompanied by two girls who were also teachers. He had told them lots about me, it seemed, and as we wound our way through peak time Dublin traffic, life was on the upswing. The music from the car radio was from one of the then proliferation of pirate stations. The Rolling Stones sang the country standard popularised by the great Gram Parsons, 'Wild Horses'. It was a good omen. I welcomed the sight of the traffic lights: each red one allowed me to drink in the great city, the glamorous girls and the buzz of urban life. Yes, this time I was ready for the move!

Next morning I got the 46A bus from Dún Laoghaire into the city centre, and as the song says, the Liffey stank like hell. The letter from the Department told me to report to Mountjoy at 9 a.m. promptly. I hadn't a clue where the Joy was. Parked in the centre aisle of O'Connell St were lots of taxis. I opened the front door of the first and asked if he would take me to Mountjoy. 'Hop in,' the driver said. As we drove, he figured out that I was about to join the service. Only years later did I understand his perspective. I could have been going up as a visitor to an inmate. It turned out that the taxi driver was an ex-prison officer. I asked him about the job. He was very fair: he had enjoyed it to a point, he said. The pay was good but he had left after a scheme he set up, according to him anyway, a

Braille shop, was taken from him and a colleague who had done the donkey work. The embryonic project was transferred elsewhere and to new actors. He took the hump and promptly left. However, overall, according to him, one could do a lot worse than join the service.

We drove up the avenue at Crowley Place that flanked the then entrance to Mountjoy. Prison officers' houses lined the avenue (they've gone now and been replaced by the women's prison). I was overwhelmed by the size of the great steel gates with no doorknobs or handles. I was flummoxed as to how to get in. My taxi man beeped, dropped the passenger window and shouted at me to press the bell, pointing towards the right of the gates. I nodded grateful thanks but had difficulty locating the bell buzzer. Finally I spotted a small nipple-sized black dot buried in the limestone. I leaned on it and instead of the great big gates opening, a small little insert of a gate within them opened. It was, I learned, called the wicket gate.

Once inside, I proffered my letter of introduction. The warder looked at it and pointed me to a bare room behind his spartan office. Inside were almost twenty other recruits. The gate warder was neither burly, big nor brutal-looking. Years later I laughed when I saw staff described in the media in such terms: 'the burly warder took the prisoner from the court.' My initial impressions were that most of the officers were small; indeed, a few looked puny. The measure I had were the Gardaí, who stood at a minimum 5 foot 8 inches. The other thing that leaped out at me was the uniforms: they were absolutely second-rate shite. Having worked for the Commissioners of Irish Lights and having been attired in the finest of blue uniforms, I was shocked at the cheap serge tat on the backs of the warders. Their caps, though like a Garda cap, were also made of cheap material and wire, and were ill fitting.

The numbers in the small, whitewashed room behind the main gate office swelled to about twenty-eight. We laughed nervously, cracked macabre prison jokes and wondered what we had let ourselves in for. Outside, the voices of returning or exiting staff filled the air. I heard the term 'dirt bird' for the first time. Though no shrinking violet in the bad-language brigade, as those who know me will attest, I have to say that rocked me. It sounded awful and disgusting. The officer on the inner gate was in banter with the main-gate guy. Apparently it related to a disco the night before. The inner-gate guy's language in the main seemed to comprise 'fuck', 'wanker' and 'dirt bird' and it was all aimed at his colleague. Worse, it was, seemingly, accepted in jest by the recipient. Looking back, I can say that it was an anomaly. We just encountered a first-class cretin on a scorching Saturday in May.

We were summoned from the whitewashed room and herded through the inner gate where the smallest new recruit was bigger than the foul-mouthed inner-gate man. Standing in front of us was a vision: a prison officer resplendent in an immaculate uniform, creased trousers, ironed shirt, a 'slashed' peaked cap, polished like a mirror, and boots that reflected the early morning sun into our eyes. He introduced himself to us and in time we came to know him as Mr Mac. My initial horrified impressions of the prison service were lifted somewhat by Mac's attire and attitude. Believe me, first impressions matter.

Inside, in an area which we later discovered was the

visiting room for prisoners, we filled in countless forms and supplied an endless amount of personal data. There was no formal induction area for newcomers to the prison service in 1978. From there, we were taken over to the stores area. Inside was a vast room that had everything from pots to teacups. We were a hindrance to the store-keepers but they lashed out by twenty-eight times one greatcoat (I will return to this brute of an overcoat), two shirts, one tie, one pair of trousers, one set of epaulettes, one cap, one tunic, a single bright silver whistle and chain plus a silver badge, and a black plastic bag to carry our belongings.

Mr Mac led us through the external Mountjoy complex and down to an area called the Training Unit. Before you logically think that this 'Training Unit' was for staff, in actual fact it was for educating prisoners in vocational skills. Within its modern confines were classrooms and areas that taught prisoners how to become mechanics, electricians, carpenters, bricklayers and so on. We, the recruits, were there on sufferance. Our access to the gym was limited to when the prisoners were not using it.

In a crowded locker room, a transformation took place. Fresh-faced young men from age twenty to twenty-five turned from raw civilians into uniformed warders. Navy-blue trousers on, shirt epauletted properly, I giggled nervously as others put them on the wrong way. My cap was big enough to cover a dustbin. I have a head the size of Daniel O'Connell's, reputedly Ireland's biggest head ever. That hat looked and felt hideous on me: it cast a circular 5-foot shadow around me. However, when I put on the overcoat, I nearly fell over. It was a beast, a bear of a thing, too heavy and uncomfortable, a back-breaker.

Mr Mac then took us to a classroom where we were introduced to our tutors. Amongst them was a Mr Davis, or 'Bill' as he was respectfully known. Bill's advice over the two-week course would hold water over my entire service. Later that morning Mr Mac took us back up to the mother jail, Mountjoy. He warned us that the prisoners would know that we were recruits but not to worry or heed them. From the bright May morning in the courtyard outside the front entrance to the jail blocks of Mountjoy, we entered a dimly lit, long, grim, yellow-painted corridor that led to a barred gate inside the cell complex.

The noise emanating from behind those bars was cacophonic. It was untamed, loud and unintelligible but it was overwhelming. It was the noise of a live jail. The walk through the check gate into the 'Circle' area was a huge leap. As the gate closed behind us, we took our first proper steps in the prison service. The Circle gave a view of all the landings in Mountjoy, but no landing could see another landing due to the ingenious way the British penal system had designed them.

The noise was omnipresent. Prisoners wandering around actually looked like prisoners due to their garb and demeanour. I was surprised as they spoke and chatted to the officers. I had assumed that they wouldn't be allowed to speak to them, but the talk seemed cordial and not confrontational. Something I wasn't able to ignore was the stench. The weather had been very warm for a few weeks and Mountjoy stank. My only comparison to the stench was Dublin Zoo, which I had visited with my mother as a young boy. The monkey house had had a horrible smell and the smell in Mountjoy that May 1978 replicated perfectly the smell in Dublin Zoo in August 1963. From one monkey house to another. I smiled wryly to myself as our tour continued.

Our training was broken into two phases. Phase One was the initial induction in the Training Unit, which actually wasn't a staff-training unit. During our training we marched, we ran, we learned basic self-defence. In addition we took classes in prison rules. Interestingly, we had no guidebooks apart from the archaic *Prisons 1948 Rule Book*. We took notes and were given copies of various sheets of paper, such as visiting dockets, report forms and the like, to familiarise ourselves with the paperwork of a prison. This was all crammed into a fortnight. Phase Two, later on, would last three weeks.

Each day Mr Mac took us up along the canal bank for a three-mile run. Being a footballer primarily, I had never run but was fairly fit. I surprised myself by not alone not being last, but actually being up at the top beside Mac. It emerged in conversation that Mr Mac was a Mayo man. Years later I also found out that Mac wasn't one bit sentimental about what we natives call the Dark County. He told me the best thing in Mayo was the road out of it.

One day as we jogged along the Royal Canal, our attention was drawn to the squawk of a Garda radio. Nearby, parked against a derelict bench, was a Garda motorcycle minus its rider. Behind the bench, fast asleep in the midday sun, resting his head on his white helmet, was a snoozing Garda. We didn't disturb him. On the way back we again took care not to be too loud lest we wake him.

Mr Maloney was our Control and Restraint instructor, an amiable guy with a beautiful Dublin accent. 'Amby', as he was known, was one of the lithest and supplest humans I have ever met. Knowing well that it took him years to reach his black belt status and that he had twelve days to knock us into shape, Amby focused on the common-sense approach. No need to be a hero, he counselled. Take stock of the situation, no loss of face by backing off and waiting for help. He made the various holds, grips, tumbles and trips look so easy but I nearly dislocated my elbow when I tried the same. 'Relax, old son,' Amby said. 'I'm at this since I was twelve and I'm still learning . . . there's no rush. Get the basics right first before you become Chuck Norris.' Amby was the epitome of the common-sense men I worked with over the years. Know your strengths, and know your limitations.

Towards the end of the course, after trips to the various jails and courts, we were furnished with a sheet of paper with the names of all the institutions written on it. We were to fill out in order of preference where we wished to work. Before we put pen to paper, we were informed that Portlaoise would take most of us as that was where the greatest need was. So I put down Portlaoise. I didn't much mind where I was sent. A few lads from around Erris were already in Portlaoise so it seemed like a good idea to go where I would actually know a few guys. We returned the filled-out sheets and then got a lecture from a psychologist. It was a tepid affair, gentle testing of the greenhorns as to what awaited them and how they might react. We didn't disappoint.

We also received our first pay cheque, called the 'Wine Docket' by staff. The cheque was attached to a counterfoil with about forty code numbers telling you what your pay was and how it was made up. The problem with it was they made it out to 'John F. Cuffe'. It's a small thing but I am actually John G. (Gerard) Cuffe. I went to the general office where they made up our wages and explained my predicament to the clerk. Sympathetically, he said, 'Son, if you want to I'll query this, but let me tell you, by the time they figure it out you might wind up getting the wrong pay. They aren't the brightest over there in St Stephen's Green, the headquarters of the Department of Justice.' I nodded doubtfully. 'Look, son. Did you get the right amount?' I nodded again. 'Good. Then do you give a fuck if they call you John Gandhi as long as they pay you what's due?' I nodded the head for the last time and left. Over time I was referred to as 'J. F. Cuffe' and towards the end 'J. B. Cuffe'. My pay number was a different number from my file number. You just lose the will to ask, and let them do what they want; it's easier, in the end.

My evenings were spent with my friend Gallagher and his pals, a group that were studying to be primary teachers in Carysfort. We'd kick a ball around Clarendon Park in Dún Laoghaire and go to the pubs at night. One of the would-be teachers who was going out with an army officer asked a rather good question. 'Johnny, how come you are all officers? In the army, the officers have men under them like soldiers?' I thought for a while and batted the ball to the slips like a good cricketer with 'that's a good question . . . I haven't a clue.' However, it was the first of many awkward questions relating to prison officers/warders/wardens, jails, gaols and institutions.

Friday was the final day after two weeks in training. No passing-out parade, no parchment, no speeches, no hats thrown in the air, no donning of white gloves, or sandwiches and tea for our loved ones. The list was read out. Eighteen of us were assigned to Portlaoise with the order to be there at 11 a.m. on Monday for those without cars (which was all of us bar one). The other six were assigned to Dublin prisons and, after a brief good luck and goodbye, we separated with a black plastic bag containing our uniforms and the thug black overcoat that felt to me like it was actually alive.

I lugged the bag onto the 46A bus to Dún Laoghaire, dragged it across to Clarendon Park and contemplated the next stage of my adventure. That night, Gallagher, his friends and I went to the *Cultúrlann* in Monkstown and listened to *céilí* music and *sean nós* singing. We were as happy there as in the Purty Kitchen down the road with its rock bands. There's a time and a place for everything. The weekend was for enjoying. On Sunday we visited a group of girls and they made us tea. One of them put on a bet with me. The bet was for £5 and it centred on how long I would last in the prison service. She said a year, I said forever, but certainly no less than five years. We both laughed. In time we met again at Heuston Station, but I declined the fiver.

2

The Bog

Going to prison is dying with your eyes wide open.

BERNARD KERIK (b. 1955)

In late May 1978 my teacher friend drove me to Heuston Station, where I caught an early train to Portlaoise. My stuffed suitcase, still with blue fisherman's rope holding it together, along with the black plastic bag full of jail uniform, was lugged aboard the south-bound train. Other lads from training were there as well and as the train sped between the green fields and past blurred telegraph poles, we wondered what lay ahead.

Portlaoise in jail language is known as 'The Bog', perhaps in reference to its rural setting or perhaps due to the actual bogs nearby. Quickly we got onto the lingo. From the train station in Portlaoise, we traipsed the rather longish journey to the prison with bags in tow. My fingers lost all circulation as the heavy black bag and suitcase squeezed the flow of blood to my hands. My fingers were a post-mortem blue and white.

The jail, on the Dublin Road, dominates the approach

into Portlaoise, with its large central building with army sandbags on the roof and walled corner sentry posts. It was then the most secure prison in Europe. We arrived and were held at an area where those who came to visit prisoners were also processed. We were told to wait until a Mr Stack, the liaison officer for new staff, arrived out to see us. I was more concerned about the lack of blood in my fingers.

Brian Stack came out to meet us. A stocky, well-put-together man, he exuded an air of one who had done this many times. He had long, neatly trimmed sideburns and piercing dark brown eyes set in a prominent face. He was serious and seldom smiled but, when he did, he transformed into a warm man, almost at odds with his jail face. Stack tersely informed us that we would be assigned lodgings in the town where we would change into our uniforms and then report back to him. Out of nowhere a fleet of cars arrived and from Stack's handheld clipboard our names and landladies were called out. Three of us were lodged in a nice lady's house on the edge of the town. After quickly dumping our bags and donning the uniform, we reported back to the main entrance of Portlaoise. The entire jail screamed 'security'. Garda vans and cars were coming and going, army jeeps too. People in uniforms of various hues, from khaki green to various shades of blue, were also coming and going. Once we were assembled, Stack arrived. He did a roll call again and then led us through locked gate after locked gate until we arrived in a small room. A single light dangled from the ceiling. The other light came through the open door. Scattered around were a handful of desks and simple chairs. No windows.

This was to be our 'classroom' for a few days until we got familiarised with the set-up. The biggest problem within that room was staying awake, not due to Stack's lectures being boring, but from the summer heat and a lack of fresh air circulating. Soon, like spring lambs, we were fed into the system and the class work was over.

Portlaoise had within its walls a number of groups: the prison and its staff, a large group of Gardaí and the army, along with various hues of republican warriors. Like the Billy Joel song 'Saigon', the army controlled the roofs and high walls, we controlled the jail and the Gardaí were there, I assume, as backup. Having a single goal – to run a secure prison – didn't mean we all sang from the same hymn sheet.

For the first but not the last time, I saw that the criminal justice system was not an interlinking network where all contributed as partners. Instead, it was like a hierarchy where some actors perceived themselves as greater than others. Hence the army had little or no dealings with us, the Gardaí stuck together, seldom mixing with us, and the jailers for their part despised the lot of them. A familiar bleat from the Gardaí was, 'If I'd wanted to work in a prison I would have joined the prison service.' The army took the view that they were wasted there. They saw themselves as babysitters. Me? Well, I'd assumed that birds of a feather flocked together but no, different strokes entirely.

The talk amongst the warders and indeed some of the Gardaí was that many of the Gardaí stationed within the prison walls were there because they had infringed rules or upset their superintendents in the outside world. Guys from stations or the traffic corps in on overtime were quick to dissociate themselves from the regulars whom we quickly got to identify if not exactly know. The army, I figured, unless they were overseas were as close to action in the prison as they would ever encounter. Apart from providing cover for bank runs, the most action they had seen up to the end of the 1970s was collecting rubbish when the bin men went on strike in the 1960s, the culling of chickens in Monaghan and the running of lorries during a bus strike in 1979. An odd bunch, indeed, and not a homogenous group, better described as apples, oranges and bananas: all fruit but all different.

Portlaoise's E Block, a large and airy building totally different from Mountjoy, housed various groups of republicans on four landings. The Troubles in the north had spilled into the south: banks were robbed, and people were killed or kidnapped on occasion, the most famous being the Tiede Herrema kidnapping. The previous Fine Gael/Labour coalition had taken a hard line on the republicans, which resulted in the IRA rendering Mountjoy unsuitable for them by rioting and systematically destroying it, thus necessitating their removal to Portlaoise.

It could be argued that the IRA modernised Ireland's prison system. Their ability to organise, to have an army structure, disciplined when needed, violent when needed, had caught the jail service and Department of Justice flatfooted. Portlaoise had seen troubled times: an escape attempt on St Patrick's Day 1975 resulted in the death by shooting of an IRA man. Trouble, strife and anger stalked the prison. Some staff were threatened, resulting in them having to vacate their homes and move into jail houses that fronted the prison. The then governor received a death threat, an attempt to blow up his car was foiled and there was a Garda presence in his garden. He was always escorted by Gardaí when he exited the jail.

The landings were E1, E2, E3 and E4. Landings E3 and E4 housed the Provisional IRA. Seamus Twomey, James Monaghan and Kevin Mallon were there at that time. The E2 landing housed the Official IRA and E1, the ground floor, housed what were termed 'mavericks'; Eddie Gallagher (of the Monasterevin siege and Tiede Herrema infamy) was there. Also, some of those 'mavericks' had reputedly lost the trust of their mentors and a death sentence supposedly awaited them on release.

The cells on the E Block were spartan, simple and reflected their occupants' views on prison life. The Republicans viewed themselves as prisoners of war, and not as 'ordinary' prisoners. The recently elected Fianna Fáil government had relaxed the stranglehold imposed by the previous Fine Gael/Labour coalition and when I arrived the prisoners, in effect, had political status in all but name. In contrast, Margaret Thatcher's Conservative government was to precipitate the death by hunger strike of ten men in the H-Blocks over the sweeping of a landing and the right to wear their own clothing. The bullheaded – and ultimately futile – evil and childishness of it stayed with me for a long time.

We, the ordinary staff, did not interact with them, even though we were on the same landings. Their landing commander would liaise with the Class Officer and tell him what requests they might have. A Class Officer generally ran a landing of about thirty cells. Essentially he was the boss. A good Class Officer was worth his weight in gold; a bad one left you with problems. The Provos exercised in one yard, the other prisoners in a back yard.

The first morning we were unleashed on the jail system we reported for duty at 8 a.m. On entering the main gate area we were searched: shoes off, pockets emptied and a pat down before admittance. Inside, we went through endless check gates before arriving in a huge assembly hall. There I saw the first indication of the hierarchy that existed between the warders. The old-timers leaned, slouched even, against the back wall with the nonchalance and lack of interest of guys who saw this as a chore. We, the newbies, on the other hand, formed three ranks about 20 feet forward from the veterans.

A Chief Officer (CO) would read the parade. Your name was called out, to which you replied 'Sir' indicating your presence. He then called out something along the lines of 'Officer Cuffe, assist E1, searches, relieve North Wall post at 9 o'clock, visits, assist E4 at dinner time.' This was too much to take in. We endured the embarrassment of asking a longer-term colleague what the hell it all meant until we had it figured out. Duties in Portlaoise were black and white, which was a good thing. We were there in large numbers to guarantee security, not to rehabilitate.

After about three weeks of being totally anonymous to most staff, I heard my name called out by an officer on the landings. 'The deputy governor wants to see you,' he said. I could feel a hundred eyes looking at me: warders distrust guys for whom the governors look, especially ones they hardly know. The term for guys about whom there might be, ahem, a certain doubt, is the age-old term 'rat'.

Jails have many 'rats', from prisoners to the odd '*francach*' in uniform. Puzzled and slightly worried, I followed the officer to a cell door on the E2 landing. The cell actually was a double cell that had been turned into a small office for the governor to hold court and listen to requests or deal with issues regarding the prisoners. I was invited inside and saw the deputy governor sitting behind an austere desk, a Manila file open in front of him.

He must have seen the slight alarm on my face as he invited me to sit down.

'Mr Cuffe, I'm looking at your file and, in the length I have been here, apart from the local lads, you are the first person to request to work or transfer here.' He paused as his finger played with the edge of my file. Was he suggesting I was a republican plant?

I explained that I didn't actually mind where I worked. The reason I'd looked for Portlaoise was that I knew a few lads from my neck of the woods. Also, any job that allowed you to finish at eight o'clock in the evening was a good job, in my book. My poor old father never finished before nine. And as a light keeper on a lonely rock I couldn't come home any evening . . . I threw that in as a kind of mitigation.

That seemed to satisfy him. He thumbed through the file again. 'I see you worked in a kitchen as a cook for a summer and have a distinction in catering from the London City & Guilds?'

I nearly died. If a Garda wished to work in a jail he would have joined the prison service and if I'd wanted to work in a kitchen then I would have continued being a chef. I love cooking . . . for myself and my family. I hated hotel kitchens; the dishcloth that cracked my jaw a few years earlier still smarted. The problem was that in the City & Guilds London I had a distinction in the theory of catering plus a merit in cooking but I wasn't a good chef. 'I think we will give you a run in the kitchens here tomorrow,' he said as he closed the file. 'That's it, you can go now.' He motioned me to the cell door.

The next morning parade was, for me, short and sour: 'Cuffe, assist kitchens,' barked the CO and nothing else. A load of officers were interested in their new 'chef'. I walked away like a condemned man. Inside the kitchen I met the real chef, known to one and all as Skipper. First thing we did was have a cup of tea, then Skipper scouted through the morning papers looking for news about his soccer teams. I'd struck gold. I loved soccer and the morning flew as I listened to Skipper talk about the Leeds 1974 team or the Man United '68 team. In essence, we didn't do the cooking at all: Skipper started it but his helpers, those prisoners who were housed in an area called the D Block, did the bulk of the work.

The inhabitants of the D Block were on half remission because essentially they were there to do the prison work the republicans refused to do. It was a win-win situation: the republicans cleaned their own cells and landings while the 'ordinaries' did the work the republicans objected to. In return, those 'ordinaries' had their one-quarter entitlement of remission moved up to a third or in some cases a half of their sentences. Thatcher and the Tories might have profited from watching that. An internal phone rang: the governor was on his rounds. Every jail has a governor's round. It's supposed to be the opportunity for the governor to see *his* jail and that all is correct. All is correct almost always because the bush telegraph has warned everybody concerned that the Gov is on his rounds. Most intelligent governors know this and it suits them. What they don't see hurts no one. Their consciences are salved.

Our governor, Mr Bill Reilly, was a native of Erris, maybe 10 miles from my village. A former Garda who resigned rather than work for their then Dickensian entitlements, Reilly was not a man who suffered fools. Hard working, disciplined and not afraid of anyone, Reilly walked with a slight limp, eyes ahead and an air of coldness. Skipper had picked out a dinner for him to sample. Reilly took a morsel and nodded his head in agreement that it was capital. He then swept out of the green institutional kitchen. He never once showed the slightest sign of recognition of a fellow Erris man. We pride ourselves on our friendship across the generations as 'townies'. I felt hurt . . . well, more annoyed really.

That afternoon Skipper broke the news to me that he was off that evening. I nearly died. I would be in sole charge. I confessed my terror to the Skipper, who laughed and told me not to worry. He called over his trusted top cat and told him what to do. A 'top cat' is a prisoner who can be relied on to act on his own initiative. They are trusted and in return get a few privileges like some smokes and biscuits. Skipper then informed him that Mr Cuffe would take care of the 'Specials'. I hadn't a clue what 'Specials' were. Skipper explained that meat, bought from the local butchers or left in, was for the republicans: steak, rashers, fish, sausages and pudding. My jaw dropped when I heard that it was the kitchen's task to cook this food.

Skipper then asked me: 'Do you want to be back here tomorrow and the day after, or do you want to be out of here for good?'

I nodded to the latter question. 'Right, I normally deep-fry the sausages, rashers and pudding. It's more efficient and quicker but you gotta keep an eye,' he said. 'Now what if the thermostat was set a tad too high and . . . eh . . . the old sausages got burned? Just saying, like.'

I smiled. That evening I turned the deep-fat fryer up to the last, till it would have smelted steel. I dropped everything in, steak, chops, rashers, sausages and pudding. I did it too well because it was no sooner in than I was rescuing charred rashers and pudding unrecognisable as food. I then plated the charred orders according to the list from each prisoner and landing that had been handed in. I stuck the list on the metal plate cover and the cocky landing officers arrived down. 'Hello, you must be the new chef?' they smirked, as they took away the charred offerings unseen to them . . . yet.

After about ten minutes the first of them arrived back. 'I think you made a mistake . . . didn't ask for that,' as a white plate with incinerated meat was left on the counter.

I apologised as the clock ticked towards night lock-up.

'Sorry about that, the deep fat fryer has a problem with the thermostat. I've put in a report on it.'

Next morning at parade I held my breath. The CO called out 'Cuffe'. I replied smartly 'Sir!'

'North Wall patrol until dinner time.'

The North Wall was the most boring post in the jail. You were caught between a 30-foot-high limestone wall and a maze of barbed wire that separated and kept secure an exercise yard. If it was dry, your trousers looked like you'd spent the day crossing a dusty desert. If it was wet, you came out of it looking as if you had been in the muddy fields of the Somme. But I was ecstatic. I had not joined the prison service to cook. Skipper had given me an out and it had worked, even though I was now walking the Portlaoise Prison equivalent of Siberia.

Over time I integrated and made my own pals. Stack was great for involving us in the local community with pub quizzes and discos. I got involved in the prison's soccer league. The only time we could play was after 8 p.m. All our shifts were twelve hours long, with no rest days, and compulsory overtime was the norm. The soccer gave me a chance to make a name for myself and I was on Skipper's team. I tried extra hard for him: I owed him big time. We lived our social lives between 8 p.m. and whatever time we went to bed. The local pubs were where we met. Some of the Gardaí who manned the jail would be there. I'd always say hello out of manners but there was an invisible barrier between us and them. I know that some of the longer-term staff hated them and it seemed the feeling was mutual.

An old friend of mine from the late 1960s was a Garda who had the bad luck to be put on prison duty. Sitting with a few of his colleagues as I passed, he lifted a finger of recognition after I had nodded to him. That pissed me off because I'd known him long before our status was predicated on different hues of blue. I went to the toilet and a moment later he arrived in. It was as if we were back in the old days. He was effusive, funny and garrulous, the guy I'd always known. Then came the cruncher: 'You wouldn't lend me a tenner until pay day. You see . . .'

I stopped him, took out a twenty and gave it to him. 'Give it back when you have it,' I said. He grabbed my shoulders. 'Fair play. It's . . . I'm just a bit short tonight. I'll get you a couple of shirts as well.'

Once back out in the bar we retreated to our respective sphere. I never got my £20, I never got the shirts and I barely got a goodnight as I left the pub. In time I accepted that we choose who we want to be. If one shade of blue or green wants to cock a snook at another, so be it.

Time passed and I did a variety of duties. Many had fancy titles but were totally opposite to that title. 'Special Patrol' was a duty that was carried out after 8 p.m. when the prisoners were locked up. The evening staff did it. It entailed walking around the landings until 10 p.m. If a prisoner wished to get out for a number two, otherwise known as a shite, you let them out one at a time, and entered their name and time of crap in a hard-backed green notebook.

One evening as I wandered around on Special Patrol, I noticed that the locked-up landings on E Block had an echo about them – marvellous acoustics – and since I'd loved to whistle since I was a kid, I whistled away the evening, lost in thought with my shite book in hand. After a while I was called by another officer who told me the ACO in charge wanted to see me. Arriving at the same door where the DG had tried to nudge me back into a catering career, I found the ACO looking slightly discommoded and thick. Without lifting his eyes from a sheet in front of him he asked, full well knowing the reply: 'Is that you whistling out there?' Cheerfully I replied, 'Yes, ACO.' Still eyes downwards, he grunted, 'Well, stop it. It's annoying the prisoners and us. Keep it quiet.'

Another duty entailed operating gates between my nemeses the kitchen and the E1 landing. A huge governor's order book lay on a table in that area. It held orders going back to the 1950s. Going through it showed me the slowly changing face of the service. One of the orders was thus: 'The governor wants it to be known that he does not expect staff to salute him up the town if they are on bicycles as this is a dangerous practice. All staff are to read this order and initial or sign same.' What a notion: to be cycling along with a bag of groceries and trying to doff your hat to your governor!

Interaction, as I've said, between staff and the republican prisoners was minimal. Their upper structure dealt with our upper structure. However, there was the odd chink of light on occasions. I was once detailed to collect prisoners for the visiting area. Often the prisoner would arrive over before the visitor had been cleared through the maze of wired and barred gates. You then held your prisoner outside until the call came from within the visiting box. The chap I was escorting was wearing Rory Gallagher attire: denim jacket, chequered shirt, blue jeans and brown Doc Martens laced forever. He was around my age and as we sat waiting, we were on neutral ground.

The Sunday before, an Ulster team had lost to Dublin in the All-Ireland semi-final and I just threw out, 'Were you watching the match yesterday?' He straightened up in the chair and replied, 'Aye, can't see them beating those Kerry boys, though.' We chatted away, simple but friendly. Then he was called in and off I went. As luck would have it, I was the one who had to escort him back to the block again. The visit seemed to have gone well and the small chat continued until we arrived at the E1 check gate. Then a thousand-yard stare spread across his face, the air chilled and I passed him on. That evening our paths crossed on E4. I, being a soft Mayo man, was about to smile but he looked ahead as if I wasn't on the same planet. It would have been hard not to feel a little miffed but even then I understood the invisible barrier between us.

The other oddity in my file was that I was a native Irish speaker. Whilst the army and Gardaí had plenty of Gaeilgeoirs, the prison service had an almost total lack of them. Once more the quest for a specialist led them to my file and I was asked to listen in on a visit that was to be conducted in Irish. Prison warders have heard all types of conversations and tend to filter out the dialogue until a key word pops up and then the ears prick up and you listen until you decide whether to intervene or let them natter away, stepping in only if matters of security are being discussed, a threat being made or staff business being given to others.

This visitor was an academic: a copy of *The Irish Times* in hand, tweed trousers, nice sweater, and open chequered shirt. Pretty soon I figured that whilst the visitor had good Irish, the prisoner being visited had not. A number of times I had to stop myself blurting out the word he desperately searched for. It was painful to listen to, the poor devil was almost physically trying to get the *cúpla focal* across as his visitor good-naturedly kept the conversation simple. Afterwards, I had to fill out a report and return it to the governor's office. I told the truth: nothing untoward discussed, and the level of Irish spoken was poor. The only threat presented at the visit was not to the jail but to our sweet language.

In a short enough time I became part of the prison's

search team for incoming and exiting army personnel. I think they did a three-week roster back then. Their knapsacks were emptied, pockets turned out, shoes and boots taken off. Forbidden were spools of thread, string, extra laces and any surplus insignia. Apparently a few years before that, soldiers had, via the thread and spools, supplied badges, buttons and insignia down to the republicans' cell windows where they were winched in and attached to makeshift uniforms for escape attempts.

Between searches we would drink tea and chat. It was out in an area called the Farm, full of stores, sheds and naturally surrounded by high walls, barbed wire and other escape-proof paraphernalia. A few of us curious ones entered a store, where literally hundreds of grey steel cell doors lay covered in dust. Stack told us that they were meant to replace the old wooden doors in the main jail but someone from the Department of Justice had measured them up wrong at the start. When the first was about to be hung, it was found to be short and too narrow, and so they were useless. Bravo, Justice.

By September I had worked virtually every day since starting in late May. Your rest days were marked out on a large wall calendar near the exit gate in red biro indicating that you were compelled to work those days. Naturally, you earned big money but conversely you had no time to spend it. Years later, I came to the conclusion that compulsory overtime was a tool to abuse us with, wear us down and avoid having to employ extra staff. The family relationships of many fine young men suffered due to the infrequency they were at home and from the high pressure and occasionally dangerous job. Some developed drink and marital problems, others had financial issues. J. J. Barrett in his book *Martin Ferris – Man of Kerry* notes:

> While Irish soldiers were suffering ear damage from artillery and gunfire, and building up compensation claims against the Irish government, prison staff were suffering psychological damage for which there may never be compensation or resolution. The negligence towards prison officers by the Department of Justice, which allowed the brutal regime to operate, has never been challenged in the courts.

Barrett wrote this after the coalition of Fine Gael and Labour once more changed the rules within Portlaoise around 1985. After the same coalition had fallen in 1977, a sea change had taken place within Portlaoise Jail. The Republican prisoners were given political status in all but name; the more confrontational aspect of jailing eased back and a calm descended. During the coalition era between 1973 and 1977, the governor's car had had a suspect device attached to it and he required a full-time Garda presence outside his house. He was assigned a full team of detectives to drive him everywhere. Some staff had to vacate their homes and move into prison houses beside the jail and some also needed a Garda escort leaving duty. The return of that coalition in 1981 once more strained relations within the prison, culminating in disturbances and escape attempts in 1985.

In training we were given one pair of trousers and two shirts. The tailor in Portlaoise sewed the initials PS (for

'Prison Service') on a circular navy blue patch against our sky-blue shirts. You stood there naked from the waist up as he sewed the shirt in front of you. The only other people who had the initials PS attached and branded to their clothing were the prisoners. The night shift was a split shift that entailed reporting for duty at 8 a.m., going home at 1 p.m., then returning at 9 p.m. and working straight through until 8 a.m. the following morning. I used to leave in my uniform trousers to the dry cleaners on my way back to the digs and would then collect them the following morning before I was back in the prison for an evening duty. The trousers were wafer thin after a few months.

Whilst initially, and due to the novelty of jail, I didn't mind the long hours, I now needed to get home to visit my widowed mother. I had worked nonstop from late May, now we were in early September. We had what to me back then looked like an old Chief Officer. Mr Weldon was his name, a Dublin man, who looked cross and grumpy. One evening as I traversed the exercise yard, Weldon made his way down towards me. 'You're the man who burned the Provos' rashers,' was his mode of introduction. All I could do was shrug with a nervous smile. Obviously he figured out Skipper's plan for me because he said, 'So you don't like kitchens?'

As we walked, the two of us, I told him of my past and the clatter of the dishcloth from a lunatic chef. He was a sympathetic man, totally at odds with his gruff exterior. In time I learned not to judge a book by its cover, particularly in dealing with staff. 'You should have put down you were a farmer that lugged logs or water butts across your land,' he said. More small chat and I relaxed. He wasn't after me at all. Before he departed I mentioned my widowed mother and would it be possible just to get two of my rest days so I could visit her.

The chief pulled out a worn notebook with turned up pages at the edges and a stub of a pencil, and asked my name again. He then left, saying, 'No promises, mind you.' The following week was to be my long weekend off: that was the Thursday and Friday from week one, tied into Saturday and Sunday of week two, thus giving you four rest days per month together. You then returned and worked ten consecutive days before your next two rest days came up. No one ever got their long weekend. On the Monday evening, the detail for the next two weeks was published at the main gate for us all to see on the way out. Imagine my shock when I saw my roster as nights Tuesday, after nights Wednesday, off Thursday, Friday, Saturday and Sunday with a 4 p.m. start on the Monday. Mr Weldon made a young Blacksod man and his mother eternally thankful and when I recall his name, it's with thanks.

October slipped into November. We passed the evening recreation time for the prisoners telling jokes, having short quizzes and picking teams to while away the time on the landings as night enveloped the town. We were now coming in in the dark and going home in the dark. Though jails are impersonal and cold places to dwell within, it was as if we were all safe within the glow of the yellow and orange security lights, and it brought a warmth to the place. As the prisoners watched TV and had their own craic, the more famous or seemingly influential amongst them were given the privilege of an officer tailing them discreetly throughout the day until lock-up.

This was a farce: a jail has a finite space and is small in

scale. If everyone is on the ball *all* prisoners' movements should be a thing of routine and easy recall. This duty naturally enough was also called Special Patrol but different than the later evening poo-and-piss patrol. Once more a green notebook was entrusted to the spying warder. The likes of Seamus Twomey and Kevin Mallon knew full well that they were being followed. Indeed, Mallon was in the habit of telling the officer following him what he had planned for the day, which was funny but made us look stupid. Both Twomey and Mallon had escaped prisons before, Twomey out of Mountjoy via helicopter. The rumour was that Mallon had allowed himself to be captured in order to stage another breakout from Portlaoise with a new bunch of guys the next time.

At night-time we walked across the top ends of the yards, the prisoners walked lengthways, ensuring each had their own space, and the cops huddled with their own mates. Sometimes we all stood in the one spot as the prisoners played football. You wouldn't want to be faint-hearted as the tackles flew in on the tarmac. Balls had the lifespan of a summer fly around an aerosol spray. If they hit the shredded wire, they ripped. The Department had deep pockets and another orange or white Mayco plastic ball was kicked into play. An old-timer, one of those know-alls, used to regale us with his witticisms (he was wasted in the prison service: his calling lay elsewhere). Once he asked us recruits, 'What's the difference between me and the governor?' We gave different answers. We knew of course that it was a trick question but we humoured him. One of us said 'about five ranks' in order to get him to deliver the punchline. 'The difference between me and the governor is this,' he intoned, a smile playing around his lips, 'I earn twice as much as him and I sleep well at night, and there's no Garda outside in my garden!' We all laughed because it was probably true when overtime was thrown in.

The old geezer also pointed out another truism: 'See that guy' – indicating some well-known Provo or other – 'that guy inside twenty years could be your minister and you taking orders from him, never doubt that.' He was not too far off the mark, out by two decades perhaps but still heading in the right direction.

Moving into late November I wasn't looking past the horizons of Portlaoise. A steady job, secure, well paid, big hours but hey, I couldn't have everything in life. On my trip home, that four-day break in September, I brought back my old Irish Lighthouse overcoat. It was a proper tailored greatcoat, unlike the thug prison one with its ugly black bull's wool. I cut off the lighthouse buttons and sewed on the jail ones, exchanging mariner gold for shore silver. Now, apart from the problem of the single trousers, not due another pair until I had served nine months we were told, I felt a lot better with a fitted greatcoat.

Then one day I was informed to report to the Training Unit for Phase Two of the training course. It was like being given an extra holiday: three weeks in Dublin, no twelve-hour shifts, and the chance to renew acquaintances with my friend the teacher. I was looking forward to it. This time I travelled light, taking my uniform and a few changes of clothes. Four of the officers on the course, myself included, stayed in a guesthouse near Mountjoy. It was adequate if old-fashioned. The landlady knew we were warders, casually telling us that her nephew was a Provo locked up in Portlaoise. She seemed a decent woman, and the prisoner she mentioned was a nice enough guy. The truth was, we were too tired to look for another place. Still, for the first night or two, I slept with one eye open!

3

Shanganagh Castle

Place me behind prison walls – walls of stone ever so high, ever so thick, reaching ever so far into the ground. There is a possibility that some way or another I may be able to escape. But stand me on the floor and draw a chalk line around me and have me give my word of honour never to cross it. Can I get out of that circle? No, never.

KARL G. MAESER (1828–1901)

Phase Two was too late to save many of us from already implanted prejudices and work practices. Our initial two-week training stint back in May had barely prepared us for prisons and I still wasn't long enough in the job to merit a second pair of uniform trousers. Now, almost six months later, we were back for Phase Two, a three-week gig with the purpose of what? The recruits that had gone to the Dublin jails spoke like veterans, calling prisoners 'dirt birds' or 'knackers'. They didn't mean it but it was to show the rest of us that they had already endured more than we had. They had aged and their uniforms looked shabby. Some even worked overtime after class. I wasn't shocked, nor did I take it seriously. I just laughed because I knew the hard-man talk was bravado. The psychologist visited us again. This time we acted the eejit, deliberately provoking him and saying cruel things. Then again, perhaps he expected that and it was him playing games with us.

I enjoyed Dublin, meeting Gallagher and his pals. I saw Mairéad Ní Mhaonaigh, and a nascent Altan play in some pub in Capel Street. I started to hanker for the bright lights. Portlaoise was beginning to look rustic and rural. The course brought us to the Dublin prisons, the courts and to an open centre for young boys called Shanganagh Castle out in Shankill in south County Dublin, not far from Bray. The break from jail life and long hours was appreciated. Soon the day of reckoning arrived and the inevitable return to our mother jails.

The previous day, the Thursday, we were asked to write a piece on rehabilitation for the psychologist. Some of the boys wrote fiction and horror but I decided to take it seriously and wrote an even-tempered piece with a bit of depth. On the Friday morning, our last day, around 11 a.m., one of the course instructors called me over. 'Would you be interested in going to Shanganagh Castle to work there?' he asked. I didn't need a second invitation. 'You've a transfer in from Portlaoise then?' he asked. Blast, my escape route blocked. 'No, eh, I haven't. I wasn't thinking of leaving down there just yet but now as the chance . . .'

He brought me to his office, placed a blank half sheet in front of me. (A half sheet is the jailer's bane and curse: a sheet of lined paper that can be used for anything, such as queries to staff as to why they did that or the other, so the words 'half sheet' can cause fear and trepidation.) 'Write out your request for a transfer and don't worry: it will be sorted,' said the instructor. An hour later I and another lad were informed we were to start in Shanganagh Castle on Monday morning at 9 a.m.

It's a small world. My boyhood pal, Gallagher, the teacher, had just been appointed to a national school in Shankill. We both came from furthest Blacksod in Mayo and now we were working about a half mile from each other. On the Monday morning on his way to work, he dropped me at the gate of Shanganagh Castle. There was a long driveway up to the castle, an impressive eighteenth-century castellated house with immaculate mowed verges, splendid trees and proper fencing. It looked more like the home of a lord than an institution for young boys aged fifteen upwards. It was mid December and the frosty cold morning added to rather than took from the scenery.

I entered by the main front door where I was met by a member of staff. In Shanganagh all staff wore plain clothes and many grew their hair long. Appearances can be deceptive, though: whilst the attire was laid back, the regime was quite strict. My new colleague brought me down to the CO's office where a Mr Dunne introduced himself to me. He was a genial man on the cusp of retirement. He showed me my detail for the coming week and the added bonus was that Shanganagh closed down for Christmas like a normal school and I was off until late December. Happy days! I spent Christmas at home with my mother and the future was bright.

The regime in Shanganagh was strict. On arrival, Frank (another new arrival) and I were shown around by one of the ACOs. It was 'those are our two new officers . . . this is officer such and such . . . hello . . . how are you? . . . see you' type of stuff and on to the next introduction. When the whistle-stop tour finished, our ACO brought us up a back stairs and into a large room that had four beds, some wardrobes and an adjoining bathroom. 'These are your quarters,' he announced to the both of us. Frank and I exchanged a glance. I thanked the ACO, saying that it would be great short term until I got a flat. Frank already had a flat in town.

The ACO sniffed as if there was a pong in the room. 'No, this is your accommodation. All single officers have to live in and can only be absent by signing a book in the CO's office. Two officers must reside and be available overnight in the Castle.' I looked at my watch, checked the time and date and yes, this was 1978 not 1878 and no, we weren't indentured, below-stairs hired hands. I asked were those officers who had to be available overnight paid or given time off in lieu. He shook his head. The look on the ACO's face showed he wasn't joking and I had a queasy feeling in my stomach. The rule was strict about signing out but, as with all rules, it seemed to apply more to some than to others.

We worked a revolving shift pattern comprised of evening duties, day duties and night duties. However, a select group of officers were permanently on day shifts, a most sought-after roster. A few of them would come into the office on a Monday morning and sign themselves out of the Castle overnight for the rest of the week. Plebs like ourselves were scrutinised to ensure two remained in the Castle thus by implication being on standby overnight.

While standby did not attract monetary reward or time off in lieu, if you were absent without permission, it attracted a disciplinary inquiry. This archaic practice lasted into the 1980s.

The annual Shanganagh staff dinner dance was approaching. Being young, eager and energetic, we looked forward to it. Our shift, the two of us, was from 4 p.m. until midnight. The supervisor that evening was a stickler for squeezing the last minute out of the shift so we both knew midnight was just that and not a second before. When he arrived up at the dormitories that we were supervising around 11.30 p.m., we assumed that, because it was dinner-dance night, he was letting us off a few moments early. The small talk dragged on for quarter of an hour until he finally came to the chase, the real reason for engaging in bullshit and pretend bonhomie: 'You're the only two left to be on standby, so I am telling ye that youse don't have permission to leave the castle and go to the dinner dance.' With that he was gone into the darkness that enveloped the stairwell.

At exactly midnight my colleague and I returned to our rooms, washed, shaved, put on nice shirts and trousers, and dabbed on the cologne. We then went to the car park, slipped the handbrake from my car and rolled it down the avenue. Once out of earshot of the castle I started the engine, careful not to turn on the lights, and headed towards Bray for the shindig. All went well to a point; you have to adjust on occasions like this, most of the guests were well oiled and in great form when we the latecomers arrived. I found it hard to get into the swing of the party and I had a nagging feeling that I actually was an escaped prisoner. Up at the bar we sipped a pint; the grub was long devoured although I would have murdered a sandwich. A friend of mine decided to tell me what he 'really thought' of me, free from the restraint of sobriety. Suffice to say it wasn't pleasant and all concerned at the bar were embarrassed, none more so than me. It became the highlight and topic of the night.

Next day it was the topic of the tea break and dinner break. I was reminded by a senior officer that I was in breach of discipline for leaving the institution and that the governor would be speaking to me. I was scared shitless. Then I rationalised it: how could I be punished for being absent when for being present I was the recipient of neither a financial reward nor time off in lieu? I wasn't a slave nor would anyone turn me into one. Also, the prisoners had committed a crime. I was here to work, not to do time. I sought a meeting with my would-be disciplinarian and made my case. He wasn't pleased but I heard no more.

The boys in Shanganagh were aged from fifteen to seventeen. In today's criminal justice system they would not be in prison. They were locked up in St Patrick's for minor crime, many came from appalling backgrounds and possibly Shanganagh was like a palace to them. While the regime was strict, it was also beneficial for those boys. You either engaged with the boys, who were never referred to as prisoners, or you didn't. If you couldn't, there was no point in being there.

The day was interspersed with class for the boys along with various work practices. The VEC had provided a full complement of teachers, two nuns provided medical care, and there was a chaplain on site. A woodwork shop, an art classroom, and a shop where they created hobby work was provided for those not at class. The vast and manicured grounds had a quota of boys who assisted in their maintenance. In addition there was a one-acre glasshouse that provided the finest of tomatoes both for the prisons and the Dublin market. No boy was idle; no member of staff was idle. The governor, nicknamed 'Black Jack', ran a tight ship. Every member of staff was afraid of him. I pick the word 'afraid' carefully, for that's the correct word: his presence in the Castle or on its grounds had everyone on their toes and fear of a scolding was the motivating factor.

He wasn't a bully, and the farther I drift from my life as a warder, the more I reflect that he was a highly clever man who had the measure of a system that was as hard as jelly to nail. Jack nailed it. You either conformed to his way or you got out. Jack saw the Castle as his fiefdom. Working with the youth brought its own issues and dangers, so he kept it simple and straight. The boarding-school setup, where single staff lived in, was austere but it was not unfair. Reluctantly, I conformed: it was easier. The evenings saw the staff engage with the young lads in the gym, playing table tennis or other games such as snakes and ladders, or by helping one or two to read.

Initially, due to the strict regime, I hated the place. I missed Portlaoise and its black-and-white rules. Frequently I had a half sheet in my back pocket to transfer out but fear and a lack of guts kept it there. My duties were banal and simple to begin with, built around being there, working with the lads and doing mundane stuff.

As I said, initial duties revolved around shift work:

evening duties of 1 p.m. to 10 p.m., 2 p.m. to 10 p.m. and 4 p.m. to midnight. You got a single 8 a.m. to 5 p.m. day shift plus a split-shift night duty. After Mass on a Sunday the boys togged out for a football match. One team wore blue, the other red. An officer supervised the match. My duty often entailed patrolling the main avenue. This was to ensure that the boys didn't stray in that direction, that their visitors were supervised and that no intruders entered. Shanganagh was run on trust: no perimeter walls, no cells, no restriction on liberty. The boys gave their word to stay there.

I watched in frustration from the roadside as the boys played. They were generally left to their own devices: the officer arrived down, tossed the ball to them, timed an hour's match and sat on the sidelines, totally uninterested. I ached to sort them out. One Sunday, the officer who was to supervise football had an upset stomach. He swopped duties with me and down I went. I had them organised from the off. I sorted out positions, encouraged, berated and romped around the pitch, whistle in my hand. When the match was over the sense of satisfaction we all felt, the boys and myself, was enormous. I was in; now I had to convince my superiors (who tended to give you the direct opposite of what they thought it was you wanted).

But pretty soon I was Mr Football. It was a brilliant way to work with the boys. I would tog out and play a half with each team and manage to referee it straight down the middle. We had a good bunch of soccer players; all they needed was guidance and leadership. Years later, my endeavours on that pitch often defused a messy situation in the closed jails. For example, while I was in Arbour Hill, we got a new prisoner up from Mountjoy. His name was given to us in Irish – a frequent Mountjoy ruse when trying to shift a troublesome prisoner well known to the wider jail world. So when this young man made his way down the landing towards us, the prisoners and jailers were in trepidation. He was a well-known hard man, a guy who would have hated Arbour Hill's stock in trade (sex offenders). However, as I looked at him, I thought he looked familiar, despite a week-old stubble. No point in waiting for trouble, I thought, let's meet it head on. I walked towards him and engaged. 'Jesus, Mr C,' he said, 'I wouldn't have known you with the cap . . . fuck sake . . . big difference from the 'Ganagh and the football you did with us, huh?' That broke the ice: a potential trouble-maker had a familiar face to talk to, we had a way in and he settled.

A Leinster senior league team in the area called in from time to time to give the boys a game. Normally it was a hiding for our lads and a showboating event for the visitors. In time I had our team playing like a well-oiled machine. Next time, we were ready for them. I played with the boys as a centre half and got a gifted midfielder to captain us. I gave a little pep talk; stuff about pride, guts and ability was the gist of my spiel. Our opponents' manager reffed the game and if they thought that the usual result was awaiting collection, they were about to be shocked. As time finally ran out and the referee blew his whistle, we were leading 3–2. At last we had beaten a big team! The buzz in Shanganagh was electric for days.

By now I had graduated to being the groundsman (the work of a prison officer is wide and varied). It entailed mowing lawns, keeping the grounds spick and span and growing flowers, literally thousands, as border plants for all the prisons in the country. Part of Shanganagh's remit was to provide all the country's prisons with flowers and, when possible, vegetables too. I always had a solid crew with me. Work was mixed with banter, a break here, a cup of tea there and a smoke for those who puffed. As spring came and the Castle grounds blossomed, my hankering for a move subsided. I was making a difference.

I was asked to organise a sports day for the boys. That entailed everything: marking out the pitch with running lines, getting it mowed, grading the different boys regarding their ability and purchasing the medals and trophies. The idea was that after the sports day a Shanganagh selection would play the Department of Justice in a soccer match and the boys' presentation would be given afterwards by some worthy from St Stephen's Green. Suddenly there was massive interest in the sports and the soccer match. Amongst the staff were some accomplished GAA and soccer players. A number of days were set aside for the sports, culminating with an afternoon of finals. We had the high and long jump. We had hurdles, sprints and cross-country. We had brilliant fun. Finally came the big match. We picked the team, starting with six staff and five boys. We had five subs to pick from as well: three boys and two staff.

The DoJ boys arrived out and warmed up at one end of the pitch, near the governor's house. We wore an old but fine set of ex-Finn Harps jerseys and warmed up at the Bray end. All around the pitch on the concrete fences sat the young lads, resplendent in their grey Sunday slacks, neat shirts and new jumpers. They were almost unrecognisable when they were scrubbed up and away from the routine. You would be proud of them. They roared for us simply because we were the only ones they knew. Early on it was evident that the Department had a few tidy footballers but our team, particularly two of the young lads, were giving them a torrid time. The tackles started to fly in and the staff members on the team responded in kind. The young lads were reticent to get involved because of their status and the DoJ lads were taking advantage.

A ball broke between myself and one of their enforcers. It was one of those tackles that if you pulled out you would wind up doing more damage to yourself than your opponent. I ploughed through and my man hit the dust. As he got to his feet he ran past me and tried to nail me with a shoulder. Then he hissed what sounded like 'fucking turkey' at me. I laughed at him and that enraged him more, once again repeating 'fucking turkey'. They were on the run and at the end we hammered them 5–2. Funny, isn't it, what stays in your mind after so many years? That evening the trophies were presented to the young lads and Black Jack was in his pomp. Nicely lubricated with a post-match drink in his office, he sternly informed the DoJ head honcho that we would retain the trophy.

That night we went to the Shanganagh Inn for a pint with our employers. We went through the match kick by kick and I told one of my friends about the 'fucking turkey' incident. My pal burst out laughing. 'Cuffe, you plank! He didn't call you a turkey. He called you a *turnkey*.'

I was an innocent abroad. 'And what's the fucking difference?'

'A turnkey must be a Mayo turkey, bud, but a turnkey is also a warder, a screw . . . geddit?'

I was outraged. So that's what the Department of Justice Prison Section thought of us. The air turned frosty as the implication swept around the tables and finally reached an actual decent guy from the Department. He came to our table after bollocking his own guy, the one who let me have it. He had the grace to apologise but I never forgot the slight.

As time went by I tried to make myself indispensible. Most of the Shanganagh staff were men who excelled in dealing with people and youth, so it was always a challenge to make your mark. In time, I took a Physical Education course, I ran the glasshouse, I learned how to run a film projector: changing the reels and setting the entire show up. And of course I was the José Mourinho manager of Shanganagh Boys FC. One evening as a treat the boys were allowed to watch a film. They had a TV and a fine snooker hall but film night was a special treat. We set the hall up with rows of chairs; friends sat beside friends, and snacks and sweets were brought out.

That night will remain scorched in my heart forever. Unwittingly, I had tempted fate. I used up every favour those lads owed me. My good friend Mac and I set up the projector. 'What's the film, Mr C.?' a voice called out. I replied, '*Breakheart Pass.*' Then the first plank on my boat was ripped away. Another voice cried out, 'Ah jeez, Mr C. We saw that three months ago!' I looked at Mac and he nodded back up at me, starting to giggle. I recovered my composure. 'Well, not all the lads saw it and as this is the only film I've got then we will watch it.' Low growling and grumbling ensued.

Lights out, the room was lit only by the projector and

the barely audible whirr of the mechanism as it purred beside me. The grumpy mood subsided somewhat and the lads relaxed. As I watched Charles Bronson, Jill Ireland and that infernal damned train chug across the screen, I lined up the second of the three reels. 'Turn on the lights,' I called out and the recreation room lights flickered into life. I was too cool, too fast and probably trying to avoid another argument about the merits of *Breakheart Pass* because no sooner had the main lights been switched off than Mac whispered to me, 'Cuffe, that's the last reel, not the second one.'

Damned if I was going to admit I was wrong, fucked if I was going to change it. Like the politicians of the 2008 crash, I was in denial. Soon a whisper in the hall grew into a crescendo: 'You've the wrong reel on, Mr C.' I sat hoping the ground would swallow either them or me. Mac was in stitches. 'Sort that one out yourself, Mr Perfect.'

I stood up and warned them that I would run them all off to bed if they didn't shut up and if they had seen it before they were now going to see it again including the end before the middle! Shock of shocks: they all sat silent and watched the entire film. I felt like a shit. Once it was over, we did a roll call and took away any matches or lighters they had before they went to their dorms. I did apologise and they forgave me. Even at this remove that incident shows what a decent group those lads were. Not so lucky was Mr Pussy.

Every year the Castle had a concert. The boys would put on a sketch, and then the stage would be taken over by various singers, actors and players who gave freely of their time. One of the ACOs had a contact in the music business and each year he managed through this contact to get some of Ireland's finest and most famous singers and performers to do a stint. We looked forward to it. For Black Jack, the governor, this was an opportunity to show the Department how well the place was run. A plethora of minor Justice officials descended on the place, supposedly to watch the boys in action but in reality to eat and avail themselves of the free beer that Guinness always donated for the occasion. One of the groups to perform was the Guinness Choir, hence the allocation of free booze. As luck would have it, Alan Amsby, better known as the female impersonator Mr Pussy, was invited to regale the audience for the night.

Mr Pussy took to the stage amid yips and yells from the boys. Black Jack was still upstairs in his office; I assume treating the more important guests to some pre-show hospitality. Pussy was a novelty to start with, the boys blown away with a man dressed as a woman but pretty soon it was evident that his humour was going over their heads. Now a sense of morbid curiosity was starting to settle in. We, the handful of officers scattered amid the boys, gave knowing looks to each other: this wasn't going to end prettily. In fairness to Pussy, a pro, he battled on but the audience was by now lost. Black Jack arrived down with wife and pet dog Pips, one of those toy dogs, under his arm, and some of the visiting committee and Department officials in tow.

As the governor squeezed his way, dog and all, into the gallery seats, Mr Pussy asked 'Ah, Mr Governor, did I give you the correct change the other night?' Instantly, Jack switched Pips from one arm to the other and started to rummage in his pockets. His wife gave him a sharp elbow as we dissolved into silent laughter. We were all terrified of Jack and here he was, the butt of a joke he didn't get but now being served as the main course in comedy.

The two resident nuns started to give out. 'Disgraceful . . . outrageous,' they hissed. That made us worse. The boys were bemused but starting to pipe up as well. Laughter was breaking out everywhere but not at the jokes, more at the circumstances unfolding. The ACO who brought the performers to the Castle now started to blush, his countenance nearly matching the maroon shirt and tie he wore. I shoved my own tie into my mouth to stifle my guffaws. Pussy battled on gamely. By now he had one of the boys on stage and was attempting to play a game involving balloons. Pussy attempted to shove the balloons under the jumper of the participant. The young fella didn't want it and Jack leapt to his feet seeking out the ACO responsible. 'Get him off the stage!' Jack ordered in his monotone accent. 'Get him off now!'

Pussy exited stage left and the place was bedlam. Soon a folk singer took over and a calm of sorts descended as we wiped away the tears of mirth. The boys settled again and Pussy was ushered into the night air, never to return again. I felt for him and I hope it galvanised him for his future career, right man but wrong crowd and venue. We will chalk that one down to experience. I assumed, wrongly, that Jack would be spitting blood at the post-concert drinks. No, he was the epitome of calm, stroking Pips as he 'forgave' Pussy and the errant ACO. 'These things happen,' he intoned, as he looked for another bottle of 'that nice Guinness'. Behind Jack's ways was a warm old devil, maybe struggling to get out at times but when it did, it was nice.

Around 1980 or 1981, I was in the habit of going to the Baggot Inn to have a few pints and listen to the music, mainly midweek when there were enough staff remaining in the Castle at night. Amongst the musicians there were Donal Lunny, Christy Moore and Declan Sinnott, all legends. Three nights a week they met at what was originally known as Mugs' Gig. Anybody in the Trad genre could turn up there, even those beyond it like Freddie White, Jimmy MacCarthy and Don Baker. Mugs' Gig morphed into Moving Hearts. They were mind-blowingly brilliant. Whilst initially loving the music, pretty soon I was exposed to the Hearts' more overt take on all things political and contro-versial. They began attracting a huge following, many from Ulster. At the time the Provisional IRA in the Maze H-Blocks were on hunger strike. Here was I, a prison officer, long-haired because I worked in plain clothes in an open prison, now questioning my very deep beliefs and being forced to question society through the music on a regular basis.

As time passed in Shanganagh I became involved in the PE classes. It was a chance to be fit myself, get paid for it and to work closely with the boys. In the gym, on the football field and in the workshops, we saw a side of those boys that society might not have. They weren't afraid to give it everything and in doing so, with our help, barriers were broken down amid sweat and graft. They saw us as human, perhaps even as guys who understood them. We saw them as kids that, given a break, were no different from any other kids. Of course there were exceptions but hey, life is full of exceptions.

In tandem with the PE I was also responsible for the

acre-sized glasshouse. Taking charge of that area meant a sacrifice that I feel guilty about to this day. Previously my shifts rotated and I was entitled to one long weekend per month, but taking over the glasshouse meant working 8 a.m. to 5 p.m. five days per week with every second Saturday and Sunday also being worked as evening duties. Now I was recalled on my midweek rest days to ensure continuity in the glasshouse. The price I paid was not getting home as often as before to visit my mother on my long weekend.

The crew in the glasshouse, the boys sent down to me, were a varied lot, those not deemed suitable for work or classes in the Castle. It was left to myself or the groundsman to knock them into shape and be of use. My principle was a simple one: don't ask anyone to do something you're not prepared to do yourself. So I learned every job entailed in running a successful glasshouse that produced tomatoes. I rotavated, manured, tied a thousand lines to overhead wires so the tomato plants would climb up to 10 feet. I fixed and attached a thousand miniature water pipes to feed each individual plant. I twisted, carefully, each growing tomato plant as it climbed up the white string.

I reeked of tomatoes, the skin on my fingers developed a green layer – I actually became greenfingered – and my clothes took on a green hue, clothes being shorts and T-shirts. I installed a huge boom box in the middle of the glasshouse so that we had music and I built a team around me. Those kids could sow, pick, side shoot and talk to the tomato plants by the time I had finished with them. In addition they assembled cartons for the ripened tomatoes that we sent to the prisons and Dublin market on a daily basis during the summer months. What did that involve? Well, on a hot June day we could pick, pack and move out a ton of tomatoes. The tomatoes for the market had to be picked exactly right, not red, just off green with a hint of orange creeping in.

I valued my team. In return I ensured they got weekends out, a few smokes, a few bottles of orange or cola. If it was too hot we sat out the back taking in the sun. No one moaned about us because they knew we were answerable to actual market forces. If we didn't move the tomatoes on time, they ripened and burst on the trees. Having nurtured those bastards from birth in late March to blossom in early June, none of us was about to let them die or rot. Working in the glasshouse might have started as a demotion for those boys but always ended up as a promotion in terms of time out or time off. It was the least we could do for them.

One year a strike occurred in the job. Well, to call it a strike is a bit far-fetched, it was more a work-to-rule. Relations between the POA and Department were abysmal. I didn't much rate the POA, truth be told, a union more driven by impulse than tactics, it seemed to me, but I adopted my father's maxim: he said he would have had nothing but for the National Busmen's Union. Our work-to-rule entailed not asking the young fellas to sweep or clean the Castle. For me, though, it would impact quite hard: the boys would no longer be allowed to work in the grounds or glasshouse. My beautiful tomatoes were now ripening on the trees and I couldn't pick them, couldn't box them or get them to the market all by myself. That didn't stop various staff slipping down to take a few for family or friends, which annoyed me. The local union took a special interest in the glasshouse as it was the only viable thing that seemed to affect everyone.

The young lads dropped down to visit me and see how I was faring. Truth to tell, I was faring badly and I was angry. I tried to pick as many tomatoes as I could, getting them boxed and into a dark spot to slow the ripening process. It was a gargantuan task for one man but I persisted. And all because I cared about plants. My mother had green fingers and we had a huge garden at home. I worked hard to keep that garden a paradise. It was in my blood to assist growth, not kill it.

One day a delegation of local union guys arrived down to reproach me: my attempts to keep the show on the road were impeding the 'go slow'. I liked them all individually but as a group they were shit-stirrers. I simply told them to eff off; I'd pick the tomatoes until I could pick them no more. Later that afternoon, two of them reappeared looking for a poke of the red lads to take home.

The 'go slow' wound up as a strike eventually. The fallout was colossal, the union miscalculated and the Department won. A walkout in Mountjoy turned into a lockout. The union had to eat humble pie and in order to regain admittance we all had to sign a form stating that we would abide by any legal request from the governor or his agents. We had now become fully fledged serfs. We would work whatever hours they deemed necessary. The fight was deferred for a few years before another battle over working conditions would redefine our conditions. What we didn't know, though, until the 2015 release under the thirty-year rule on Government papers was that the

Department of Justice feared total anarchy in Mountjoy. It had been neglected too long and the system was smashed.

My mother passed away in September 1983. She was in Dublin for routine tests. She wasn't in great health but no one anticipated her demise. The Monday she arrived up to Jervis Street Hospital I had to work a fifteen-hour shift. The next day my sister visited her and asked me to come in on the Wednesday when she would have gone back to work. On the Tuesday evening I returned to the Castle around 9 p.m. where there was a phone message for me to go to Jervis Street. Our van was returning a young fella who had previously run away back to St Patrick's Institution so I hitched a lift to town with the staff. They told me they would collect me around 10.30 p.m. on the way home. I suspected nothing.

I asked at the desk where Mrs Cuffe was warded. St Anne's on the third floor, I was told. St Anne's was a good omen, Anne was her first name. Getting out of the lift I met a nurse. 'I'm looking for St Anne's ward, my mother, Mrs Cuffe, is a patient there'. The nurse replied, 'Oh, you're too late. Your mother died a half hour ago.'

Had you picked up a hammer and hit me in the forehead with full force, I would not have felt it, such was the shock I got. I followed the nurse into the cordoned-off bed area. My poor mam: her twenty-a-day affair with Mr Gold Flake had hardened her arteries and, in the end, the heart had given up. Her face was now free from pain, no wrinkles and pure white. She lay on the bed, arms folded and a rosary intertwined in her fingers. Her face was as cold as a marble slab as I stroked it. I thought of the times we'd had, the times we hadn't and the times, always, when she stood by me. Now it was over. I was on my own. I was crushed.

The Castle staff were good; they even came to the funeral in Mayo. For weeks afterwards I got cards and condolences. Still something major in my life had been stripped away. A young lad long since gone from Shanganagh must have seen a death notice somewhere because a letter was dropped into the Castle with a Mass card from him for me. It meant a lot. Other young inmates in the Castle sympathised with me. It made them feel that perhaps their mothers and fathers mattered in a way that they hadn't noticed before. I travelled west a good few times, to rekindle something I had lost.

What was I looking for? A connection, a vision, anything to explain her quick departure? The scent of her still filled the house. I drank it in. Her plants and flowers refused to die in sympathy and I watered and repositioned them every time I came home. The hospital had sent on her travel bag and when I opened it her perfume escaped once more, having permeated the towel, the nightdress, her little prayer book and notepad. That scent was the closest I could get to her and it unlocked a torrent of tears. Somehow or other I felt her presence. 'Continue on' was the message that filled the air.

Back in Shanganagh I applied for a promotion to the next step in the job. It was for the rank of Assistant Chief Officer, once deemed a managerial post but as time went on in the job it was redefined as 'supervisory'. I was always ambitious, not power for the sake of power but a step up because it was a logical step. That attitude wasn't always welcome in the prison service. ACOs were neither management nor the basic-grade officer. They trod a narrow path where one poor decision could haunt the remainder of one's career.

I was reluctant to go for interview. I had gone a year earlier and it left a sour taste in my mouth. It felt as if I was wasting my time and the interview board seemed preoccupied. A year later, at the last moment I was approached by a senior member of staff to put in an application. I did, figuring I had nothing to lose. John Lonergan, governor of Mountjoy, the deputy governor of Portlaoise and a Department official were on the three-person interview panel. I was confident but not arrogant. Lonergan asked, 'What if you have to discipline a staff member that you just worked on the floor with and he replies, "Who are you to tell me what to do?"' My reply ran along the lines of 'this is now and that was then', that I wouldn't be fazed once I was doing it for the right reasons: easy to say at an interview, though.

Sometime later the results came out. I was placed fourth out of a panel of twenty-eight. Four of us from Shanganagh were on the panel. Other lads who applied weren't so lucky and an air of celebration was mixed with disappointment. I was delighted and proud. My regret was, of course, that my mother wasn't there to share my good news. The panel was announced in June 1984 and the first three promotions were instantaneous. I was next. Part of me had now moved beyond Shanganagh. I wanted out and to get on with the next phase of my career. It was hard to concentrate on the glasshouse and the PE. It was hard to concentrate on anything.

That summer the chaplain invited a team of student

priests out to play the boys. In my five years in Shanganagh over the boys' team, we had never been beaten. I was determined that my 100 per cent record wasn't going to be snatched before my departure. We togged out, went down to the pitch and I went through a warm-up routine with the lads. As they kicked the ball around I eyed the opposition. You would be surprised what you can glean from body gestures and reactions. This was at a time before the dam-burst of clerical scandals, when the Holy Show, a group of singing, joking, dancing priests were selling out concerts around the country. Their stock had never been higher.

Our opponents were of the Father Trendy type: long hair and big attitude. One in particular, a fuzzy-haired guy, hand aloft continuously looking for the ball to be passed to him, reminded me of Uli Hoeness, from Bayern Munich and the West Germany World Cup winning team of 1974. One of our boys was the captain so he went for the toss-up. He extended a hand but their captain merely ran his fingers across the tips. The game kicked off with our captive support sitting on the concrete fencing around the pitch. They looked like vultures waiting for dinner or birds massed on telegraph poles. That's what I wanted.

Soon the challenges were flying in and it was my boys that were on the receiving end. The referee wasn't doing us any favours. I whispered to him that the boys wouldn't retaliate because they feared some form of sanction. I was wasting my breath because, next thing, one of our lads, a gifted footballer, was flattened. I moved up the pitch and picked him off the ground. As we took on water, I spoke to the tackler and pointed out the need to keep to the football.

'Hey buddy, it's a man's game. They shouldn't play it if they can't take it,' he replied, to smirks from his team mates.

My lads heard this, as did the vultures sitting on the fences and the watching officers. I had been challenged on my home patch. What was I going to do about it?

This time I didn't drop back to sweep: no, I played at the top of the midfield diamond. Even though I was thirty-two I was as fit as I'd ever been and had legs well tuned from hundreds of miles of running. Soon I was near the tackler when a ball broke between us. Possibly he had me marked for execution too but perhaps he didn't have the real killer instinct. I ploughed him into the ground with a sickening tackle, the ferocity of which shocked even me. As he screamed and held his leg, I caught him around the neck and snarled at him, 'Now, you prick, how do you like the man's game?' What snapped me out of my attack was the roar from the sideline vultures of 'Give it to him, Mr Cuffe! Give it to him!'

We were separated and I trekked back to centre back, angry but elated. I had stood up for us as much as myself. The knowing winks and nods from the team as I jogged back made my day. We ran out comfortable winners and the opposition simply melted away. Coming off the pitch I was surrounded by the young lads, they clapped my back and told me, 'You're fucking mad, Mr C. Fair play to you, though.' My colleagues thought me mad too and advised me to apologise. I swallowed my pride and went into the opponents' dressing room. I said all the right things and received a round of watery applause for it but I didn't actually mean a word. I had put them in their boxes and next time out they'd respect their opponents. After all, it's a man's game.

That was my testimonial match. I wanted out. The guard was changing and other lads were moving up the chain. Still the panel failed to move until the following February. Finally, in response to a joyriding crisis in Dublin, the then Minister for Justice, Michael Noonan, had Fort Mitchel in Cork Harbour taken over as a prison. Spike Island, the prison home of the patriot John Mitchel before he was transported to Australia, would now once more become a jail. This meant that staff were needed and the promotion conveyer belt would restart.

I was offered a choice of Spike Island, Mountjoy, St Pat's or the Training Unit. I opted for the Training Unit on the basis that it might be similar to Shanganagh due to the class of prisoner it accommodated. The Castle staff made a presentation to me, a clock and a pen. The governor said nice things to and about me, seeing this as the first of many promotions. I was delighted, revelling in the attention. I took a week's leave, bought myself some new shirts, shoes, trousers and ties. The Unit was a plain-clothes institution like Shanganagh. The next time I would return to duty it would be as a supervisor. That promotion, though, would prove to be my high-water mark.

4

Promotion Premonition

Do you want to know who you are? Don't ask. Act!
Action will delineate and define you.

THOMAS JEFFERSON (1743–1826)

Back in February 1985 they simply promoted you. They didn't prepare you, train you or advise you how to behave and react as a manager. As with basic training, there was no manual to turn to. One day you're a warder/officer, the next you have a stripe and you're a supervisor. Mentally, emotionally and physically, I would be tested. Weight fluctuations – moving from 11 stone to 17 stone and back – would now dominate the rest of my life. Healthy as an Indian guru for a while and then bingeing on junk. Life was changed forever. But was I ready for it?

Though the Training Unit was a closed jail, staff wore plain clothes. I topped off my new clothes with a Crombie coat that I bought in Moons in Galway. So desperate had I been to buy – you know that feeling when you must have something and you must have it now – I bought an overcoat that was at least two sizes too big for me. What was the real difference between a blue Crombie overcoat and wearing a blue jail uniform overcoat? None, when it was all boiled down.

This was the same Training Unit where I had done my Phase One training. I reported for duty feeling important. I was an ACO, the kind of guy that I had been in slight awe of when I joined the job five and half years earlier. I was somebody. The usual introductions, the usual trip around the workplace: 'This is Officer Blah . . . this is our new ACO Cuffe . . . hello . . . welcome . . . thanks . . . hope you're happy here.'

The first thing I noticed about the Training Unit was that it wasn't Shanganagh with its 30 acres of green space, old castle and high ceilings. The Unit was built like a rabbit warren, corridors like tunnels, low ceilings, institutional breeze block with cream-painted walls. Despite it being relatively new, already it had a tired, worn look about it. A good wash and a lick of paint might have sparked some life into it. I was shown around the place but not shown how to supervise or manage its staff. I was expected to hit the ground running, to make decisions and give answers. Most prison staff are aware that the new guy isn't an oracle so they cut him some slack but there are always one or two that will gently lob a pin-pulled grenade towards you.

The rooms in the Unit, not cells, resembled the rooms you would get in any modern low-budget motel. The prisoners put their own stamp on their abodes. Walls were covered in posters, pictures and slogans. The prisoners wore their own clothes and attended the various workshops in the Unit, which ranged from block laying, car mechanics, plumbing and electrical through to drama and music classes. Despite this, a large proportion of the prisoners seemed unemployed; certain areas seemed top heavy with idle inmates. The number of prisoners in the Unit was around 110 but the landings and room areas appeared to have too many cleaners. Despite this plethora of cleaners the place looked seedy. It also felt enclosed and claustrophobic to me. Once a superficial cleaning was done, those cleaners seemed to loiter around the passage-ways, watching and smoking. Unlike Shanganagh, this place seemed adrift and without focus.

My first role as an ACO was to count. Counting prisoners is the daily staple of prisons. Across our jails, our prisoners are counted umpteen times a day, from first thing in the morning to last thing at night, with counts during breakfast, dinner, tea and supper. The bottom line is that the numbers must tally. The Numbers Book is the road map of a jail. A glance tells you the inward and outward movement of the jail, as well as the internal movement, those who might be in a strip/padded cell, a cell for prisoners who self-harm or who may have attacked a staff member or another prisoner. The problem with counting at times is that prisoners constantly move as you try and tally, sometimes in a deliberate effort to confuse you.

The Training Unit was a nightmare for counting. Unlike most closed prisons, the prisoners all ate communally in a dining room for their meals. Lunchtime was particularly hard to count as guys went up to the serving counter for extras or were emptying their plates, etc. The officers would count with me and we would agree a tally but essentially I was the one that carried the can. One day I had tallied and assumed all correct. It was lashing rain outside and all the prisoners were indoors and accounted for. A loud banging on the fire escape doors caught my attention. It was two drenched prisoners looking to gain admittance. They had been playing squash or badminton on an external court but I had assumed all were inside . . . yikes!

Time taught me that the ability to supervise and manage was a learned experience. Most of the staff I encountered in the Training Unit were actually longer in the job than I was, which presented certain issues. A younger, cocky ACO telling old salts what to do tends to rub certain guys the wrong way. Also, the officers stationed in the Unit worked an unusual shift pattern. Its main thrust was aimed at maximum time on and counter-balanced with maximum time off for staff. So staff started work at 8 a.m. and finished around 10.30 p.m. Note I use the twelve-hour clock. Most services operate under the 24-hour clock, including my old lighthouse service. The Prison Service didn't give a toss about the 24-hour clock so staff didn't work until 22h30, they worked until 10.30 p.m. For accurate recording of events in services like the Garda Síochána, army and navy, they use the 24-hour clock. It is clearer and simpler.

The problem with that shift pattern was simple: there wasn't enough manpower to cover the rest days. So staff were then recalled to cover the days off. This resulted in most of the discipline troops working savage hours six and seven days a week. Shanganagh saw all officers on parade at 8 a.m., no late arrivals for duty and few or none on sick leave. In contrast, in the Unit a handful of guys perpetually arrived in between 8.30 and 10 a.m. Sick and uncertified ill days were common. The reason was simple: the daylights were worked out of the troops available.

The ACOs had a different work pattern. Just to be awkward, the CO worked 8 a.m. to 5 p.m. The ACOs were spread across 8 a.m. to 5 p.m. along with a 1 p.m. to 10 p.m. and a split-shift night duty from 8 a.m. to 1p.m. and resuming at 10 p.m. until the following morning at 8 a.m. For some reason, I seemed to pick up an inordinate amount of the 1 p.m. to 10 p.m. shifts. It was a rotten shift, the morning rendered useless because of the impending 1 p.m. start, the evening gone by the reason of such a late finish. My getting overloaded with this shift meant the staff saw me treated differently by management and perhaps a soft touch. It was easy to give out a shift like that to a newbie because a newbie might be reluctant to complain.

So my eating centred on nearby McDonald's, Big Macs, chips and a bucket of diet coke. My waistline expanded and soon I was a fat, pudgy-faced young man. While the staff in Shanganagh interacted with their charges, the disciplinary staff in the Unit, particularly on the landings, mostly hung out together once their prisoners went to work. This concerned me. I felt that their areas were not supervised carefully enough. My real fear, of course, was that I couldn't cover every eventuality and early on in the Unit I saw the place as being full of booby traps.

The Training Unit staff there weren't stupid. They were sharp and clever but they had become institutionalised and were working hours that were too long. Hence by stretching bodies over twelve-hour shifts five and six days a week a certain degree of laissez-faire had crept in. The warning lights I saw weren't registering with them. One morning on one of my rare day duties I spoke to an officer who was off his 'class' (prison terminology for a landing or unit of around twenty cells separate from other units or landings). It was an awkward moment. I said something along the lines of 'Really, shouldn't you be up on your own landing rather than down here on the ground floor?' His reply was, 'Well, if that's what you want, Mr Cuffe, I'll head back up there.' The chill in the air was palpable. When a colleague calls you 'Mr' and no prisoners around, it tends not to bode well.

Ten minutes later that officer knocked on my office door and handed me a written half sheet for the governor. It said: 'Sir, I wish to be relieved of my duties as class officer because Mr Cuffe apparently is unhappy with my ability to run the class.' You didn't need an abundance of intuition to get the message. As I read it, two things became very apparent. First, the warder was alerting me to his ability to put me in my place and secondly, the governor would be alerted to the fact that he had a troublesome supervisor in his jail. The outcome would be all the staff casting a wary eye on a guy who had notions.

I placed the half sheet on the desk in front of me. I asked the officer to come in and close the door. I told him that the half sheet would be in the governor's office in a few minutes but asked him if he was prepared to speak off the record. Sitting down, he nodded. I believe in truth and laying the cards on the table. So I told him of the way

Shanaganagh was run, how I felt the Unit was a notch away from a catastrophe; I told him of my own fears and, if the truth be known, my own inadequacy in my new role. Reaching across the table he took the sheet, tore it in four, dumped it in the bin and walked out after saying 'OK'. That was a close one and a lesson learned for me.

My first night duty was an eye-opener. At 10.30 p.m. the officer in charge of each landing locked the prisoners' room doors. The ACO then turned a master key on the same door. The usual: 'All right there . . . you ok for everything . . . goodnight' with the replies of 'Sound . . . yeah, all fine . . . goodnight' from the locked-up. Finally, we arrived at the last two rooms on a landing. No prisoners in them. The class officer explained to me that those two prisoners were working below in one of the training shops, a steel fabrication one. I hadn't been told about this and the officer knew I was perturbed. If in doubt, play it safe. Looking at me, he said, 'Well, John, I know it's unusual but that's the way this place operates. They know about it.' 'They' being management.

I firmed up and asked him to go down and return them to their rooms. He actually seemed relieved to do that. As we locked them up, I told the warder that I was simply covering myself and that a prisoner locked where he should be made all our jobs easier. He nodded in agreement. A few days later when I returned for my usual buzzkill evening shift, the conversation in the ACOs' office centred around the nocturnal habits of the Lesser Spotted Prisoner. Boiled down, the indirect message I was being sent was that the senior staff hadn't any great issues if a prisoner or two wanted to do a bit of extracurricular activity in the ample workshops. As long as they were all locked up around midnight, what harm was there? Like any coded message, it was broadly aimed and utterly open to interpretation.

To tell you the truth, I felt a bit of an eejit. My biggest fear was that the staff I worked with would see me as watery and a worrier, fretting about covering my back all the time. That is a fate worse than death and some supervisors carried it with them their entire careers. The troops don't like working with a fusser and don't feel confident with him around. Soon the prisoners get the vibe and then you're in a joyless place. That, in conjunction with my eternal 1 p.m. to 10 p.m. shifts, was taking its toll. I pined for Shanganagh and its ordered life. The seeming chaos of the Unit was now playing tricks with my mind: was I imagining bogeymen where none existed? Was I actually cut out for the role of supervisor?

One evening I drove back to Shanganagh, to touch base maybe, to recalibrate, to get the vibe back . . . I'm not sure why. I was welcomed like a prodigal son. The first thing that leaped out at me was how clean the place was and how quiet and mannered the young lads were: the atmosphere was good. Driving down the long avenue I enviously glanced across at the two sets of teams playing on 'my' football pitch. I knew there and then that I had made a bad mistake. The following day I was due on in the Unit at 1p.m. . . . . again. As I arrived at the main gate I was surprised to see it open and a big red fire truck narrowly squeeze itself out like escaping toothpaste. A fire drill, I assumed.

Inside the gate, I got the distinct odour of acrid smoke, the smell of burned plastic dampened and fused as water hit the blaze. The gate officer told me that a fire had occurred in one of the prisoners' recreation rooms. Arson, it seemed: tables and chairs deliberately set on fire on the very landing that I had expressed my concerns to the officer about. The very landing of which the officer requested that the governor relieve him of his duties. I went up to the landing and the stench of burned plastic was everywhere. The officer involved came towards me and muttered, 'You were right.' This wasn't an exercise in glory for me. It just confirmed to me what a dangerous place the Unit was. I told him that any one of us could have been caught out. I privately thanked God it didn't happen on my watch.

The Unit had a drug problem but it wasn't visible to me. Yes, I heard the rumours and staff were vigilant, once finding a cache of high-quality heroin in a ceiling. The trouble was that, although the place was closed, it was run almost as an open centre, except the inmates were not compliant kids. Many were hardened and wily serious offenders working the system.

By their very nature jails are small places: there are not many places to hide, nor many places to retreat to. Your countenance, feelings and moods are an open book to the alert watcher. And yet, in my thirty years, I never ceased to wonder how governors and senior staff managed to fly so low below the radar that we scarcely detected them as part of those very places.

Possibly it was an inherent institutional subliminal agreement. Governors would keep out of sight from the floor staff and, in return, floor staff were spared senior scrutiny. What the governor didn't see, the governor didn't have to worry about. This wasn't just in the Unit: it was in all my jails, with the exception of Portlaoise and Spike. Of course, it ensured that no *Brubaker*-style governor emerged, to inspire us with reforming zeal. And the governor can only run with the length of rope the Department cuts him. Hence, if he hasn't got the manpower and space and the end of the line beckons, what's to be obtained by kicking over the traces?

In the Unit visits were in small booth-like rooms. Trust was the key. The Unit was supposed to be for prisoners wishing to pursue a vocational trade but a burgeoning growth in crimes like joyriding and drugs was straining the system to the last. Prisoners considered most likely not to reoffend or deemed as non-risk were released early to make space for the intake. And places like Shelton Abbey, Loughan House, Shanganagh and the Training Unit now had to take in a calibre of prisoner for which they were simply not suited and which they would not have had to take in before. This created a revolving-door system, as prisoners saw that they could also misbehave, secure in the knowledge that jail space was at a premium and so docking them ten nights' recreation or a fortnight's remission was useless because overcrowding now changed the entire dynamic.

Walking past those visiting booths, it wouldn't have surprised me if a Panzer tank was passed over in small parts over a period of time. Drugs would have been no problem. A single officer trying to cover those visiting booths without the aid of a central surveillance system was as useful as a farmer minding mice at a crossroads. The Irish Prison Service was at boiling point but those in charge in the Department weren't at the ball game. Their match revolved around taking on what seemed to them a militant POA. Reform wasn't on the agenda. Judges, theoretically, could lock up 500 prisoners in a day, highly unlikely but not impossible. The prison governor, regardless of space, prisoner safety, staff safety and infrastructural support, was legally obliged to accept any prisoner delivered to his gate under warrant.

It seemed to me as if some of the governors themselves were in thrall to the Department. Many governors merely rubber-stamped rather than governed. Whose fault was that, you well may ask. It is my belief that the Department of Justice kept the governors on a tight leash, but those in the DoJ were not on the floor of the jail to see reality. Or perhaps governors were simply tired of telling the facts as they were and being ignored at the other end of the phone?

By now the Training Unit seriously spooked me. I was looking for a way out. Once more I was picking up an inordinate number of evening duties even though I had secured a promise that this would be rectified. And once more I turned up, unenthusiastic for my shift. On this particular evening, the place had a surreal feel, but this time it was not the scent of burned rubber and plastic. This time the scent was human and it smelled of panic and arse-covering. Two prisoners had absconded.

For all the fine talk and aspirations about rehabilitation, education and opportunity in jail, the escape or loss of a prisoner is a disaster: a disaster for the staff directly involved, their immediate supervisor, management and the rest of the staff. It's a bit like 'accidents happen', it's easy to say but we all know they don't. Accidents are caused through carelessness of some sort, not intentional, often inherited work practice and methods. There's also a belief that 'accidents happen to others, not me' and, strangely, prison staff have a capacity to separate out an incident that does not directly concern them. I couldn't. To me, this was a disaster.

The escape? Simple, really. Remember the two guys who were out of their rooms on my first night duty? How I sent for them and locked them up, how a few days later the general talk in the staff room was along the lines of, 'Hey, those guys are basically doing us a service, no need for overkill'? Well, the two prisoners were allowed out again, obviously on nights 'Nervous John' wasn't on. On this particular night, the staff worked away as normal. The ACO in charge possibly had a cup of tea with the two officers, small talk exchanged and sometime after midnight someone would say, 'Time to return the two lads to their rooms.' Off the officers would go to the fabrication shop, whistling or singing, their 'time to finish up, lads' greeted by silence. No need to panic: they've probably gone back to their rooms by themselves.

The trip up the stairs, the mind not yet engaging with reality, the two room doors open, now a slight stir, a mild wobble in the tummy. 'Best have a look in the jacks or showers,' one officer might say to the other. Doors of toilets and showers opened. The sounds of a dripping tap and filling cistern signal no one there, back to the room, down the stairs, possibly met by the ACO. 'Well?' says the ACO. The officer holds the arms apart, 'No one upstairs in the rooms.' Now nausea replaces the butterflies in the tummy. Back down to the workshop again. Silence but now someone perhaps spots a fire exit door slightly ajar. A trip outside reveals nothing.

The entire Unit is quickly scoured but the truth is already dawning in the minds of the staff. Their prisoners are gone.

Later on, in daylight, a search outside the Mountjoy walls along the bank of the Royal Canal found a full-length fabricated tubular ladder with a curved top designed to fit the sloped jail wall. The prisoners had been making plans for an escape for ages. They had also been making a ladder and no one had noticed. Now the three night-duty staff found themselves in a harsh and unforgiving spotlight. Sloppy perception and basic housekeeping duties had allowed the situation to develop into the catastrophe. Everyone, including me, felt for the troops. Everyone, including me, thanked whatever god they believed in that they weren't on duty that night.

Once more the tearoom talk in the supervisors' office was about the incident. This time, however, certain voices were of the opinion that they were unaware of this practice, and that the governor too was certainly unaware of the practice. Already the drawbridges were being raised. Young and green as I was, I remarked that the last time we spoke about the escaped pair of prisoners, the feeling I took from the conversation was that the senior staff *were* aware of the Corinthian and valiant attempts those prisoners were making in order to further their vocational ability. If there was going to be a hanging then there was going to be a defence. Easily I could have been on that scaffold and let through the trapdoor. If management was on the ball NO prisoner would be out of cell after lock-up time. This was a systems failure across the board, not simply the three scapegoats on that particular night.

Around this time I rang Assistant Governor Mannix in Shanganagh. A big fine man, I recalled him outside Mountjoy once looking every inch the leader in his Chief Officer three-bar uniform. An ACO wears a single gold bar on his shoulder to signify his rank, a chief wears two, but places like Mountjoy, Portlaoise and Castlerea had chiefs who wore three bars. Personally I believed it to be a superficial rank that simply put another layer of insulation between a governor and his charges. That said, however, if such a rank existed then Mannix was the poster boy for it.

In Shanganagh he was assistant governor, having arrived in the early 1980s. A warm and engaging man, he gave me great confidence and I was proud to be in his circle. My father had died when I was twenty-one and despite having a mother who had the guts of ten men, I missed having an older man to talk to, to guide and advise me. Mannix, in a way, was a substitute father. He quickly figured out my problem. And as quickly he didn't sugarcoat the solution. 'There will be no vacancy here in Shanganagh, old son, for at least two years and my advice to you is simple: get out of that kip. Go anywhere, go to Spike Island if you have to, but that place will be the finish of you if you stay.'

My own thoughts exactly. That evening I rang Spike Island and spoke to an ACO colleague there. He wanted out and if I moved down it meant he was free to return to Dublin. I didn't tell him about the Unit and he didn't tell me about Spike. Both of us were using each other to sort a problem. I submitted a transfer request; one of the Unit governors spoke to me and expressed a disappointment at me leaving. I lied about needing space and being unable to get used to the enclosed buildings of the Unit. Well, it wasn't really a lie: it was part of the reason I wanted out, but the main reason was that my bottle was gone; I didn't trust the Unit and feared more shit hitting the fan. I operated best under clear rules and instructions. Those were absent there.

To push my transfer I also rang a senior officer in Spike. We had worked together in Shanganagh and had got on well. I knew he rated me and I rated him. He told me that my transfer would come through almost immediately and that he was looking forward to seeing me.

Word went around of my impending departure. The Unit staff had never really taken to me, nor I to them. Years later, I would recognise them as top-class, but poorly led. They possibly saw me as a brash buck with the minimum service in charge of them at the coalface. At the time I saw them as possibly incompetent, and not aware of the mayhem that surrounded them. Where they saw normality, I saw trouble. Both of us were partially correct. In later years and with confidence I would have been a better asset. In later years I did work with many of those troops in other jails and we worked really well together. Once away from the Unit and on a different team we got the best out of each other.

Typical of prison staff, they threw a going-away party for a pair of other lads who were transferring out as well. I was included in the presentation and night out. I felt like a thief. I didn't merit a farewell do and I was embarrassed.

I finished my last day in the Unit and that afternoon collected a full uniform from Mountjoy stores for my forthcoming trip to Spike. In my room I tried out the new uniform. The last time I'd worn a uniform was back in 1978. The same pig of a greatcoat, black and made of bull's wool and weighing a ton. I cut the stripes off it, the gold harps that were on the sleeve, and stuffed them under a bed, never to be used again. The tunic was like what the guys in *Porridge* wore, a throwback to the 1920s. The officers wore a belted tunic, and the ACO wore a cross between a shortened soutane and an undertaker's jacket.

Still, it has to be said, with my head of curly hair, big moustache and eyebrows, I was a passable Tom Selleck of *Magnum PI* fame. I never turned up for the farewell do. I didn't think I'd be missed. However, about a year later at a nightclub in Dublin, a Unit officer accosted me and gave me both barrels: my rudeness for not turning up wasn't forgotten and my badmouthing the Unit to others on my departure was also noted. I had to plead guilty on both counts but apologised, and truthfully I wasn't berating staff *per se*, but a chaotic system where we were all victims. It didn't cut mustard that night. (Twenty-five years later it did: we discussed those pitiful days in the neutral territory of Castlerea and he conceded I was right after all but still a bollox for failing to turn up for the farewell do.)

I packed my life's possessions into the boot of my car. In went a cardboard box full of football trophies and medals, books, notebooks, old school play scripts and programmes, my plain clothes and uniform. Heading down the Naas Road on a beautiful May morning, I reminisced on my years in the job. Starting in black-and-white Portlaoise, then

Shanganagh from 1979 until February 1985. Now inside five months I was heading to my fourth institution. This wasn't good. It was too much movement, too unsettling. 'Be careful what you wish for' goes the Chinese proverb 'lest you get it.' I had wanted to be promoted. Now that I was, I was taking in water. This wasn't how it was supposed to be, but as I drove southwards the clouds lifted as the sun lit up the impending summer and the buds blossomed on the trees.

Nearing Cobh I recalled a conversation my mother had with me as a child. She told me that the biggest mistake she ever made was to leave Dublin. She was a native Irish speaker who first spoke English at nineteen and who came from Gweedore, Donegal. I'd assumed her wish was to get back to her native home. But no, it was the leaving of Dublin that troubled her. I recalled her wistful look as she spoke about the Gaeltarra headquarters on Westland Row, O'Connell Street and the dances with Misses Barrett, Butler and McGee, and Paddy McGowan: the craic and camaraderie of the lost 1940s. Did I detect a loss in the romantic sense, a decision made in haste and forever regretted as she moved to Galway and Connemara initially, before meeting my father and settling in quiet Blacksod?

Driving down the hill into Cobh, I spotted Spike Island nestling in the middle of Cork Harbour. It looked like a John Hinde picture postcard. As a former lighthouse keeper, a man who was raised a kick out from the ocean, this was more to my liking. I banished my mother's words from my mind: Dublin, for me, was in the past, and this was the future. Carefully I nudged the car into an empty space and got out. My new black jailer's shoes hurt; the leather around the ankle seemed to have been cut from a rhino. Still, the tang of the salt on the air was good. The next stage of my career was about to unfold.

5

Spiked

You'll never find out about yourself working in some
fucking factory in Ohio.

CAPT. BENJAMIN L. WILLARD, *Apocalypse Now*
(dir. Francis Ford Coppola, 1979)

In Ireland we do things differently, politically, institution-ally and economically. We often reach out for a blanket called 'An Irish solution to an Irish problem' as first suggested by Charlie Haughey in relation to the Health (Family Planning) Bill in the late 1970s. Recently it manifested itself by means of the 2008 bank guarantee bailout, which guaranteed one thing: you and your children will be paying for it until you pass on to the great bailout in the sky.

Spike Island, also known as Fort Mitchel, was an Irish solution to an Irish problem. To be more specific, Spike came into being as a solution to a particularly Dublin problem. Joyriding, a rather cute name for car thefts by disaffected youths, was becoming a blight on the city and a danger to the populace, with crashes, hit and runs, kids themselves being killed in pile-ups. Something had to be done, they said. Demands for it to be stopped were a daily staple in the media. No one looked at the underlying causes, the deprivation, the falling attendances at schools and the lack of meaningful work.

Michael Noonan, the then Fine Gael Minister for Justice, had ridden into town and 'saved' the nation from Garda excesses in encroaching on civil liberties. The previous Fianna Fáil administration had engaged in tapping the phones of journalists, amongst others. Paranoia was rampant and Noonan made capital. I have to admit that I was initially beguiled by him, his methods and his concern for the nation. Fine Gael was always the Law and Order party and gave short shrift to any mollycoddling of miscreants. Paddy Donegan, a former Minister of Defence, had seen the fall of a president over his intemperate remarks (when he called President Ó Dálaigh a 'thundering disgrace' for referring a contentious piece of legislation to the Supreme Court rather than rubber-stamping it for the government). Fine Gael's dealings with the Provisional IRA threat in the mid-1970s were steel-tempered and Portlaoise prison was on the front line.

Noonan clashed with the POA, and it's fair to say he gave them a bloody nose. His remarks about striking staff as they broke off from the dispute to aid a riot-engulfed Mountjoy would not be forgotten by the troops, nor by me. By 1985 the Irish prison system was in chaos. It limped along, with overcrowding, poor equipment and demoralised staff. Of course, as a staff member working within it at the time, my view and education didn't extend to an overall appraisal of the service, and so, along with my colleagues, I just accepted my lot. What we didn't know until the release of government papers under the thirty-year rule was that the Department itself feared the entire system caving in over Mountjoy. Judge Michael Reilly, Inspector of Prisons, recently noted that it was run by a small, select group within that Department. That report confirms what many staff assumed over the years anyway.

Spike Island was created to make space in the prisons, alleviate the revolving-door syndrome that more than anything else undermined jails. Staff knew prisoners could now not be kept to discipline if they knew that very system was failing in its basic tenet, the ability to keep them locked in. However, instead of the joyriders or older compliant prisoners being sent to Spike, the jail got some of the biggest troublemakers within the system. Governors and Chief Officers across the nation took advantage of clearing out the 'troublesome lags' that polluted their jails. So Spike wound up with a ragbag assortment of miscreants and thugs.

Initially the numbers were low, the regime was relaxed and the outlook good. I arrived in May, two months after the island had opened up, and I wasn't prepared for what awaited me. Around midday on my arrival in Cobh I crossed to the small pier and boarded the ferry to the island. On board was an officer to whom I introduced myself. On arrival at the pier on Spike, after passing Haulbowline naval base, we were taken up to the prison in an old, battered blue Landover left behind by the navy. A deep overgrown moat encircled Spike; its main gates looked old but imposing. Once inside the main gate I gave my name and crossed the enormous marching and parade square.

The sun shone and for a moment I felt transported back to the British Raj in India. Those massive barracks, the huge square, the high walls with their powerful gun emplacements, were a reminder how Britannia ruled the world. My leather-soled shoes were no match for the asphalt-covered square. The young prison officer (they were all young) brought me over to the CO's office. He was expecting me, a small, swarthy man. He looked very fit and was full of energy. Quickly it was evident that there was one show in town and he was the ringmaster. 'You tell me what happens, I tell the governor if he needs to know and that's that . . . ok?' was his opening line after shaking my hand.

I nodded. In my twenty-five years as a supervisor/senior officer only once did a governor sit either me or my peers down to outline his vision, praise or reprimand us. Generally, governors didn't want to know, except for a handful of exceptions. They didn't 'do' micromanagement meetings and left the running and 'dirty work' to their chiefs.

We walked around the inner walls of the fort. It was imposing, if tired and worn out. The government had put nothing into it since the British had left. Sailors lived in dorms that had open fires. Toilets were outside and were basic, smelly and cracked. The bottom line on Spike was this: what the sailors and navy had endured would not be offered to prisoners.

Surrounding the huge square were four barracks. One had been burned out during the Civil War by republican prisoners. One was now in use for the current prisoners, one was the administration block and the last was used for staff accommodation and canteen. To the front were solid bunkers that had once stored ammunition and ordnance.

The staff were mainly young recruits, with a few older troops who, like myself, were trying to reboot their careers in a different environment. Spike certainly was that: a very different environment.

Interestingly, my arrival on Spike saw me jump from bottom-of-the-pile supervisor in the Training Unit to second in seniority amongst the Spike ACOs. The CO left me to wander around for myself. I crossed to where the dormitory was, passing groups of work parties. A concrete set of stairs led to the dorms within the old barracks. The officer in charge of one of the dorms welcomed me on board and gave me a guided tour. The block was broken into four occupied dorms with about fifteen prisoners in each dorm, sparsely furnished with a bed, a simple locker and a few chairs for each inmate. The doors of the dorms resembled the type of door you might have on your garden shed: you could drive it in with your shoulder; you might even put your fist through it. A circular hole was cut out for observation and a cheap padlock kept it secured when we locked up for the night.

The mix of prisoners was not good. They ranged from a few heavies doing life for serious offences like murder to spaced-out drug addicts and prisoners more suited to a psychiatric setting. In their midst were the usual number of 'good guys', prisoners who accepted their lot and just wanted to do their time, pay the debt to society and get out in one piece again. Unlike other 'closed' prisons, the inmates on Spike ate communally in a kitchen-cum-dining hall in the administration building. Spike was set up to fail, but I was too green to see the early signs of mayhem.

That evening I went to a local hotel where staff hung out. Prison staff quickly accept newcomers unless and until they prove they should not belong to the flock. Being an ACO, a supervisor, meant that you walked a tighter rope than the rest of the troops. You were neither fish nor fowl, not a 'manager' but also removed from the basic officer. In time I learned how to walk that tightrope, but not without a few tumbles. The people of Cobh, the ones I met, more or less accepted us. The mid 1980s were glum and Cobh had lost its late nineteenth/early twentieth-century grandeur. Anything that brought a few bob into a once-booming town was to be welcomed.

The town had a history of naval service and many of its occupants served in Haulbowline. They wore their uniforms with pride and, initially at least, viewed us with suspicion. We were also uniformed but not as proud of our cheap serge outfits. We were, however, paid substantially more than the average naval sailor. In time they simply did what they always did and we respected their status. We weren't there to take anything from them; we were there to provide a suitable and safe jail. Boiled down, even though we were all fruit, the prison service was a pineapple to the naval apple.

Cobh more or less closed down around 6 p.m., apart from the hotels and pubs. I missed being able to buy the *Herald* or *Evening Press*. In a way the early experience brought me back to my lighthouse days, except this time instead of tending that great beam that loomed across the oceans, I tended humans. Spike was full of work parties. One group was employed in renovating more dormitories; another, 'armed' with slash hooks, scythes and rakes, cleaned out the overgrown moat. Other groups, with sledge-hammers, jimmy bars, spades and shovels, were engaged in removing galvanised Nissen sheds that spread across the once great square. A massive coal bunker stood to one side and the area that once held John Mitchel, the great patriot and after whom the fort was renamed, was now a shower facility.

As I settled in, the numbers correspondingly grew. So did the trouble and incidents. Over a very short time, much happened. We had escapes, breakouts and damage done inside the dorms. Initially, we recaptured those who broke out. The island was a kind of Alcatraz and my seafaring background made me appreciative of the swift currents that separated Spike from the mainland. Apart from sharing a house with some colleagues on the mainland, I also had a room on the island. It was spartan, white-washed and cold, with a locker and a mattress on the floor. If I worked a late shift I overnighted in that room; other lads did the same.

One night I was roused from bed when there was another breakout. This time, though, four of the prisoners made it off the island despite us being on the scene quickly. Next day we collected a pair of them from the Gardaí in Ringaskiddy. It was embarrassing, but the numbers kept climbing as more prisoners were committed to Spike Island jail. Politically, the revolving door had to be seen to stop even though Spike Island was not a secure prison. Now a new problem was being created, a powder keg was being packed and the fuse just awaited a match. The night of the European Cup final in Brussels' Heysel Stadium between Liverpool and Juventus of Italy more or less encapsulated the descending gloom and danger also settling over Spike. In Brussels, large numbers of troublemakers mixed in with fans who just wanted to see the match. The 1985 Heysel disaster saw the deaths of thirty-nine people, with 600 injured. As the bodies were piled up at the side of the stadium, and as the match progressed even though death stank in the air, I knew we were living in a changing and dangerous world. Spike was on a different scale but also explosive. It took Hillsborough in 1989 and wrongly maligned Liverpool followers before the British government made their football stadiums safe and meant for football, not war. Prisons needed the same inclusive government response to put them on a proper footing.

As time passed we were in emergency mode most of the time, reacting rather than being proactive. We were finding lots of hacksaw blades left behind from the previous occupants. The Mitchel Block where cleaning equipment was also kept became a brewing house for home brew called 'hooch'. This was the prisoners' concoction of apples, fruit, yeast from squeezed white bread and God knows what else. Once consumed by already half-mad inmates, the sky was the limit as inhibitions were discarded. We stamped that out as soon as we detected it.

Another issue then raised its head. Having been 'protected' from reality in Shanganagh I was shocked to see the amount of medication that the prisoners on Spike were on. Valium, sleeping tablets and other pills were dispensed in a nightly ritual as we settled the prisoners down and locked the henhouse doors on the dorms. Spike's inaccessibility meant that we hadn't access to the doctors and infrastructural medical care that Mountjoy had, for example, with the Mater Hospital nearby. We were an ocean apart from medical support.

On night duty once we encountered a prisoner who was unable to sleep because he needed a sleeper. On checking the medical book I found out that he wasn't prescribed any medication. This was like talking to a child who wanted an ice cream on a sunny day and wanted it now! He moaned and whinged to such an extent that he was now waking other prisoners and using up too much of our time. The officer in charge of the dorm looked at me. As we walked back to our basic surgery he said, 'Why not give the fucker a sleeper, John? Otherwise he'll break our hearts all night long.' My own thoughts exactly except, generally speaking, I was one of those guys who tried to keep between the red and blue lines on the copybook. Passing the kitchen area, I paused for a second. I picked at a piece of whitewash that bubbled from the wall. My days as a child in Blacksod where Ted, our light keeper, gave us barrows of sludge to whitewash the village houses, and my time as a light keeper where I once whitewashed the tower on Inis Tiaracht with nothing but a piece of rope tied to my waist as the raging Atlantic rumbled 300 feet below, had taught me one thing: whitewash and lime won't kill you. I had got it in my eyes over the years, swallowed it as the wind lifted it from my paintbrush and spat it out again.

'Yes, this will do,' I said out loud. Taking the flake inside the surgery with me, I sourced a small brown dispensing pot. Crushing the flake of whitewash and filling the pot with warm water, I shook the daylights out of it. Then I made a beeline for the dorm, officer in tow.

'Here you are,' I said. 'I shouldn't be giving you this, I'm not covered and you're not on the doctor's list. Swallow it down . . . quickly.' He gulped down from the brown plastic pot, turned over and slept like a king.

The other aspect of Spike was that newly arrived officers, new recruits who had no training whatsoever, were now landing on the island to be trained by us. Some stepped off the train in Cobh, lugged their suitcases across and were kitted out in new uniform that afternoon on the island. A pair of instructors arrived down from Dublin and I was more or less seconded to them as Liaison ACO with the brief to bring both the instructors and the new recruits up to speed with Spike's rather special systems. I still shudder in horror at the thought of those young men thrown in at the deep end, untrained and ill equipped. It was utter madness. In addition we were given lads who were awaiting a call to Templemore to join the Gardaí. I smiled as I recalled Portlaoise and the Garda whinge, 'If I wanted to work in a jail I would have joined the prison service.' They became known as 'mules': neither a Garda nor a prison officer.

About twelve to fourteen officers from Loughan House, an Open Centre on the Cavan/Fermanagh border, were also seconded to us. They were great guys: a gang of pirates glad to be away from home on full subsistence and travel allowance for a number of months.

One night we had a serious incident. A group of prisoners barricaded the dorm, seemingly full of hooch, tied other prisoners to the beds and generally created mayhem. Our instinct and first call of duty was simple: prevent an escape. This was a different challenge, though: those guys were about to go on a rampage.

I phoned the mainland and Cobh for any available officers to cross over. Some senior management also arrived after I apprised them of the facts. Eventually we settled the place down and the danger abated. I kept my duty journal and report book up to date regarding the facts and occurrences. Next morning as the sun rose I issued the keys to the staff for unlocking and then collected the report books from them. On looking through the journal from the troubled area, I noted that there was no mention of the previous night's mayhem. It had been logged as a normal night.

Some days later I was driving to Dublin for a weekend away. The POA Union's annual conference was on, in Kilkenny, I think. As I drove through the countryside the news on the radio nearly made me drive off the road. In a report from the conference, the journalist referred to a statement made by the Spike union delegation and mentioned the latest incident from the night I was in charge when we'd come close to big trouble. What they said was more or less the facts; the problem, though, was that the journals on the night didn't reflect those events, apart from mine.

On returning to Spike, I discovered that all the journals had been taken away for examination. I already had written a report concerning those nights' events anyway. The Department of Justice had been embarrassed and were looking for blood. One officer in particular whose version of events to the assembled troops didn't match the version he wrote up in his journal came under scrutiny from the annual conference.

I suggested to senior management that statements be taken from all concerned to put the mess to bed once and for all, but this didn't occur. Now I was on a collision course with that officer, even though my report vindicated him, while his own report had put him in a pickle. Around this time events moved quicker than ever. The Loughan House group were sent on to Mountjoy because the Dublin jail was experiencing its own troubles. A meeting had been called on Spike where the POA, the Department of Justice, the local POA and the governors would sit around the table. The governor had requested my presence.

Before the meeting the POA top brass had walked around the area and were not impressed with what they saw. I watched the various factions as they sat around the table, and instead of a group wishing to see a solution to a problem of mutual interest, saw that each faction was protecting its own version of events and status. Spike was broken and this was the time and place for straight talking, not for settling scores. The POA, I have to say (and I was never an adherent of theirs), were the most realistic at that meeting. A POA official stated to a Department official that Spike was not going to become the new Training Unit.

My ears pricked up. A union man said that everyone knew the Unit was seen as the heroin capital of Dublin and that the Department bore a major responsibility for that. The Department people nearly blew a gasket. I had been there a few months previously and the whole drugs issue had gone over my head. Did anybody in the prison service at the higher level actually talk to their staff or even amongst themselves? We had denial then from the Department but little actual contribution as to how to sort Spike's issues. One of the Justice officials was writing copious notes even though they weren't saying a huge amount. 'They're very interested in this argument,' I thought.

A knock to the door stopped the conversation. My boss nodded to me to check it out. As I squeezed past the Justice note writer, I sneaked a sly peek at what was being written: the sheet was full of doodles.

Nothing was resolved at that meeting. Nothing could be unless all were big enough to simply rip up the plan and start again. Little did we know that afternoon, but soon enough the plan would be ripped up: not as we might have envisaged, though.

Amongst some of the bric-à-brac dumped out to us on the island was a box of small blue-covered bibles. I brought it to the dorms and asked the officers to issue the bibles to whoever wanted them. I tucked one into my left-hand top shirt pocket. The right-hand pocket held my work diary. Occasionally I took out the little bible and read passages. I was looking for messages that this hell would soon end.

As time passed on Spike, the bible took on a different function. That little blue book was to serve as a small but effective cover over my heart, a vital organ. I realised then that if 'war' broke out amongst the prisoners and we were to intervene, some of those guys didn't care how or where they might hit you. From that day in 1985 until I retired in August 2007 I carried that bible in my breast pocket, more for physical than for spiritual protection. I hadn't known the meaning of stress before, but now it was kicking in. I was putting on weight, eating rubbish and no longer exercising. The truth was we hadn't the time or the energy for a normal life. Arrive ashore from a twelve-hour shift, sink a few pints, buy a takeaway, wake the next morning, trudge to the boat, climb the hill to the jail and remount the treadmill after a handful of aspirin for the hangover.

'Fuck this,' I thought. I hadn't signed up to a life of misery. I'm as loyal as the next guy – in fact I took my job very seriously – but it didn't take a rocket scientist to figure that Spike was going to get much worse and, like a runaway train, no one was prepared to put on the brakes. The then acting governor was a colleague of mine from Shanganagh and we had a great working relationship. His problem was that he was prepared to go the extra mile for the Department. He had the backing and belief of the troops, including myself, but the Department were acting the bollocks by permitting totally unsuitable prisoners to be transferred to us, and also not providing him and us with a safe jail or enough manpower and equipment. In essence they had a good guy in situ but weren't prepared to back him properly.

I told him I wanted out. Even though I had been around a short time, it felt like years, such was the mess Spike was. I hadn't the heart to tell him the real reason lest he take it personally. So I lied, I told him I had a girlfriend that wanted me back and she wasn't prepared to move south. We agreed that the half sheet for the transfer would be submitted and I agreed to remain until the autumn. In the meantime our numbers had risen inordinately. We had close to 120 prisoners without the infrastructure for them. No worthwhile schooling, gym, welfare or medical backup.

Trips to the island naturally entailed a boat journey. Simple things became problematic. Trips to courts, hospitals or other escorts were timetabled to the boat. We didn't control the boat, so anyone could arrive on the island. It was a joke: we had tourists and chancers coming across to look at Ireland's Alcatraz, as the press had titled the place. If they knew that it was more kindergarten than concrete and iron perhaps they'd have used less fancy language.

Towards the end of August, so much seemed to have happened. The Air India disaster impacted on Cobh as the navy retrieved bodies and debris from the Atlantic. Barry McGuigan had beaten Eusebio Pedroza in Loftus Road as we cheered him on from a pub in Cobh. I had taken to the road and lost three stone, gone off the drink and junk food.

There was almost an acceptance that we had hit a glass ceiling. We were where we were. Many of the staff were like me, happy to do the work but also happy to get off the carousel when their number was called. At this stage our young staff had become quite good and were in tune with the peccadillos of Spike. Also we had a great group of young ACOs. I have to confess here: even though I was the number two ACO, the guys behind me – Sully, Pencil and Red Eddy – were top class. All had served in the Joy and all had been well tested in a 'real' jail. So even though they were young as ACOs, they were assets to Spike and the young staff they oversaw. Bluntly put, they were better than me for those very reasons.

Towards the end of August, on an unremarkable evening, I was the duty ACO on the late shift. At 10 p.m., I went ashore and all was well. Young Sully was taking over from me and a safer pair of hands didn't exist. I went for a Lucozade: I was determined that the weight shed would stay shed. I went back to the house we shared, and as I was to be up early in the morning I went to bed. I always went to sleep with the radio on, listening to one of the Cork pirate radio stations. Soon I was out for the count. I woke around three or four: I must have been dreaming, I thought. In my sleep I had imagined that the jail was on fire, that the army had been summoned, that extra staff were being rounded up.

I went back to sleep as Phil Collins soothed me with 'Mama'. 'Fucking Spike,' I thought, 'it's invading my dreams now.' I awoke around 6 a.m., and the news came on. 'More Gardaí and army personnel are being drafted in as prison officers try to contain what's left of Spike Island. Fires have raged on the island all night . . . ' I flew out of the bed. 'Fucking hell!' I thought 'I wasn't dreaming . . . O Christ . . . fuck it . . . fuck it . . . fuck it!' as I pulled on my shirt, tied my shoes, buckled my trousers and looked for my car keys in the same panicked moment. I tore into the town; the horizon over the Cobh of Cork was glowing red, like a scene from *Apocalypse Now*. Coming down the hill I espied abandoned Garda vans, cars and army trucks along with police motorbikes. This was a living nightmare. I felt shit: the lads had been out there and I in my bed.

Spike resembled a battle site. Rocks, stones, smashed timber, broken glass and debris were strewn everywhere. It turned out that the staff had prevented the prisoners from leaving the island via the incoming reinforcement boats earlier that night. Climbing the hill with some urgency, I spotted the red Moog van we used to deliver stuff around the jail. Its windows were smashed, its doors pockmarked as if it had been used as a battering ram. A dumper, now abandoned, had been driven through the gate with the oak-panelled doors; the doors were hanging limply.

As I picked my way through the wreckage I had a panoramic overall view of the inner Spike. To my right was the old, already burned-out barracks. Ahead was the barracks that had until the previous night housed the bulk of the prisoners. Now it was a smoking shell with the odd flicker of flame licking the windows. The upper floor had collapsed onto the ground floor and contained a mass of mangled steel beds and lockers. Across from it was the smashed general office and the looted kitchen, its butcher's knives and victualling equipment stolen. The governor's office had been burned along with the prisoners' files and warrants. The surgery had been looted and its stock of Valium, sleepers and medication distributed amongst the baying mob.

As I walked and tried to take it all in, my eyes picked out the night crew. They were in a tight knot, looking at the roof of the staff mess and locker rooms. They still had their blue helmets on. The prisoners were now on the roof of that building, wearing stolen prison officer uniforms. Some had towels and tea cloths as masks around their faces; others simply wore our uniform hats and didn't care about being recognised. A torrent of abuse rained from the roof. Making my way into the knot of staff I felt like an intruder. I hugged one guy, patted the shoulders of others. Their eyes were tired, tormented and puzzled. One, a young guy, had a huge gash down the back of his helmet. (As the escaped prisoners were pushed back from the pier, they drove a vehicle through the broken front door of the prison and attacked the defending staff who were trying to keep the non-rioting prisoners safe. In attempting to hack their way into the visiting area where staff had barricaded themselves, one of the attacking prisoners had slashed the partition, hitting the back of the officer's helmet and splitting it. He didn't realise how close he came to being killed.

I spoke to Sully, the night ACO. He had done a great job, as had all the troops. He apologised for not contacting me: as the prisoners went on the rampage the phone lines were severed and he had just enough time to get through to the Gardaí. It was I who should have apologised. I felt like the guy who turned up after the big match ended and watched as the worn-out, injured and tired players cooled down. I was part of the troops but not part of the horror visited on that particular crew. Whilst I could empathise and sympathise, at the end of the day, all I was doing was using words.

Around us stood Gardaí; a few soldiers were setting up a field kitchen. We persuaded the night crew to go home. Reluctantly they departed, afraid to leave the scene of the nightmare lest they dream about it at home, perhaps. Soon different personnel started to arrive, men in plain clothes who looked sombre and important. I assumed they came from the Department of Justice: I never found out. I did notice a Garda in plain clothes with a flashy raincoat. He didn't seem popular with his cohorts, because none of them hung around him too long. Looking up at the roof full of uniform-attired prisoners, he remarked, 'I don't see any Garda uniforms up there.' He then looked around him, leering, for a response.

I moved closer to him. 'Sorry . . . I didn't hear you,' I

said. A few months earlier two Gardaí had their uniforms taken from them at gunpoint and were locked in the boot of their car: a reprehensible act and traumatic for the victims. The gaberdine-coated dick repeated what he had said. I replied, 'Bet you won't find any prison officers locked in a car boot anywhere around here either, though?' A sergeant standing between us burst out laughing. I moved away and closer to the rooftop lined with rioting prisoners. We were told that we might be in for a long siege. Nobody was going to rush the roof. That made sense.

The POA arrived and, correctly, they were livid. The Department had feared that Mountjoy would collapse inwards; instead the collapse occurred in the south, where the resources and infrastructure were limited or non-existent. The army gave us a welcome lunch and the wait went on. The prisoners were still giving us dog's abuse from the roof, but the lack of food meant that the adrenaline-fuelled ecstasy from the previous night's escapades had to be slipping. As the afternoon wore on a plane flew low overhead. The rooftop protesters cheered. We cringed, as no doubt the entire mess was now fodder for the evening's news, complete with aerial photos.

On the roof I watched one prisoner in particular. He was wearing a distinctive-looking tunic. I figured it was mine. I'd had mine taken up somewhat, and this one looked very much like it. In order to get my tunic he would have had to rifle my locker door open. Inside the locker on the shelf were a memorial Mass card and a pair of rosary beads belonging to my late mother. I kept them close to me in a locker always for luck. I had the west of Ireland's islander pagan superstition about me. A red band of anger swept across in front of my eyes. If that fucker had looted the relics of my mother, then he had better not be recognised as he came off the roof. This was personal. A line was crossed, and it pricked a boil on my soul.

I spotted a different Garda sergeant walking towards the mess roof with a ladder. We hadn't been told about this development. Word quickly spread that one of the prisoners wanted to come down. In a way we were disappointed: we wanted a war to repay the shit we had endured. Giving up now would rob us of that. The sergeant shouted up as the prisoner hesitated. Obviously a debate was going on on the rooftops as well. Some prisoners wanted to come down; more did not, it appeared from the signs, shouts and body language. The guy, the prisoner who had one foot on the top rung, shouted down to the sergeant again. 'I want your word that those cunts over there won't be allowed to attack me . . . ' We were 'those cunts over there'.

The Garda gave his word and the prisoner tentatively put a foot on the next rung, almost the way you'd dip a foot in the water before diving in. Then he placed the other foot on the rung below. Finally he hit the ground. We took him to an old gym and searched him for weapons. He smelled rotten: a mixture of sweat, smoke and fear. Then another was delivered to us; soon the hall was filling up. The problem now was that we had no place to put them: remember, the dorms were burned to the ground. A solution was found: the dark dungeon ammunition bunkers with their six-foot-thick roofs would have to suffice. Once searched and frisked for weapons, the prisoners were transferred into those rooms. Needs must.

So how did prisoner number one decide he had had enough? Simple really: his mother heard about the riot on the radio. She crossed over on the boat, and spoke to a guard she knew. He escorted her to the outer wall where the rooftop was clearly visible. At first she couldn't pick out her boy, so she roared out his name. Sheepishly he came towards the section of roof closest to her. There was no negotiation. 'Get off that fuckin' roof, you pup!' she bellowed. 'Mam . . . !' he replied, as if wishing she would stop embarrassing him. She wasn't for turning. 'Get off that roof now!' Hey presto . . . rooftop protest over. Pity we hadn't had her on the island for the six months previously!

I worked a twenty-four-hour shift, as did every other officer. That night we had emergency lighting installed by the army. We were issued with torches and all the prisoners were locked up in the magazine stores. Around 10 p.m. I wandered off around the jail. Embers from roof beams still glowed in the dark; hot, twisted metal looked grotesque as my torch picked the awful shapes out. The scent of burning and acrid wreckage was in the air. I entered the wrecked general office, then the shell that was once the governor's office. Burst and heat-tempered filing cabinets were piled on top of each other, their contents long dispersed into the flames. Two safes, however, were intact and welded together in the heat.

I crossed into the mess area. Above me was the roof that the miscreants had squatted on. Inside the kitchen had all its sharps, cleavers and cutters long gone. The huge fridge door was ajar, milk cartons and uncooked chicken all over the place. The food stores and bread bins had been rifled. No point going on a rooftop picnic if you don't have a few sandwiches. I picked my way carefully, as strewn furniture, burst lockers, upturned beds were everywhere. My torch picked out my locker: to my surprise it was one of three that still stood upright; I recognised it because of the Mayo sticker on its upper door. I took my bunch of keys from my pocket. The door opened and my mother's Mass card and prayer beads and my tunic were intact, untouched. I ran the rosary beads through my fingers a few times. I then kissed the photo of my mother and placed it inside my top pocket. I put on the tunic: the night would be cold and long.

The next few days on Spike were a blur. The stench of smoke was everywhere. The sun shone but our bodies didn't feel the early September warmth. Everywhere was destroyed but slowly we eked out personal spaces, putting broken chairs beside broken tables for our cuppas. Busloads of jailers from Dublin and Limerick arrived to take away the miscreants who burned the jail to the ground. It was an impressive sight, I have to say. Each prisoner was handcuffed to a warder; on a given signal they all marched down the hill to the pier where some of the riot debris was still visible. They passed the wrecked Moog van, the smashed dumper and battered navy jeep. The handcuffed prisoners cheered before getting on the ferry: this was their last hurrah. Might as well let them have their moment. For some reason we retained about ten of those troublemakers and housed them under close confinement for a few weeks more.

I spoke to the deputy governor and withdrew my transfer until the place was resettled or closed down. I couldn't imagine that the Department would keep it open, seeing as they had made a total mess of the entire project. The next few weeks saw us convert the magazine cellars into secure accommodation. The non-participant and 'good guy' prisoners, some of whom the rioters actually wanted to kill, started to put an air of normality on the place. We had a kind of bond with them: they chose not to act the thug, and we appreciated that. There were, however, one or two whom I doubted. I felt they were part of the mob but had switched sides during the musical chairs of fireworks.

The kitchen became the focal point for meeting up. A functioning kitchen is vital to any institution. No grub, no deal. We were left with about forty prisoners from a population of about 120. The sound of shifting debris, scraping shovels and hammers was the music of choice on Spike in that early part of September. One morning we heard the sound of a helicopter. We were told that the minister was going to visit. The Air Corps Alouette roared onto the massive marching square and a diminutive man emerged, lost in an overcoat topped with a bald head.

I didn't like Michael Noonan: not since he accused prison officers of being drunk outside Mountjoy during an early 1980s dispute. Perhaps some had drink on board, but Noonan stereotyped a group of us that were already at the bottom of a pile. Nothing in the intervening years, to this day, could warm me to the man. The deputy governor brought him to the kitchen, where a massive pot of water was always boiling to make tea and provide sustenance and normality. Noonan stood near the boiling pot and for a moment a cartoon comic image crossed my addled mind.

I imagined him trussed up and being boiled in the pot. After he shook hands with us all, I rubbed by hands against my tunic.

Our employer had flown in after the battle was lost. Soon the whirling blades swept him into the Cobh sky. Good riddance. I watched the helicopter disappear and got lost in nostalgia. As a former lighthouse keeper I was flown into and out of rock stations around the coast hundreds of times. The contrast was stark. Lighthouses give out light and provide security for the mariner. Spike gave out light that burned it to the stump and didn't provide security to anyone, least of all those whom it should have held and those who worked within its thick British-built walls.

The third Sunday in September is All-Ireland football final Sunday. My beloved Mayo was in the minor final and I was on duty in Spike. Calm had prevailed due to the small numbers, and a perverse sense of normality existed even though six of the rioters were still under close confinement: a reminder not to get complacent. To us they were like an itch that irked. After lunchtime, as the jail more or less dozed, I tipped around checking all was correct. I timed my tour of inspections so I would arrive at a well-positioned TV screen in the mess. We had been given two TVs, one for the prisoners in a makeshift recreation hall down at the magazine cells and one in the mess for the staff during breaks.

I watched as our minors dismantled a good Cork side. I even had a few words of difference with an officer from Cork over a hefty tackle on one of our guys. We were returning to normality if we could argue amongst ourselves over sport. My radio splattered into life. 'ACO Cuffe to the exercise yard please', it robotically spat out. This was not good news. Firstly I was going to miss the closing five minutes of the minor match. Secondly the exercise yard at that time was in use for the remaining rioters. 'What the fuck is up?' I thought as I headed down to the site. On arrival, it became clear as day.

Two officers stood near the door of the magazine/cell area and a single prisoner stood at the back wall. In his hand he had a shard of glass. I looked at the warders. I wasn't impressed. How had the prisoner gotten the piece of glass? They read my eyes. 'It must have been hidden near the wall,' one said. Possible, but not the reply I wanted. A cursory check might have located anything loose and dangerous lying around. We were in danger of slipping back into complacency, and the scent of burned steel was still in the air. I fixed my eyes on the prisoner and his extended hand with the projecting shard of glass. I walked towards him.

'Put that fucking piece of glass down now!' I barked. I was in no mood for negotiation, nice guy, pretty-please and 'think of the consequences' shit. 'No!' he replied, shaking his head. I moved closer, taking the radio from over my shoulders and wrapping the strap around my right hand, allowing the radio to drop about eighteen inches towards my knee. All the time I watched not the piece of glass but his eyes. In sport it's not always your feet, your hands or strength that wins the day; sometimes it's what the eyes see. The message the eyes relay to the brain gives the edge. This guy's eyes weren't for war; they were eyes of tiredness and despair, eyes that were pissed off, walking a small patch of concrete and sleeping in a dim former ammunition store.

Still watching his eyes but now taking in the extended hand and glass, I struck. The radio was a blur as it came down on his wrist, knocking the glass out of his hand. He put his hands to his face and I told him to relax. It was over. While I escorted him back to the cell area he said 'Sorry.' My thoughts were elsewhere: had Mayo won or lost? I looked at the officers again and we didn't need words to communicate. Returning to the mess, the sight of a green and red jersey, cup aloft, made my day. Life did exist beyond those walls after all.

In time, we refurbished part of the place. Tradesmen quickly turned four walls and concrete into smart cellular space. Spike might have a future after all. Night duty was an oasis of calm. No baying prisoners, no junkies looking for Largactil, sleepers or painkillers, no whitewash scraped off the wall and mixed with water. All slept solidly under the cold November night sky. A roaring coal fire warmed my office, to the extent that I had to vacate the room: it was more like a furnace. I stepped outside and looked into the heavens above. The stars, shielded from light pollution within the fort's high walls, twinkled; a meteor flew across the sky. For a brief few seconds I was a light keeper once more. My radio emitted a quiet 'All correct here, ACO' as one of the night guards checked in. 'Sound,' I murmured as I headed back to the office. We were in recovery.

My friend the deputy governor sent for me one day. We spoke about many things. Staff had been interviewed by the Gardaí over the riots. He spoke about the future, the present, his hopes and aspirations. We had worked together in Shanganagh so we knew each other in a different way. I could speak freely to him. Even though he might be restricted in what he could do by the Department of Justice, he was a clever man who knew what the troops endured. 'Your transfer?' he said. I knew what was coming. 'Yes?' I replied. We didn't beat about the bush. 'Are you going to stay or do you want to go back to Dublin? I want you to stay.' 'Fuck it,' I thought: I didn't know what I wanted. A big part of me wanted to stay: staying meant I probably would go up the ladder fairly fast; staying meant I would have a say in the rebuilding of the place and making it work. I had the youth and the hunger.

Another part of me – the part that's not rational – swung into action, silently saying, 'But what about not being able to buy the *Herald* and *Evening Press*, Dublin's cinemas, buses, traffic lights and life . . . what about all that? Remember your mother: the biggest mistake she ever made was leaving Dublin.' That little guy on my shoulder whispering in my ear won the day. 'Sorry, governor' (and I was) – 'sorry, but I have to go.' The deputy governor made one more effort to keep me but my mind was made up. He sanctioned the move, leaving me with a heavy heart.

That was early December. The other ACOs had moved up a gear. They were competent, confident and wanted to make the place work: my kind of boys, except I would shortly be leaving them. I had slipped in the pecking order, no longer deferred to when decisions were being made, and that's how it should be. They were the future, not me, but I have to admit that it did hurt. Seeing their ideas come into action was an eye-opener; none of us possesses all the answers and none of us should impede fresh ideas. My role now was that of an honorary ACO, there but not to be troubled. Out of the blue one day, an episode from the past arrived to waken old ghosts.

The Department were back for their pound of flesh. They were continuing their investigation into what was said at the POA AGM union meeting in Kilkenny back in May, focusing on the officer who stated the place was in chaos (true) but whose report journal on that night didn't reflect his statement to the AGM. This time they decided to take statements from all on duty on the night: my own suggestion months earlier. I was outraged. Our prison was burned from beneath us due to gross incompetence and no inquiry was instituted. Staff had been viciously assaulted, abused, traumatised, but now we were back to investigating a building that was a pile of tangled rusting steel, and an officer who told the truth but stupidly didn't write it in his journal. This was madness.

I got a query and gave it short shrift. I replied along the lines of 'check my report of such and such a date; I have nothing further to add to that report . . . J. Cuffe ACO'. The officers who were on duty that night came to me and asked my advice, which was simple: 'Lads, tell the truth, tell it as it happened, tell it from your eyes . . . don't worry about me . . . I have written what I have written; it's the truth and I won't be adding to it, do that and we will all come out of this fine.' The reports were written and I never heard another word. That episode confirmed to me that the lunatics were running the asylum.

As I worked on this book, some state papers from thirty years previously were released. Many of the same actors are still at it, wreaking havoc. What we were enduring wasn't in our minds. The Department of Justice was fully aware of the mess the entire prison system had descended into. They chose to ignore it, like a child, hoping the 'bad thing' would go away. I then got access to another document, the Eleventh Report of the Dáil Select Committee on Crime, Lawlessness and Vandalism. This report was commissioned on 12 September 1985, a mere fortnight after the riot and burning of the jail.

The Dáil Select Committee was chaired by Dr Michael Woods; Gay Mitchell was Vice Chair. On the committee were Bertie Ahern, Brian Cowen, Liam Cosgrave, Mary Flaherty, Alice Glenn, Mary Harney, Willie O'Dea and Mervyn Taylor. It included two future Taoisigh, a future Tánaiste and a future Defence Minister. Reading through the report, one admires the way they teased out the abysmal selection of prisoner policy. Reflecting the report's seriousness, the committee wrote to the Minister for Justice, the Garda Commissioner, the POA and the Association of Garda Sergeants and Inspectors. All replied bar one unit: the Department of Justice and the Minister.

The Minister for Justice, Mr Noonan, refused to attend for questioning, refused to attend in private and refused to give a written account to the Dáil Committee. Furthermore, the Minister instructed his officials not to attend even in private. 'The Committee was extremely disappointed with the response of the Minister', they wrote in paragraph 1.5. I could not put it better myself, bearing in mind that it was the lives of my colleagues, myself, the prisoners and others that were on the line during that chaotic episode. They added 'they were particularly disappointed that the Minister did not allow his officials to attend a meeting even in private'. Why did he not, I wonder?

The Dáil Committee were advised on an earlier visit to Spike that it was an 'open' prison. That was news to me and the rest of the staff. The Committee were told that the Defence Forces in the event of a riot would be on site within five minutes. That was an assurance given to the POA and themselves not once but twice. The Dáil Committee noted that it took the army eight hours to get on site: only seven hours and fifty-five minutes late. No wonder Mr Noonan found silence the best way forward both for himself and his officials. The Dáil Committee started work in early September 1985. As you can see from the above, it was in early December that the Justice Department came looking for their own pound of flesh.

The entire episode strikes me as rather rich. Those culpable for opening a matchbox jail – the Minister and his officials who deemed murderers, armed robbers and bank robbers suitable for Spike – chose to take a vow of silence. On the other hand, the members of staff who raised concerns at a union conference were pursued up to that Christmas even though what they predicted was now reality; Spike was burned and smashed to the ground.

Soon it was 'crying time again – I'm gonna leave you'. I had a few drinks in a local hotel in Cobh. It was a pissy, wet night, the type of night that you wouldn't put the cat out. A few of the lads dropped in, had a drink, wished me well, got up and left. Truthfully it was more like a wake. No speech, quick handshakes and good luck to one and all: the perfect way to end my time on Spike. I arrived in the glowing sunshine of May and departed in the sheets of hail and rain of December. But my conscience was clear; I had given it my best shot and had worked with some great young lads. Next morning I packed my car with all my earthly possessions and headed towards the big smoke. 'What could possibly be worse than Spike?' I asked myself as I saw the island in my rear-view mirrors for the last time. Arbour Hill would be a doddle.

6

Out of the Fire

At the beginning of the fourth decade of the HIV epidemic, profound stigma and discrimination is a fact of life for those with the disease – not just socially, but within our legal system.

SEAN STRUB (HIV activist, b. 1958)

Driving from Cork to Arbour Hill, I tried to recall what I knew about the Hill and its staff. I had often seen them at discos and dance halls across the city. They came across as a very intelligent lot: almost intellectual when compared with some of the rougher, louder Mountjoy staff. Of course I am stereotyping, but all we can judge people on at times are sample lots.

At inter-prison quizzes the boys from the Hill seemed a tight bunch, cocky, confident and loud. We played them in the Civil Service soccer cup once: they were a top team, and we in Shanganagh were in the bottom tier. Four divisions separated us from them and their smattering of ex-League of Ireland footballers. After a tight battle, which they won 2–1, my abiding memory was a running verbal battle I had with one of their forwards. We abused each other disgustingly. Today as I type those words, I cringe.

Why did we do this? Perhaps in the shallow pool of people we came across and who understood us, we wanted to show off to each other that we were the real deal. Was he still working in the Hill, I mused as the Laois countryside swept by. Finally I arrived, after going up and down Montpelier Hill and Manor Street numerous times. Arbour Hill was tucked between those streets, with no sign to mark its presence. It had been refurbished in 1975 and its main inmates were sex offenders and murderers of women and children, plus an assortment of informers ('rats'), along with middle-class prisoners who would be targeted in the main jails. The criminal Paul Ward, in a phone call, said the only people that go to the Hill are 'Hairies' (sex offenders) and rats. He added that his associate Charlie Bowden (arrested after the murder of journalist Veronica Guerin) was not a 'Hairy'. Arbour Hill had come into being to segregate and protect sex offenders because in the 'normal' jails they were open season, and I don't mean saying nasty words to them: they would be violently attacked.

Formerly a military prison attached by tunnel to Collins Barracks, it was now an institution designed to hold about 120 prisoners. At the time we didn't see it because we were in the eye of the storm, but the entire prison system was in chaos. Spike was the answer to the 'revolving door' and joyriding problems, but it didn't solve them. Arbour Hill had a fully functioning education set-up behind its limestone walls. Those in power turned many of those classrooms and much of the infrastructure into sleeping accommodation. Hence the principal's office could hold two sleeping prisoners and the art room up to ten: now the Hill could hold 160 prisoners, but with the loss of the educational unit, which housed forty prisoners.

A jail is not built entirely around warehousing prisoners, but when the blowtorch licked the arses of the Department officials, their first reaction was simple. Pile them high and stack them up. Fuck rehabilitation, fuck the staff that work there and fuck those who do time there. (Well, it looked that way to me, and I have no cause to change my mind.) An ACO – the acting chief but de facto ground-floor boss – introduced himself to me and showed me around. An imposing man who carried himself with confidence, with a clipboard under his arm, Big Tom was the master of all he surveyed.

After the tour he took me to the staff mess and gave me a room. The mess had about twenty rooms for staff accommodation along with a canteen. The room was simple, spotless: breeze blocks painted in antiseptic white, just like the prisoners' rooms in the Training Unit. Compared to Spike and St Muredach's College, Ballina, where I served five years' hard time as a starved boarder in the mid 1960s, it was like the Hilton. I hung up a few pictures, placed my football trophies on a desk, stacked my travelling collection of books on the window, placed the memorial photo of my mother on my bedside locker, and finally lay on the bed and closed my eyes. I was tired.

Next morning I reported for duty. There were the usual introductions. In the Unit I was bottom of the supervisory pile; on Spike I had been near the top but it was plain here that the Hill had a very senior officer staff along with supervisory staff. The one man I did not meet was the governor . . . strange in such a small area. I saw him but wasn't introduced to him, nor did he seem keen to acquaint himself with his latest supervisor.

The jail was busy. Apparently they were moving out up to forty prisoners and replacing them with forty more. The replacements were not like for like. The chosen deportees bore the faces of men going to the gallows; the staff something similar. They dreaded what was about to be unleashed on them. A scourge called HIV/AIDS was sweeping the drug-taking part of the nation. No surprise that many of the chief junkies were already within the confines of the penal system. Mountjoy had begun a testing regime and up to 100 of its inmates tested positive for HIV/AIDS. Naturally those weren't the brains trust of the criminal population. They were the ones you crossed the street to avoid, with their yellow skin, tinny, drug-addled voices and eyes long dead in their sockets.

Soon the outbound prisoners were dispatched to the Joy. I was basically useless to the staff because I hadn't a clue as what to do or how to do it, so like a well-trained dog I followed different ACOs around all morning. We adjourned to the prison kitchen for a cup of tea. Imagine my shock when who appeared in chef's whites but the officer I had clashed with all those years earlier on the soccer pitch. We both thought the same thing: 'That's the bollox who abused me on the pitch in Shanganagh.' No point in getting high and mighty now, I figured: this was his patch. Extending my hand, 'I suppose better late than never . . . sorry about that shit and mouthing years ago in the Ganagh.' He shook my hand and laughed. 'Forget it,' he said.

That evening it was dark early, and foreboding. One could almost hear the clocks tick. Word came that three vanloads of AIDS prisoners were parked outside, awaiting admission. They were not to be processed via the main gate and reception area. No, this crowd were to be isolated on the two landings of the East Wing: East One and East Two. They were to be taken through a side entrance. However, there was a delay because we weren't fully ready. Meanwhile the prisoners in the vans were getting more agitated. They wanted to go to the toilet, they wanted their medication, and they wanted a new one to me: their 'Phy'. 'Where's me bleedin' Phy?' became a mantra to we who served through that hellish time. Phy was a substitute heroin weaner properly known as Physeptone.

These drug addicts had serious health issues and little comprehension of their medical situation. They were diagnosed with this HIV/AIDS disease, their life expectancy would be reduced, and they were to be isolated in Arbour Hill and away from their mates. Great . . . not alone were they designated as seriously ill with a limited lifespan but, worst of all, they were now sharing a prison with sex offenders and child molesters.

Finally the Mountjoy AIDS prisoners were filtered through the side entrance to the East One landing. Like young calves seeing the first spring grass after being released from their winter sheds, they raced down the wing towards a gate that opened onto the Circle area of the jail. We got it locked just in time. Like monkeys they climbed on to the bars that separated them from the rest of the prison. They shouted and screamed. Those weren't just sick people: those were seriously disturbed people. After much chaos we got them into cells. Clearly many of them were strung out. Medical files had to be raced through to figure out their medicine. More than likely the Hill hadn't all the assorted coloured pills this mob needed. That led to more friction.

We then took twenty of them up to East Two. That entailed letting them onto the Circle area with its access to the remaining two blocks of landings, the North and West Wings. Once out on the concourse some of them made a run down those wings, clouting any other prisoner they saw: 'bash a Hairy' seemed to be a rite of passage to this lot. Finally we got them into their cells. It was quickly evident that some of the Hill staff hadn't the stomach for the 'Antibodies', as we quickly christened them. And I don't blame them; those officers had operated under a different regime, dealing professionally with a different category of offender. Now they were asked to take a massive step in another direction.

Ah yes, the Department of Justice in its wisdom decided that Mountjoy prisoners affected with HIV/AIDS would be segregated and shifted to a wing in a totally settled and successful jail: possibly one of the few prisons in the country that actually worked as it should. Minimal medical and psychological education and information seemed to be given to them. Even if it had been, most of it would have gone over their heroin- and cocaine-addled heads. They had been given an hour to pack their meagre belongings, shunted onto a bus and held for three hours outside the Hill until it was finally ready for them. In this time they could not access a toilet. And let's not forget the converted classrooms for 'normal sex offenders'.

The staff in Mountjoy for months after rejoiced in the noise levels being reduced, the drop in aggression and the relative calm that descended on that kip after the Antibodies were transferred. The staff in Arbour Hill were not briefed as to what to expect: what HIV/AIDS exactly was and how it might affect them, their families, their friends, their colleagues. At the time there was a media frenzy about AIDS and its effects on the gay community. I recall about six weeks into the unfolding mess a doctor coming and speaking to us for about twenty minutes about AIDS, but I don't recall a word he said.

The prison descended into a form of hell on earth. One officer whose wife was a nurse told us that the Blood Transfusion Service refused to take blood from her because her husband worked with AIDS-infected prisoners. That fairly focused us. We, a service already bottom-feeding in the metaphorical seas, were about to be shoved into the leper desert. As a sop we were issued plastic gloves, the ones you see sandwich makers use. Your hands sweated within them and the prisoners objected to us wearing them. Quickly Arbour Hill fragmented into a number of new units. We now had an East Wing devoted to the Antibodies. The West and North Wings were for the sex offenders, middle-class killers and robbers along with an assortment of 'rats' and protection prisoners. The School Unit doubled as a school, of course, but also held about forty prisoners in classrooms and recreation areas, as I have mentioned. We had the ingredients to pack into a powder keg. All we needed was some clown to provide a lit match.

So here we are: you'll note that we have slipped into Arbour Hill without too much detail other than that things are messy. Every day was a work day. All shifts were twelve and a half hours long . . . at a minimum. I got to know staff by working on the front line with them: this was no gentle introduction; this was a continuation of Spike, only worse. This place was confined; Spike had acres and a sky over it. January melded into February. To cut out the assaults and attacks in the 'normal' part of the jail, it was decided to install a stairs at the bottom of East One that facilitated an entrance up to East Two, at a stroke removing any interaction between the competing groups.

An Antibody had sneaked onto the West Wing and was found in notorious double killer Malcolm MacArthur's cell. He wasn't calling to wish MacArthur a happy St Patrick's Day. That speeded up the process of isolating the Antibodies further; hence the introduction of the new stairway. The affected prisoners weren't provided with any infrastructural support. No school, no gym, Mass was held on their landing; their recreation, TV, snooker and other games were also crammed onto that same ground floor landing. When tension rose, often a snooker ball was put through the TV. We stopped that by putting Perspex in front of the screen. They responded by tipping a bucket of water into the back of the gogglebox: fun and games for all.

Not a day or night passed that didn't have a cutting, a cell fire, a broken cue, a chucked snooker ball or some drug-addled junkie wandering around in a daze. Trips to the Mater were de rigueur, staff wearing hideous white boiler suits so they wouldn't get infected by a stray squirt of blood. The prisoners now took to a new game: after acting the bollox but pretending to be sorry and 'We won't do it any more, mister', they would extend their hand. Did you now shake a hand that carried a potential life-ending disease? Such was the shit we dealt with on a daily basis. It couldn't last, and sure enough in late January all hell broke loose. The East Wing 'went up' – jail parlance for a riot. The check gate was rushed, forcing the officer outside to lock it, thus locking in the landing staff and catching all by surprise.

Quickly they stacked furniture, lockers, tables, chairs, bed heads into a corner at the gable end of the landing. They climbed up, smashed through the thin layer of plaster on the ceiling and got onto the roof. From there they made their way to the highest point on the complex: the army church next door. Staff had to ensure that the rest of the jail was secured before tackling the East Wing, lest we lose the entire jail. One correctly assumes that the oversight on the main jail had diminished, such was the pressure exerted by the Antibodies. By the time that was done, most of those involved had wrecked the entire landing: dismantling fluorescent lighting and smashing sinks, toilets and anything else that could be pulled down or out.

A group of us surrounded the church area as the slates rained down. We were ill equipped. Word had gone out to Mountjoy and other jails to send reinforcements. Some of the prisoners had already escaped by jumping off the twenty-foot-high walls and had scarpered into the gloomy Stoneybatter streets. Two had remained, crippled, at the bottom of the external wall. They broke ankles in the fall, and the raining slates weren't going to discriminate between warder and prisoner. We formed a turtle with plastic shields and carefully moved across to remove the two injured prisoners. Finesse wasn't our calling card because we were under attack from slates hitting the plastic shields and we needed to move them quickly for their and our safety.

We moved to the rear of the church with fire hoses. The idea was to drench them so that the oncoming evening cold would hasten their departure from the roof. Cars drove slowly by on the main road, their occupants aghast and agog at the unfolding madness. Now a new problem emerged. The roof of the church was pitched very steeply. The cascading water made it treacherous, with a danger of some prisoner slipping to his death. We decided to pull back, and as we did I marvelled at the sight of slates like snowflakes descending towards where we sheltered. One of the slates crashed behind me, severing the hose and drenching us in the spray. This was madness, this was not cool and this wasn't a movie.

Prisoners shouted from the rooftops, alleging that they were victims, that they were sick and that they were poorly treated. Some truth in that: we could have shouted the same from the ground. They weren't physically maltreated by the staff; if anything they were treated with fluffy cotton wool, but we had an understanding of their plight. The gazing crowd wanted more. A snooker ball hopped off the tarmac nearby as the Gardaí moved the onlookers away from the perimeter wall. Eventually the industrial manager, a guy who did care for the welfare of those prisoners, cajoled them down. Then the usual 'look at me . . . I've no marks on me body and I don't want those screws with the billiard and snooker cues to kick the shit outta me.' A ladder was gingerly extended and the coming down was more dangerous than the going up. The only cues and snooker balls were the ones discarded by the rioters.

As I entered the main gate a squad car was ushered in. Two Gardaí got out and threw three prisoners towards us. They had dragged them from under cars on Manor Street. As quickly as it drove in, the squad car flew out. We marched the would-be escapees back to their cells. To them it was a caper, a laugh. To us it was an ongoing disaster. The one thing that surprised me was that by seven o'clock that evening both East One and Two looked as if you could eat your dinner off the floor. The place was cleaned, swept and debris removed. Physically the jail recovered very fast; mentally, the wounds were crusting.

One day in March I was covering the Cage area, a place originally created for a troublesome prisoner called Karl Crawley: a Mountjoy prisoner who had a myth attached to him on account of his rebellious ways. The Cage was a foolproof exercise area with very narrow mesh that supposedly couldn't be climbed. Eventually it was decided to let Crawley live out his own movie in the Joy, and a Portacabin divided into a number of rooms was placed within the Cage area. This area was now a make-shift school and visiting area for the Antibodies. It was totally impractical and should have been scrapped. It was pokey, manky and full of nooks and crannies. A bazooka could be passed in, such was the chaotic layout of the visiting box.

Word came through that the governor was on his rounds with some Department officials. They appeared in the Cage area. He chatted to the officials, ignoring me. Suddenly one of the Department men recognised me; I had spotted him earlier. We had battled on the soccer pitch a few times and he was a decent guy. 'Hi John, long time no see, not much football here I'd say,' as he shook my hand. The governor suddenly noticed me. 'And who is this man?' he barked, looking around at his Chief Officer. I was 'this man'. The CO replied that I was the new ACO who had arrived from Spike on . . . January the second. The Department man and I exchanged looks and slight smiles. 'I must see you in my office later for a chat,' said the departing governor. I have yet to make that trip or have that chat.

By now the HIV/AIDS prisoners – forty at the max, sometimes down to thirty-six – were draining our resources and energy. We had got a new CO: Big Bill, a Mountjoy chief and a jail legend who engendered respect from staff and prisoner alike, and who was a badly needed asset. I remembered him from my training days. Tall, angular and confident, he exuded calm as he gently puffed his pipe and often pulled his long stockings as he took tea with us. I asked Big Bill had he ever seen such stress, tension and hassle. He told me that he often had in Mountjoy, but had never experienced ongoing intensity like that in the Hill. This was a first for him, and that gave me confidence: we were in this together.

As per the norm, we couldn't get a rest day off. This was taking a huge toll on the staff. You cannot work 24/7, day in, day out, without something giving. Family life for the married men was put on hold; single men's lives were on hold too. Some of us took to exercise and a run at lunchtime in nearby Phoenix Park to relieve the stress. Others had a few lunchtime pints to keep in touch with normality. The wages were high but the cost exacted on staff will never be recouped. We lost months of our lives never to be regained, fighting an enemy that wasn't for defeating.

It got to the stage that thirty to forty Antibodies exerted such a hold on the penal system that Arbour Hill had to take in extra staff from Mountjoy, themselves under immense pressure, the Training Unit, Shanganagh, Limerick, Loughan House and Spike. I had memories of the Loughan lads on Spike and I knew that they weren't going to be there long-term. However, the lads from Limerick, I have to say, were exceptional. Nothing fazed them: the bigger the hassle, the better they reacted. They were a godsend. Spike gave us a top-rated ACO who also relished getting stuck in. He knew most of those junkies and trouble-makers. By now there was an acceptance amongst us that this was to be our lot, our way of living. Transferring was out of the question, my roaming days were over, and this one had to be seen to the bitter end. Leaving, in the circumstances, to me would have been akin to cowardice and desertion.

Life had to go on, and within the chaos we tried to do normal things. We ran our annual Arbour Hill 10K in the Phoenix Park and over forty staff took part; a couple of undercover Garda cars patrolled the area discreetly. Credible information had been proffered that suggested an attack on the Arbour Hill staff at this event. Some of the HIV/AIDS guys had influence that extended beyond the limestone walls. We also had the final of our inter-staff soccer tournament. My only recollection is that I was sent off. I had moaned and bitched my way through the match, and the referee finally had enough. 'You!' he barked. 'Off!' As I walked the path of shame, some of the players said, 'Aah Rocky, for fuck's sake, leave him on.' I don't know why: perhaps playing football was a surreal act for us and they wanted all twenty-two of us to see it out to the bitter end. Actually being able to tog out was an achievement, considering the rock and hard place between which we resided. I apologised, the referee accepted and he's my best friend to this day.

Easter week arrived. The chapel in the jail was for the 'normal' prisoners. As I pointed out earlier, the Antibodies had Mass on the landing. Only a handful ever bothered attending, perhaps five to eight. We still required a huge presence of manpower. This was what sucked the air from us: their ability to keep us on our toes and our stress levels through the roof. In mitigation, I wonder whether, if I was in their boots, with an infection that led to death within five years, I would want to play happy families inside a prison. On that particular Easter Sunday morning I recalled, briefly, how my father would wake me as a child to see the dancing sun and give me my Easter egg. This particular morning I was with five officers behind the priest and the makeshift altar but in front of the plastic-screened TV. Other staff sat on the snooker table with the balls removed (nothing like a flying snooker ball to show you how fragile your skull is).

The rest sat each side of the landing. The priest's theme that morning was forgiveness. Amongst his flock was a prisoner who had had half his ear bitten off in a row in the outside world. When not fighting us and the system, he was actually a funny guy, popular with the older staff who knew him from about the age of seventeen in various jails over the years. The AIDS had addled his brain and though he gave us a hard time, we felt that his heart wasn't really in it; he was playing to the gallery a bit. The priest gave Jesus and Peter as an example. In a fit of anger Peter had severed the ear of a Roman centurion, but Jesus restored the stricken soldier's ear: a miracle. This was too much for those of us attentive and awake. All eyes went to the prisoner with the deformed lug. He started to blush, and one of our more senior staff muttered loud enough for us all to hear, 'Jesus must have forgotten poor old Buddy here, he didn't cure his ear.'

For a moment we thought the place would explode in anger, but instead everyone, including Half-an-Ear, roared laughing. The priest then sped up the rest of the sermon and we survived. That evening, I was still in charge of the Wing. We had over fifteen prisoners on lock-up for various infractions of the regulations: smashing a TV, throwing a snooker ball, abusing staff and disobeying an order. As luck would have it, most of them were on the first floor up on East Two. Around 6 p.m. an officer from that landing beckoned furiously to us beneath to come up. On arrival we spotted and smelt smoke coming from under various doors. The locked-up prisoners had set fire to their cells with them within. Looking through the spy holes we saw that some of them had also deliberately cut themselves and had pulled down the light fittings, clutching broken fluorescent lamps.

Quickly we started to unlock the burning cells. A large number of officers had arrived. The bottom line in jails is simple. The only viable deterrent is the presence of staff, better if in reasonable numbers. Staff, regardless of personal feelings towards each other, always respond to a colleague under attack. A batch of orange rubber balaclava-type fire masks arrived from the ACO's office. We had never been shown how to use them, don them, or work in them. In fact I wasn't even aware they existed until the smoke was billowing around me. Opening the first door I came to, all I could see was a haze of grey smoke. A cell is a small area, but with smoke it takes on the vastness of the ocean bound up in fog.

I couldn't see the prisoner, I hadn't a clue where he was: was he armed, was he dead, was he slashed, was he waiting for me with a length of glass? What I was certain of was that he was within that area and I had to get him out. All this was happening in seconds. I donned the orange mask, dropped to my knees and felt my way into the cell along the ground, banging my head against the bottom of the bed. Slapping my hands ahead of me as I felt the ground and surroundings for direction, I got a sensation of being unable to breathe. The more I tried to suck in air through the mouthpiece, the wider my eyes seemed to bulge; I was getting no air. As luck would have it, I caught the prisoner's foot: he had gone to the ground for air. I backed out and dragged the foot with me. Outside the cell I was helped to my feet and the prisoner taken away. As quickly as I could, I clawed at the orange mask, trying to pull it from my face before my head exploded.

My eyes were the size of golf balls, my nose streamed and I gulped in air. Looking inside the mask and feeling around the mouthpiece, I was shocked to find a plastic cover over the mouthpiece, in order, I assume, to keep it hygienic before it was put into action. I hadn't removed it because I never knew it existed in the first place. I felt like a fool, but the real fool was the person who brought them to the jail and never trained us in how to use them.

We went from cell to cell. We were met by violence, spitting and blood being thrown at us. One prisoner had a shard of fluorescent bulb at the back wall of his cell and dared us to take him out. We had no choice but to remove it from him for our safety and his. At this stage adrenaline had kicked in: the torture of the previous three months, the feeling of not being in charge of the mess we were gifted, abated. For those few minutes we were expending pent-up emotion. Inside the cell CO Bill rushed the prisoner with a full-length shield, pinning him against the wall. His arms were trapped akimbo like a crucifixion stance, his face squashed behind the shield. One of us got each side of him and took the shard from him. He then gave up the fight and we removed him from the cell. All our shirts were splattered in AIDS-infected blood, but at that stage we didn't care.

That fight, that riot, seemed to draw some of the poison out of the air. The Antibodies saw another side to us, a side that said, 'OK, act the bollox to a point but go beyond it and we will do what we have to in order to keep hold of our jail.' We got our message across. Summer turned to autumn. In the meantime I had got engaged, but still hadn't got a rest day. Word went around that the whole of Arbour Hill was going to be turned into an AIDS prison. More and more prisoners were presenting with the symptoms of the disease. This deflated and worried us. A jail full of them made our future look like we'd be working in a dead or zombie zone. Then out of the blue word came that they were returning to the Base area in Mountjoy. The grand experiment had failed.

We had gotten on to our union about what we were enduring, but at a well-attended meeting the reply we got was this: every jail has problems and problem prisoners. Arbour Hill simply had to take its share of the problems. We reacted badly to that, pointing out the stupidity of dealing with a medical problem through isolation and ignorance. The Hill had functioned successfully as a sex offenders' jail; why not leave it that way? Now it appeared that everybody agreed with us. There would be a sting in the tail that would almost bring down the entire prison, but not for a while.

It was with a degree of disbelief and huge relief that we packed and got rid of the Antibodies. As they left they gave us the fingers and clenched fists, like the prisoners who earlier burned Spike: those guys felt they had won a battle. Certainly we felt we had been in a battle. Such was their mark over the nine months that almost twenty years later, the East Wing still brought back bad memories to the staff who endured that trauma. In place of the HIV/AIDS mob, Mountjoy didn't pick forty sex offenders or return to us the sex offenders we earlier had transferred out. Instead they picked forty of the roughest and toughest jailbirds they could muster.

Serious drug pushers, murderers who had killed on robberies and an assortment of up-and-coming thugs arrived in our small jail. Most were settled on the North Wing, as we had earlier cleared out the East Wing and restocked it with our own compliant inmates. An assistant governor returned from a meeting at the Department and even though I was on the fringe of the conversation, I could tell he was spitting fire. Apparently in the discussions about the Antibodies' transfers, Arbour Hill was deemed not to have performed to the Justice Department's satisfaction. We had, as it were, let the side down. He had tried to explain the situation but found that no one wanted to listen. A side had been let down all right – the staff of the Hill and the prisoners who had this awful affliction – and those who let them down weren't the prison officers.

John Donnellan, Galway three-in-a-row All-Ireland winning footballer and TD, once described a colleague of his thus: 'If it was raining soup, he would be out gathering it up with a fork.' Those words described for me perfectly those who ran Justice. How could any senior official, governor or administrator permit a jail to select some of the most inappropriate prisoners to be sent to another jail: not once, not twice, but now for a third time? Had they learned nothing from the burning of Spike and the destruction of Arbour Hill by the Antibodies? Obviously not: those newbies were heavies. They had clout and weren't shy about using it. Some were suspected of being part of the Prisoners' Revenge Groups (PRG), a group of ex-prisoners who had burned down a prison officer's house and who attacked another on his way home at the Strawberry Beds, battering him senseless with iron bars and pickaxe handles. As is the norm in those situations, both officers who were attacked were easy targets: two men who devoted their careers to doing the right thing for their prisoners.

Fatigue had taken its toll on the staff. The long, relentless hours dealing with the Antibodies had drained us emotionally and physically. Having got rid of the

Antibodies and seen the return of what we assumed were 'normal' prisoners, psychologically the guard was possibly dropped. Staff assumed that the Hill would revert to its old status of generally compliant jailbirds. This didn't happen. Big Bill, having steered and guided us through hell, returned to the mother ship: he was always a Mountjoy man. We missed him, a good guy who gave real leadership. Early November 1986 I was sent to Dún Laoghaire District Court with a criminal up on some minor charges. He was serving time for serious robberies but I wasn't made aware that a further trial lay ahead for him, for a robbery where a sawn-off shotgun was discharged. He had a sallow complexion, pockmarked skin and dark greasy hair. He was also non-communicative. Most prisoners once away from a jail setting tend to open up a little. Not this guy.

The courthouse was packed with petty criminals, trivial dealings, and the usual mob scavenging off the criminal justice carcass. Bringing a prisoner already in jail for another crime to a District or indeed a trial court requires you to play a game. Everyone pretends that the person under escort is blemish-free. Hence you are under pain of death (joke) if you allow them to be seen in open court in a set of handcuffs. Our guy I didn't trust, so I ordered that the handcuffs be kept on until the last possible moment. I threw my civilian jumper over the cuffs, covering the officer's hands and the prisoner's. Finally we were called.

As our prisoner went into the witness stand to give evidence, the solicitor from the previous trial stood up and asked the judge for further clarification. If I was the judge I would have said, 'You had your chance: now fuck off' (politely, of course). However, their exchange became lengthy and as the low November afternoon sun beat through the high glass windows directly behind the judge's bench, it was starting to put me to sleep. 'Drone, drone, blah, your honour, your worship, lick my arse, if it pleases the court, my good man, yak, yak yak' lulled me to the Land of Nod. Suddenly my prisoner leapt from the stand, sprinted past me and was out the door.

Forcing myself to wake, with the added disadvantage that my foot was asleep, I chased after him, my mind desperately trying to engage with the present and reality. As I ran from the court, a woman stood up and shoved me across the benches, thus allowing the escapee further ground. On reaching the front door, not a trace of my prisoner was to be seen. Did he go left, did he go right or did he sprout wings and do a Batman? I tossed a metaphorical coin in my head and raced to the right. As I turned the corner the guards had my man in a head lock and were taking him back to me.

'Take a look at my face and see there are no marks on it, I don't want this cunt to give me the digs for running off,' the newly returned lag bleated to the cops.

One of the guards looked at his face: 'Seems it's already full of marks and scars.'

'Yous are all the fuckin' same,' the prisoner whinged.

My job, shitty and all as it was, was never going to be ransomed for handing out a gratuitous slap, no matter what provocation. I operated under a strong guiding principle that kept my conscience clear and my morals intact: 'Use the minimum force necessary.' That ranged from strong verbal force to actually killing someone if the need arose. Thankfully I never used the latter. Inside the courthouse I ordered the officer to keep the cuffs on the prisoner, even in the witness box. Our case was called again and this time I stood in front of the box; the officer was handcuffed to the prisoner and we awaited the trial.

The judge peered over his glasses as he adjusted his wig. 'Is this man handcuffed in my court?' the wigged one boomed. My mind went, 'No, he's not, you stupid pompous prick, he's having an ice cream and we are going to the cinema after.' Before I was tempted to retort, a Garda sergeant replied. 'Eh, judge, this man tried to escape from lawful custody and was recaptured outside the court precincts.' I was outraged: the fool on the bench had seen the prisoner run because he, the judge, was ranting and pontificating over an already finished case. He had also seen me knocked over a bench in the court by a woman who, incidentally, was still in the courtroom, and he asked a question that he already knew the answer to.

The judge peered out again. I didn't get a chance to talk. My opinion wasn't requested. I was the monkey among many organ grinders.

'Well, on this occasion I will permit this . . . but it's not something I'm happy with.'

My mind raged: 'It's the likes of you and other gobshites that probably have contributed most to the daily erosion of respect for law and order. We are the victims here, not the scrote who ran away from *your* court, and what about the woman who aided and abetted an escape and prevented an officer of the court and state doing his duty?' The sergeant read my mind and pointed out what I thought. The judge just asked if the defendant's solicitor was in court.

Back in the jail we settled in with our new chief, but a malaise was creeping across the landings. Whispers of escape attempts were gaining credence. Mountjoy had both an inner and an external wall. The newcomers quickly figured out that if the Antibodies managed to get to the roof, then fully fit and clever prisoners like them could figure further exit strategies. In the North exercise yard stood a sentry box. Behind it was an alcove-type area. A wall had been built in that area which hid a key cell window from view. That worried me. I wrote a half sheet about it to the governor and showed it to a senior officer. After reading it, he dropped it on the tea-room table and said, 'You're what the governor calls an alarmist, Cuffe.' That was telling me. I took back the half sheet and tore it up and tossed it into the bin, wondering what else the governor thought of me.

Early December saw me in charge of a trip to the Mater Hospital with a prisoner. This guy, from Northern Ireland, was an affable lad, and for some reason he figured that I was into fast cars and stuff like that: a petrolhead. I wasn't, but if it meant keeping the place calm and normal, I felt no urge to deflate the boy. Prior to the escort he was as talkative as a pumped-up parrot, but on the trip to the Mater the cat seemed to have got his tongue. My gut kicked into action. Things weren't right. As he lay on the hospital bed the doctor prodded and poked at his stomach: was there a pain here, a pain there? My colleague and I made eye contact. No words were needed. This guy would run if given a chance. The doctor looked at us and his eyes sent a message: 'Nothing wrong here, chaps.' He wrote a note, sealed it in an envelope and gave it to me to take back for the Arbour Hill doctor. We attached the handcuffs and I made small car talk but the guy was elsewhere, or wished to be elsewhere.

A few nights later I was in charge of exercise. The northern guy and his cellmate hadn't availed of exercise; they remained in their cell, talking or doing hobbies. As we gave the prisoners their supper I glanced through the 'Declined Exercise and Back in Cell' book. This showed the officers keeping an internal watch which prisoners remained in cells (checks were needed only on occupied cells). Our 'friend' and his cellmate had remained on most of the recent nights. I was suspicious. Our biggest fear in the Hill was the cell windows. They had a pair of parallel quarter-inch iron bars. A hacksaw blade would go through these fairly quickly, so we depended on regular checks to ensure no tampering. Those nights spent in the cell might be for a reason, I surmised.

When he came down the stairs with his tray to collect his supper, I made sure I was at the foot of the stairs for his return trip. 'You must have the bars out by now, Georgie,' I pretended to joke (though serious). He looked at me, picked at a bun and said, 'Jesus, Mr C, you're paranoid. I could get the vibes off you below in the hospital last week, you think everybody wants to run away, get a life man, I thought you were OK . . .'

I laughed and walked away as he trudged up the stairs. The words of my elder colleague rang in my head: 'You're what the governor calls an alarmist, Cuffe.' Now a prisoner was telling me the same. Maybe I needed to lighten up; maybe I needed to get a life and cop on.

Two mornings later as I arrived for work there was a damp buzz around the place. I knew something had happened as we made our way to the staff parade from the way little knots of warders whispered together. There had been an escape during the night. Two prisoners had gone, including our northern car freak. I was right all along, I wasn't an alarmist, I wasn't imagining it, and my gut was alive and functioning.

An escape drains and kills a jail. Rehabilitation is a desirable but frequently unattainable ideal. Security is an expected norm: a bottom-line requirement. You open in the morning with 120 prisoners and you lock up that night with your tally correct: that's how you're measured; that's how you're successful.

You lose a prisoner and it's a stain on your copybook. Initially destructive and corrosive, it shreds your confidence. In time, if you are lucky, people might make a joke about it: rarely, though. Our hearts went out to the night staff. There but for the grace of God go we, and that type of thing. An examination of the bars showed that they were bent sideways, not hacksawed. That puzzled us: how in God's name could they be bent like that? What was used to do this? Interestingly, the departing offenders had left two short ropes tied to the bent bars, suggesting that they had been pulled apart. Having once watched as a curious child a score of my village's strongest men try to pull iron bars from the coastguard boathouse window with a rope (the only things dislodged were their spinal columns), I knew that whatever forced that steel apart, it wasn't a stray rope.

The night staff suggested that the escape occurred shortly before unlock: that the prisoners were correct and present on the earlier check. Nobody disagreed; we weren't there . . . thank God. An officer who was aware that I had written a half sheet expressing my concern about those windows now came to me seeking a copy of it. Sheepishly, I told him about being called 'an alarmist'. We both shook our heads. Coming up to Christmas, the confidence amongst the warders in Arbour Hill was badly shaken. We were poorly led. I didn't see any inspirational heads at the top, just those of my fellow officers who hadn't the power. We had endured twelve months of abject misery. Surely 1987 would bring better days?

On night duty there was a practice of leaving out a few prisoners to tidy up the kitchen after lock-up and prepare for the next day. Around ten o'clock they would be locked up for the night. They were regarded as trustees, and often they would deep-fry a pot of chips for themselves: a kind of bonus for the work they were doing. I wandered into the kitchen around 9.50 p.m. and was given a bowl of the most exquisite chips ever: large, brown, tasty . . . a meal in their own right. The 'top cat' – the prisoner deemed within the system to be the most trusted and senior – offered me vinegar and salt. He then beckoned me to the back kitchen for a chat.

'Time to head off for the night boys . . . thanks for the work!' I said to the rest, as a hot chip set fire to my throat. I was handed a cool glass of milk to put out the fire. Sitting down, the prisoner – a likable rogue, adept at keeping both sides of the house onside, regarded well by the staff, trusted by the prisoners – looked me in the eye. He was a camp drama queen, but had a hard centre. 'Mr C . . . this place is gone to the dogs!' he exclaimed dramatically. I nodded, dipping a chip in salt. He looked out the door to ensure no one was eavesdropping.

We talked: well, he talked and I listened. He was

alarmed at what was going on. He told me that a group of prisoners were plotting to escape; lowering his voice, he gave me the names. What was in it for him? Truth be told, not a lot. But most prisoners like a jail to be settled, like to get on with staff and do their time and 'bird' as peacefully as possible. What he told me confirmed what I already thought. Now I had names to go with it: the very names I also suspected. I thanked him. He put his finger to his lips and whispered, 'You didn't get this from me.' I nodded, muttering, 'Of course.' That night I drafted a half sheet with the information for the governor's attention. Next morning I took the CO to one side, told him what I had heard and gave him the half sheet to give to the governor.

The next week went by and nothing happened. In the meantime staff recovered twenty feet of rope jammed into a pair of Doc Marten boots with a sock on the top. Things were hotting up. My next tour of nights brought my 'camp kitchen friend' and I together again. Once more I came scavenging for chips. Once more I was beckoned into the back kitchen, door gently closed. 'What the fuck are ye up to Mr C . . . this is going to happen, there will be an escape and I'm putting myself in danger by telling you lot, but nothing is happening.' I nodded and told him what I had done, but he didn't seem impressed. Next morning I reiterated my worry and the CO agreed with me, but he had passed on the information and was hamstrung from the top.

An ACO colleague asked me to accompany him to the North Two toilet area a few days later. Having ensured that no prisoners were around, we lifted the stainless steel toilets from their base and found more rope and a number of hacksaw blades. The ACO wrote out a report; we once more added the names I had already given plus a few suspects from my colleague. We then went to the governor's office, and left with a promise that this group would be transferred before that afternoon was out. They weren't . . . fatally.

Two Sundays later, during afternoon exercise, we had the second escape. I think about eight to ten prisoners got out. Catastrophic is the only word I can use to describe the sick feeling and gloom that descended over Stoneybatter that day: it was late January, grey and gloomy, a typical lazy jail Sunday. The afternoon was wet so we decided to exercise all the prisoners in the recreation hall. Mid-afternoon I left the hall to relieve my colleague in the Circle area of the prison for his tea break, leaving the spare ACO in charge of the recreation hall. A prisoner made his way down the stairs from North Two towards me with a slight smirk on his face. I expected bad news.

'Mr Cuffe . . . you better come up to my cell . . . something has happened,' he said. My stomach turned: his cell was the very one I had written a half sheet about: the one not visible from the ground, the one screened by a high dividing wall. The earlier escape had occurred from an end-of-building cell. Stepping into the cell I saw a sheet tied to two bent bars: bent the exact same way as the escape five weeks before. I turned and headed down the stairs, head spinning: 'How many have escaped?' was my first question, quickly followed by, 'Where do I stand in regard to this: am I covered?'

As I hit the bottom step the assistant governor arrived over, rubbing his hands together as if fending off the cold. 'All OK, John?'

'No,' I replied, 'we have a problem . . . we might have lost a lot of prisoners . . . the bars are bent on the cell on North Two . . .'

Suddenly we had prisoners streaming back from the recreation hall, smiling and high-fiving. This confirmed what we already guessed and feared. We had our own *Midnight Express*. Once they were locked in cells we awaited confirmation of who had escaped. It was devastating: gone were guys we already had tagged and reported, guys who should have been transferred out. The good news? We were lucky that we didn't lose eighty prisoners instead of eight. Some of us went to the back gate area looking for clues: we had resigned ourselves to the fact that they were already a long way off. More tied sheets hanging limply from the wall made my stomach heave once more. We were a disaster.

How did it happen? Well, the easy and simple solution was to blame the staff who were on that day, principally the staff who worked in those immediate areas. Scapegoats were easy to find if we were looking at the final act of this mess, but this escape had its roots in months of ennui and mayhem, and the blame rested squarely with the Department and those who ran the jails. Staff work with the cloth that's cut for them. They expect that those charged with running the jail will do what they should. Of course basic supervision and surveillance were not at the desired standard that Sunday, but if the escape hadn't happened then, it would merely have been postponed.

That evening as I went home, I feared for us all. My position wasn't in jeopardy because my duty centred elsewhere, but I was guilty by association. I felt angry and helpless: angry that this was preventable, helpless because no one heeded me or the other staff who saw the dangers. Next day as the staff who had been off duty that weekend returned, their mantra was, 'Thank God I wasn't on yesterday!' Still, that escape wasn't concocted and executed inside a single day. Others were culpable by omission, carelessness and poor judgement but weren't on duty when the shit hit the fan.

We turned over the entire jail. Every cell was searched; beds, lockers, sheets, personal effects were dumped onto the landings and what didn't fit on the landings was dumped onto the wire mesh that stopped items being flung down on us on the ground floor. Staff moved like men possessed. Prisoners glared silently, afraid to open their mouths lest our anger and shame be visited upon them. It was tense. Anything not officially allowed was dumped. Then someone on North Two started to rip open a mattress on the landing: inside was a steel clamp. The curse of our careers was found. An expanding clamp had been placed between the parallel steel bars and widened the space between them, allowing prisoners to slip out. Obviously this was the same clamp that facilitated the December escape.

Our problem was that in dumping all the mattresses and bedding onto the mesh, we didn't check what cell that particular mattress came out of. So we didn't know who had been holding it: typical of the mayhem in the place. In our anxiety to find a solution, we didn't use best practice. How does a clamp get into a jail, a clamp that facilitated two escapes? Now that's a good question. A search of the workshops showed that all their clamps were in place and accounted for. The mystery remains to this day.

In tandem with the searches there was a Departmental Inquiry. Two Justice officials took over the assistant governor's office and began interviewing staff. The blame game and scapegoating started: who was where, who was supposed to be where, who told whom what, who locked or didn't lock the cells, who locked or didn't lock gates? That is normal: the will to survive and be seen as having done one's job is in us all. Eventually I was summoned into the inquiry. The assistant governor's office was small, with opaque windows looking out to a courtyard. I was neither greeted nor invited to sit down.

As I pulled my chair closer to the table I surveyed my inquisitors. The nearest guy – the real boss – slouched on his chair, slightly grey-flecked dark hair falling over his eyebrows. His eyelids reminded me of an iguana: they seemed to coldly open and close, giving off no warmth. His sidekick was bespectacled and equally morose. It was of course not a time of celebration and jollity. Pushing a sheet of paper in front of him, Iguana-Eyes asked what the hell was going on. I answered as best as I could, listening carefully and more interested in saving my own bacon than anything else. The questions didn't directly pin me, which was a relief, but the tone was as if those two guys were dealing with something that stuck to the bottom of their shoes. It ended inconclusively: I simply got up and walked out with a word of farewell from them.

That night at home my mind raced. In bed I recalled all the times we had brought this entire mess up the line, the information given to me in the kitchen, the finding of the rope, the finding of the hacksaw blades, the sending up of forty totally unsuitable prisoners to an equally unsuitable jail. The inquiry was to nail a few scapegoats and hang them. Keep it local, keep it focused on the low-grade staff and let the culprits at the top away with it. I felt from the meeting with the Department guys that we were seen as basically idiots. I reached under my bed and brought out a handful of photocopied half sheets: the ones with the information on who might escape and a few others.

Next morning I asked the governor if I could be interviewed again. This was a gamble: I was in the clear, but I also was part of the jail that this had happened to, and with the stroke of a pen and a different job description that Sunday, I could have been fighting for my job over an issue that extended beyond the local. I was called back to the assistant governor's small office. Nothing had changed in the previous twenty-four hours. Once more, no invite to sit down, no 'Hello, John.'

'You looked to see us again,' said Iguana-Eyes.

'Yes,' I replied.

'Why?' he asked.

'Because yesterday I got the feeling that you lot thought that we were like Keystone Cops here . . .'

He fiddled with a piece of paper, saying, 'It looks that way, doesn't it?'

'Well, that is wrong: we are run off our feet here, we report anything and everything that happens and it's not our fault that people choose to ignore what we are saying.' With that I passed him a number of photocopied half sheets. He studied them, without interest at first, then slowly sitting higher in the chair. He gave the first to his colleague and started to read the second before passing that one on as well. He read another. He looked me in the eye.

'Who got those . . . who did you give them to?' I told him the CO, which was true, because it was countersigned by him with a note adding 'to governor'. Looking at the one regarding the rope and hacksaws along with the names of the potential escapees, he asked: 'And nothing happened?'

I nodded my head, adding, 'We can only do what we are allowed to do.'

He once more looked at his co-inquisitor and back to me. 'Can we keep those?'

I stood up and went to leave. 'Yes . . . I have further photocopies of all of those,' and gently closed the door on my way out.

I didn't save the day, but I certainly presented another side to the story. Still, it didn't save me from being a scapegoat myself, as others tried to paint my return trip to the Departmental Inquiry as an exercise in self-preservation. My conscience that day was as clear as it is now. I did the right thing for all of us, but a few tried to construe a different angle that saw a few people never speak to me again. Eventually change came: a number of transfers for staff. It could have been worse; they would live to fight another day. We got a new governor and a new chief. A chapter had closed on the travails of a tired and much abused jail.

For the first and only time in my supervisory career, this new governor brought the ACOs over to a meeting. We sat around him on a ring of chairs as he placed his bum on the large desk in his office and sought to reassure us. Gradually, he said, we would regain control of the prison. He was true to his word.

The new CO wasn't a warm guy. I had worked in Spike for a while with him, and initially he saw his transfer to Arbour Hill as a poisoned chalice: it had become a graveyard for a few COs. His attitude was that he wasn't going to be the next victim, so he had no favourites and it was his way or else. Whilst I never warmed to him, looking back, he was what the doctor ordered.

We clamped down on everything. No stray movement or wandering around. All gates locked, cell doors locked and a strict enforcement on unaccompanied movement. One Sunday I was in charge of the inner jail. All prisoners were in the exercise yard, recreation hall or locked up in their cells. The check gates on the landings were all locked. You are of course as strong as your weakest link. Some 'nice guy warder' – the type who can never say 'no', the type who passes the buck until it nearly catches fire, the guy who wants to be the prisoners' friend – was in charge of the north yard exercise gate. He let a prisoner through unaccompanied who wanted to go back to his cell. This wasn't allowed: the prisoner should have been turned away at the gate.

Now he was my problem. I told him to return to the yard but he simply walked by me and tried to get into West Two, finding the gate locked. I called up to him, 'Get off that fucking landing and back to the yard.' I still see him ignoring me, looking up at the skylights. My teatime relief arrived to let me off. I filled him in on what was happening and once more ordered the prisoner from West Two. As he came down the stairs I was putting my civvy jumper over my shirt before I left the jail for my tea. Through the jumper I saw him pick up pace, ball his fists and drive towards me. As he left the last step, not realising I could see through the jumper, I rugby tackled him around the ankles, sending him over my shoulder, whereupon my colleague got him in a head lock. We took him to the strip cell amid a flurry of 'fucks' and 'cunts' aimed at us.

Next morning he was before our new governor. The riot act was read, severe punishment dispensed. 'How dare you assault one of my staff . . . who do you think you are?' the governor demanded. The prisoner apologised, and he meant it. I was impressed by the governor, not because he took fifty-six nights' recreation off the prisoner but because he spoke of 'my staff'. It was nice to be part of a team. About a month later my attacker approached me. You don't keep grudges in a jail, it would paralyse the place. 'Mr C, do you mind if I go in and ask the governor to suspend the rest of the lock-up nights?' I actually didn't, and I was impressed that he had come to me first.

There was, however, another reason that I was happy for him to go in and look for a suspension. Each prisoner by law is entitled to an hour's exercise. Failure to provide that can lead to a High Court habeas corpus. We exercised our punishment prisoners from nine in the morning until ten. The problem was that we hadn't always got the staff, as work was about to commence within the prison for the inmates, as well as visits and reliefs for staff. Throw in a court escort or a hospital escort and you were in real trouble. So getting two officers for exercise was a bit of hassle. My prisoner's long punishment cycle meant we were under pressure every morning to find available staff.

I told him to see the governor on his morning parade and if he wished he could tell the governor that Mr Cuffe had no problem with it. This he did, and ten seconds later he was out the door, glancing at me before looking up at the ceiling, face blushing. When the parade ended the governor summoned me to the office. 'Mr Cuffe, when I give punishment for one of my staff being assaulted, when I give an order, I mean that order to be carried out to the full . . . do you understand?' It was my turn to go red. I nodded, apologised and slithered out the door, jaw on ground. Never again did I interfere in justice being dispensed within the jails.

As we surfaced for much-needed air around mid 1988, a long-festering boil needed lancing. Relations between the POA – our union – and the Department of Justice were low. Noonan had short-circuited the 1984 industrial dispute but the rancour had lasted. The union had one of the best public speakers ever along with a mixed crew of different talents. I could take them or leave them: I possibly leant more on the 'leave them' side but I always heeded my father's advice about unions (he was a bus driver). He believed that without the union he and his comrades would have had nothing at all, so he gladly paid his subs. I concurred.

Negotiations broke down time and time again, and as the union had called for a strike many times, this time they had to go through with it lest they be seen as the boy who cried wolf. Despite the POA representing all grades up to assistant governor, I always believed that the only ones they could represent adequately were the officers. I was an ACO – neither fish nor fowl, a strange breed indeed – and if I had a dispute with an officer and he sought union support, it left me in a strange place because the union also purported to represent me. Thankfully I always managed to avoid such a scenario, but it did trouble me.

I also felt that the union was too militant: don't ask me why, but I wasn't a fan of theirs. And I didn't want to go on strike. I spoke about this openly and often to all grades across the job as the D-Day loomed. The evening before the strike I was in a quandary: I felt they were going the wrong way about it, but I couldn't see any other solution. We gathered up the keys and vital jail documents and lodged them in the general office. I had taken a few phone calls from well-placed people whom the union trusted urging me to support the strike, saying that I was well regarded and that whilst people knew of my difficulties, my support would be welcome. That night I discussed the issues with my wife and decided I wasn't going in. A weight lifted from my mind.

Next morning I was awake as usual at 7 a.m. I felt strange but I also felt released; I had done the right thing and was actually happy with my decision. I went out to cut the grass and thought my car was a bit lopsided looking. I glanced at the right rear wheel and spotted a puncture. As I took the spare out, I then noticed that the left rear wheel was flat too. Coincidence? Subliminal messages, perhaps: a reminder in case I needed any convincing about where I stood regarding this dispute? I shall never know. It turned out that I was the only ACO to walk on the picket with the Hill staff. I did feel for the guys who for one reason or another chose to pass the picket and go in. It wasn't easy; indeed I would say they mainly were brave but ultimately foolish.

The strike lasted a full month. I used the time to train like a demon for the 'Dublin Millennium' marathon. We got tax money back, along with a few bob from the union. Financially I was as well off as when I was working. Once freed from my conscience, I enjoyed the month. I roamed the country roads and climbed hills. My wife and I ran the Sugarloaf hill climb, winning silver medals. We should have a strike every year!

No, not really. Whilst some guys, the stronger ones who came in during the strike, were ignored but not harassed, others – guys who were previously seen as the 'in men', guys who were the life and soul of the party – were treated as lepers, boycotted and verbally abused. They had betrayed their colleagues and they would pay a price. Years later their main tormentors, sadly, were younger officers who weren't even in the job during that strike.

The day before the strike was officially over we went to a mass meeting in the Adelphi Cinema. We were fairly ebullient and happy at the thought of going back. A new roster was being introduced for the staff and we were getting a grand for our troubles. The fine print was laid out for us. Basic grade officers would get a new work roster with three eleven-hour days on followed by two days off, rotating to two on, three off. However, this new roster or work plan was only for the basic grade officer. It did not cover from the rank of ACO upwards. This shocked me. I had – reluctantly – gone on strike for a better work schedule and now we were left behind. It was to take five years before my rank finally was accorded the same status. But the best part was to come. It was customary and respectful to answer your name for the morning roster with the word 'Sir'. You might not mean it, but it acknowledged you were present and ready for action. Now a cock-a-hoop union grandee shouted into the microphone that no longer would the word 'Sir' be used: it would be 'Present' or *Anseo*.

This was childish and almost anarchic. Decent staff had no issue with the word 'Sir', and now they were being put in a position where they were bringing politics into the morning and afternoon roster calls. Next day we went back on duty. I met the handful of lads who remained at work during the strike. Openly I shook their hands and told them I bore no grudge. Quite a few of the staff did likewise and some didn't. That was understandable, and for those men, life was actually changed forever. Gradually we resumed and regained control.

The roster calls were chaos, though: a Babel Tower of 'Yes', 'Here', grunts and *'Anseo'*. Once I learned not to take it personally I actually didn't care: if a guy replied *'Anseo'* I addressed him and called out his duty in Irish. I'm a native Irish speaker from a granny who had no English. Soon, though, I got tired of it and reverted to English. In time the guys with balls reverted to 'Sir', almost to prove that they were their own men. The old timers were happy with 'Sir'; the younger guys clung to multilingual replies: childish but, in the end, irrelevant.

In late October of that year we had three very disruptive pups. I normally don't refer to prisoners in such disparaging language, but this trio were acting the blackguard big time. Two I knew from my Shanganagh days, the other they recruited in the Hill. They figured that if they acted mad enough they would be transferred to the Central Mental Hospital in Dundrum and effect an escape from there.

One of them in particular was the harbinger of bad luck. Three of his former acquaintances had either been killed in stolen-car crashes while with him or committed suicide. He was a bad one: one of the few I would describe as such. Most people have some redeeming features. This guy struggled in that department.

One evening they tried to treble up: two were in a double cell, the other in a single cell. They asked me and I refused, correctly. They were a danger to staff and putting all three together was asking for trouble. A day later one of them committed suicide: the assumption was that it was an accident. However, needless death in jail is severe and painful for all. That evening jail life continued as normal. We are always extra alert in case of copycat attempts, but the jail seemed at ease. We were still wearing cheap rubbish as uniforms and a slight chill had entered the yard. Rather than go to my locker for my tunic, I borrowed a long raincoat from the ACOs' control room. On returning from the yard after exercise, I assisted supervising for the late supper. From the corner of my eye in the very busy Circle I saw someone heading rapidly in my direction, a jug in hand and a look of deadly intent in his eye.

The next sequence happened in a blur. He broke through the other prisoners and let fly with the two-pint jug of boiling water, laced with sugar to do maximum damage, straight at my face. Forewarned is forearmed: the corner of my eye had given me a vital second. I quickly turned my head away, brought up my shoulder and squeezed my head towards my chest. My raincoat took the brunt of the steaming water and the jug bounced off my ear, sending the rest of the water down my neck. The steam rose from my coat as I lunged at my assailant, who squealed like a pig when he realised I was not disabled. The troops ran in, outraged, but I had him in a headlock, one arm up around the back of his neck, as the steam still encircled the two of us. I took him to the padded cell saving him from a fate he might not have wished.

I was shocked, though, as the water cooled and I saw the effect it had had on the raincoat. Had I not worn that coat, I would have been severely disfigured. I put him on a P19: a form that's used for discipline. One of the senior staff took the place of the governor for the report to be dealt with. It was written fairly and described the circumstances. The result was a week's loss of recreation. I thought my ears were deceiving me. As the prisoner was removed he looked at me and apologised. I ignored him, my eyes instead focused on the judgement deliverer. The CO – the one whom I saw as cold – looked equally shocked. 'I was severely assaulted, I could have been disfigured for life and you think that a week's loss of evening Rec will settle it?'

A stony silence ensued before the senior official cleared his throat and said, 'Well, I have to take everything into account and the circumstances are we had a suicide and feelings are raw.' I was more aware of that than him: I didn't need telling. I was angry now because the implication was that I brought this on myself by not allowing them to treble up. I said as much, and a rather unconvincing 'No' finally emanated. I recalled the last time I refused treble-up, on North Two the night before the first escape: a prisoner who had painted his cell wanted to go into the double cell from which the two were to escape. Had I permitted it, three would have gone that night. I solved that one by telling the painter to place an onion in his cell that would absorb the smell of paint.

So I bleated on but was never going to win. 'I see this as a reflection on me, that I'm to blame for the suicide . . .'

The senior official was getting impatient with me now: 'Nobody is blaming you, you did your job and the right thing but that's it: one week lock-up.' Gathering the single report form, he got up and walked out. The CO wasn't impressed and knew I was angry. The staff didn't take kindly to it either but that was that; nothing would change. A week later the CO had my assailant transferred to Limerick. Down there he started stirring the shit with other Dublin prisoners. They attacked him, slashed him and, ironically, poured boiling water over his face.

He was promptly dispatched back to us. I reported for evening duty totally unaware that he was back. A colleague caught me by the arm and said, 'I've someone here I'd like you to meet.' With an evening shift ahead, I was in no form for banter or bullshit. Reluctantly I followed him down to the end cell on East One. Opening a door, I espied a prisoner with a scarred face. It was my old adversary, but I didn't recognise him for a moment. 'Hello Mr Cuffe . . . I'm back . . .' Walking away as the door closed behind me, I thought one word: karma.

Going away on my summer holidays that August, I was by now a married man with a beautiful seven-month-old daughter. When I came back to work we had another new Chief Officer. Inside three years and eight months we had four governors and five COs. This guy was to top them all and dominate the next decade.

7

Sledgehammer

Courage is fire and bullying is smoke.

BENJAMIN DISRAELI (1804–1881)

Late August 1989, back from our holidays, I was refreshed and ready for the rest of the year. As I walked towards the main gate the usual banter was taking place: 'Mayo for Sam, John?' being the main currency of my workmates, referring to my native county's first All-Ireland senior footbal final appearance since 1951. I gave as good as I got, and as we walked we discussed our latest Chief Officer.

Inside the ACOs' office I spotted a young, fit-looking man sitting near a radiator. I was introduced to the new boss, and was met with a warm handshake and called 'John'. We had met, briefly, over the years, mainly passing through Mountjoy as we turned around our prisoners. All Arbour Hill prisoners returning from court had to go to Mountjoy first, as the Hill wasn't a committal prison: a technicality whereby we lodged them and, once the paperwork was sorted, took them back 'home'.

The new chief, as 8 a.m. approached, jumped up,

grabbed the morning detail roster and went out to face the assembled troops. His reputation as a fearless warrior had gone ahead of him, such were the loud 'Sirs', *'Anseos'* and 'Heres' from the troops as they acknowledged their attendance and duty call. Quickly the CO gathered a few nicknames, but the one that stood was 'Sledge' as in Sledgehammer. Nothing was impossible to him within the confines of the jail. He brooked no opposition and quickly showed one and all his confidence and capability.

Years earlier, as the staff in Mountjoy were under external attack from a group of thugs who labelled themselves as the PRG (Prisoners' Revenge Group), Sledge's name came up as being under threat. Earlier, as I have mentioned, two very prisoner-welfare-conscious and decent senior officers had been attacked: one had his house torched and the other was dragged and beaten with iron bars on his way home near the Strawberry Beds. Sledge heard of the threat towards himself, found out where it originated from and calmly walked into the fabric shop in Mountjoy with two batons stuffed down the back of his trousers, past forty hard chaws, and demanded that the hardest come up and take him on, there and then, in front of everyone. Not surprisingly, after much looking at the floor, there were no takers.

Put bluntly, you didn't fuck with this guy. Behind his tough demeanour dwelled compassion of sorts: sometimes very warm, sometimes quite practical, but with a granite force that feared nothing, including Satan (that's not a joke, by the way). In time we would all feel his presence and his power. The next ten years of my career were to be determined by this man, with widely different outcomes.

Initially he was a breath of fresh air. He cleared out all the debris Mountjoy had earlier sent us up; more than likely he played a huge part in selecting what we actually got. In the end only one of those troublesome prisoners survived the cull. Prisoners gave him a wide berth, as did certain officers, such was his decisiveness. You either marched to his tune or you found another band in another town. A number of staff decided to further their careers elsewhere. I myself welcomed him, his ideas and his clear-minded way of running the jail. In addition he was a long-distance runner and had completed many marathons, just like myself. In time we started to run together in the Park, mile after mile ground out. This brought a certain amount of slagging on me. I was seen as his 'pup' and his 'man' because I ran with him. In truth, over the years I ran thousands of miles with the man but you could compress what he said on those runs into a single sheet of paper. He was a deep, silent, morose runner. Still, I was framed as having some special relationship with him. That brought a touch of the 'green eye' out behind my back.

Around this time, possibly due to a rise in high-profile murders and sex cases, Arbour Hill's prisoners started to fill the media. One of the first to get wall-to-wall coverage was a prisoner called Vinnie Connell. He had been arrested and put on trial for the murder of a woman at the Fraughan Festival near Johnnie Fox's pub in Glencullen, County Dublin. Connell was a former prison officer; he spent a week with us in Shanganagh on job familiarisation at one stage. He was also a noted DJ, hence the Hill staff christened him 'Fab Vinnie'. He told me he had been a member of the Merseyside Police. Part of him appeared

Walter Mitty-like, but the charges he faced were very serious.

Much of the evidence was circumstantial, and almost ten years had lapsed since the crime. It was a difficult trial, and dragged on and on. Prison staff, though bottom of the totem in the courthouses of the land, have a unique front-row seat during trials. Connell wasn't your ordinary subservient 'lag' trusting implicitly in his defence team and their expertise. Vinnie, on my observation, called the shots and drove the agenda. Mild-mannered and calm in front of us, he was forceful and determined to the point of bullying in laying out what he wanted from the defence team.

Vinnie was always immaculately turned out in suit, waistcoat, pressed shirt and matching tie, and had long piano-playing fingers. One morning he was in particularly good form going down to court. He explained to me, 'Mr C . . . today I am going to land a big blow on those fuckers.' 'Those fuckers' were the prosecuting Gardaí. Connell hated them with a passion. As the trial resumed, former Superintendent Courtney was called to the witness box. Courtney was a member of the Murder Squad and had a high reputation. He came across as matter-of-fact and to the point. This guy was no pushover and had been in bigger court battles. His Kerry voice would have made a great Bull in John B. Keane's *The Field*.

Vinnie's barrister had in front of him a piece of paper that he fondled carefully. Connell himself, in front of me, purred as the paper was twisted gently between the brief's fingers. 'Superintendent Courtney, you believe that my client here committed this crime of which he is charged?' Courtney grunted and nodded in agreement. 'How come, then,' continued the brief, 'how come, then . . . years later you signed a form of good character for my client to go to South Africa if you deemed him such a threat to society?' The air was sucked out of the courtroom. The presiding judge played a bit with his wig and we were all on our toes, ears cocked. Courtney was nonplussed. 'Can I look at that signature?' The document was passed to the court clerk, then to the judge and rather gingerly to Courtney. A quick scan from the eagle-eyed Kerryman before the document was passed back to My Lord. 'This is not my signature . . . that signature is of another Superintendent Courtney, not me.' A sound like air escaping from a tyre hissed from Vinnie.

Eventually Connell was found guilty and, as he trooped up and down the stairs to his new home on North Two as a prisoner, he cut a forlorn sight. Head bowed, shoulders like a drowned duck, feet trudging, tray almost carrying him instead of the other way round, his attempt at getting some fraternal sympathy from his former colleagues was wasted. A senior officer moved closer to the stairway and as Vinnie moved over to receive words of comfort he was instead met with, 'The first five years are the hardest . . . ha ha ha ha ha!' I was coming down the other side of the stairs and heard Vinnie reply, loud enough for the bearer of 'good news' to hear: 'Cunt'.

If anyone thought Connell would lie down and accept his sentence, they were wrong. He badgered the courts until he was released over a legal point that was in his favour and the gates swung open for the Fab One. Was he guilty of that murder? Will we ever know?

When he got off, I was there, and I was appalled and disgusted that a technicality bore such a high return. I was also institutionalised into thinking that the Gardaí were always correct. Today with the benefit of hindsight, having seen what other credible witnesses said in statements to the Gardaí, I am not so sure that it was merely a technicality.

Initially Sledge and I got on famously. I looked up to the man. A gradual freeze was drifting in, though, and I was the last to notice it. We still ran in the Park but there was something I couldn't put my finger on. What little conversation we had became stilted. Like sailing in a fog towards a lighthouse and the first indication you have of it is when the foghorn blows, so it was with me. I didn't see it coming, but when it arrived it was hell. Looking back, I am still flummoxed as to how and why it happened and the wounds, though covered, are never far from the surface. Something that happened to other people was now happening to me. I was being bullied, and it wasn't nice: it was horrible.

The first thing you feel when you are being bullied is pain. The next thing is shame. You doubt yourself, you question yourself, you are in an almost out-of-body frame of mind, constantly asking why, constantly making sure you don't give your tormentor the chance to humiliate you. You can actually smell the transfer of power as it slips from you to your torturer. He knows it but, worse, you know it. That silent sly smile, those eyes telling you one thing: 'You are fucked, a beaten docket . . . worthless.' The natural default setting within most of us, and especially within me, is to try to please the aggressor, try to do what you think they want you to do. It doesn't work. You are now going against your own instincts, those very instincts that made you what you are in the first place. But the worst feeling is knowing that all your workmates are aware of the place you're in and no one can help you. Those who like you feel for you; those who saw you as a cocky little bollox now have their moment of joy.

Bullying is hard to quantify: one man's 'He stared funnily at me' is another's rolling of the eyes and a silent 'He's going fucking mad' look at the person who tries to get to the bottom of the allegation. Decisions I once made easily now became arse-covering exercises because, depending on Sledge's mood, no matter what way I called it I was wrong. Worse, staff who had time for me saw the toll this shit was taking on me, and I hated their pity. Sledge would confront me in front of my colleagues with a question that he already knew the answer to, secure in the knowledge that his audience weren't going to defend me as he tried to belittle me.

I used to sometimes get the 7 a.m. bus to work and, though not suicidal, I wished a car would knock me down and lift me from this Garden of Gethsemane I dwelt in. As I walked to the bus, I ran scenarios over and over in my mind. Indeed, sometimes I plucked up the courage to confront my tormentor, but when I was in his presence that bravado slipped away like sand through the fingers. One ACO told me that my only hope of redemp-tion was to transfer out. 'You know,' he said, 'once Sledge takes a dislike to you, you are fucked.' 'Who are you telling?' I silently thought. Nowhere in the conversation was a smidgen of 'Maybe Sledge is a bully or Sledge is wrong.' He put the fear of Christ in prisoner and staff alike.

At home I couldn't escape him. Rest days were a rarity and I treasured them. We had two children by now, and on a sunny summer's day I took our phone off the hook as I played with the kids in the back garden. A good friend of mine who was also on a day off arrived at my house: he had to cycle two miles to pass me a message. I was to ring the jail. I did. Sledge answered. 'I want you to come in . . . such and such an ACO has gone sick and you're needed.' I protested meekly, imploring that it was my day off, that my wife was at work and I had nobody to mind the kids. 'That's not my problem,' he said. 'The jail has to run and you're to get in here.' He then slammed the phone down.

To cut a long story short, I did. Logistically I had to move heaven and earth. Mentally I felt two foot tall. Today I would have used two words to Sledge: 'Fuck off.' And I have to add that until my dying day I will never forgive myself for going in. I was a wimp and let myself and my family down.

In February 1992 I embarked on an Open University course. I wanted to do it, and many of the staff were interested in how I would fare. However, Sledge took it almost as an insult, along the lines of 'Who does he think he is . . . a governor or more educated than the rest of us? Education and degrees . . . they won't lock up many cell doors.' Some of my colleagues fed him plenty of fuel along those lines.

Coming into the summer it was customary for us to flag our holiday intentions. As I was junior ACO, I allowed the senior men to put in their choices first. A window for two split weeks opened up: the first and last weeks in August. I wanted the first week for family holidays and the last week for travelling to Durham University for a compulsory OU school.

I logged those into our roster book beside all the other men's. That evening when I returned I saw both had been Tippexed out. I knew Sledge did it. I had to meet the devil in his office and ask why. 'You're not the only family man here,' he attacked. I tried to reason, pointing out I had allowed everyone else to have first pick: those dates were available. 'It's make your mind up time, John,' he said (I hated when he called me 'John'). 'You can have one of those weeks, not the two . . . take your pick.' Coward that I was, I opted for the OU week: once more, like Peter, denying those I loved.

A week later a strange thing happened. An ACO who had pencilled in his name for the first week of August Tippexed it out. Two ACOs were allowed time off on holidays at the same time. Now the first week of August, prime holiday time, was available once more. The other ACO possibly never wanted it in the first place, but pandered to Sledge to slice me. (As my tormentor, Sledge had an accomplice or two.) Big Jim, my good friend – we had worked together for many years – didn't spare me. 'Stop feeling sorry for yourself and stand up and be counted' was his advice, cold and true but well meant. Truth was, I wasn't capable of doing it. In late July I asked for the spare week . . . if no one else wanted it. Sledge neither said yes nor no; a day later I saw my holidays stuck into the sheet. I had got what I wanted, but at an enormous price.

Writing this chapter saw me refer back to old work notebooks and running logs. The work diaries mainly referred to hours worked and shifts done. However, the running logs paint a picture of my turmoil during that time. Selecting a few examples I can now track the change in temper and manner towards me.

26/4/91 – 'Polo. Temper . . . recalled*.' That notation refers to the morning I was ordered in to work despite it being my rest day and having no one to mind my kids.

1/5/91 – 'Pressure at worst . . . God be with me.' A call for help?

30/8/91 – 'Tough @ work.' Not the prisoners.

15/3/92 – 'Rough day Thur Sledge Pig.' Heat is rising.

31/3/92 – 'Another week. I find it hard going.' Not referring to running or prisoners here.

9/8/92 – '40 years of age on 7/8. Some week at work, a disaster.' Happy fortieth, John.

27/9/92 – 'Long run on Wed. Good week. Work s**t, God bless us.'

22/11/92 – 'OK. Bad @ work . . . Surviving.' *Surviving* written in margin. Barely, though.

Mid August saw an intensification of my pain. The hot weather had addled the prisoners and they were getting giddy. We had an upswing in cutting and acting the blackguard. This mainly stemmed from a small corps of younger sex offenders who were a long way off maturity. Night after night we had self-inflicted cuttings, almost as if rehearsed, one trying to outdo another. When you come on nights, generally you hope to have a quiet one, especially in a non-committal jail like Arbour Hill. Sometimes, like Forrest Gump, you don't know which chocolate you will get from the box. I was to stumble into one of those nights.

Around 10 p.m. I heard an almighty smashing in a cell. The noise when I reached my office on the ground floor left me in no doubt that somebody wasn't best pleased. On investigation, the bright light of the cell showed smashed delph all over the place: smithereens, smashed to dust. Not alone could you see it, you could smell it and watch the tiny delph particles floating in the light. The prisoner had a leery look on his face. Normally composed, he was now full of hooch, a form of home brew concocted by prisoners. I don't know if he had read Sledge's mind or seen his actions towards me, but this guy gave me a look of contempt. In addition, he had deep lacerations on both arms.

We removed him to the strip cell while he called us every cunt and fucker he could think of. The medic examined him and decided he would need hospital treatment. That was a nuisance, because we already had a team out with an earlier cutter and we were short of staff. Anyway, I phoned for an ambulance and a fire brigade one arrived. Then the prisoner refused to go out if he was handcuffed. 'You gotta be joking, pal,' I said. However, he dug in. I now made a call: a big call. I sent away the ambulance after asking the prisoner umpteen times. He deteriorated somewhat, so we got an On Call Doc in. The On Call Doc told me that this prisoner needed urgent treatment in a hospital or the consequences would be dire. I recalled the ambulance, went to the cell, handcuffed him myself and saw him escorted from the jail by two officers.

A few days later I was back on night duty. A prisoner, Anthony Cawley – christened 'the Beast' by the media but whom I found easy to handle – cut himself, hitting an artery. Cawley was well known, a survivor of abuse in Trudder House for young travellers. He cut a strange sight: pale, bordering on pale yellow, wired to the clouds, arrogant, aggressive and trouble personified. Behind all that lay a gentle boy, a kid once chained naked to a wheel by an abusive alcoholic father, a boy abused in state care. But he always fought the system: you never beat him; you agreed parameters. I, luckily, had an insight to his soul, gleaned from conversations and trust built and broken over time, then rebuilt again. With Anthony you had to reset the clock often. He spoke to me when he felt the heat coming on. Once when he was really cocky and on his way back from the workshop, he grabbed the tea urn full of boiled tea. He started to shake it violently. Health and safety, injury to himself, injury or assault to another prisoner or staff member flew through my mind. He was doing this on my patch and in front of me.

I shouted at him; gleefully he stared back at me and gave the urn another hug and shake. I marched over, caught him by the scruff of the neck and flung him towards the East One gates. 'Get back to your cell, you fucking eejit!' I roared at him. He grinned back at me, as if almost in shock. As we fed a prisoner from the East Wing, a guy who kept me informed on events sidled up to me. 'Mr C . . . mind yourself, Anto is put out that you showed him up in front of the other prisoners . . . he's going to do you.' I made sure my back was against the wall: I had a clipboard in my hand and I waited for Anthony to come out for his grub. He flew out like a chicken from a coop, glanced over at me, but then went and filled his jug full to the brim with boiled tea, got bread, his sausages and beans, and made straight for me.

Inside I was relaxed. I knew the lad, and showed no fear. 'Anthony,' I intoned, 'we aren't going to fall out over a tea urn . . . are we?' He looked at me, picked up a slice of bread and whispered 'Jesus, Mr C . . . you showed me up there . . . in front of all the others . . . what am I going to do?' I looked at him and actually understood his position. Eyes watched from the landings; a few staff hovered near me, smelling the danger. 'Ant . . . just look at me,' I whispered, 'then walk away and as you are half across the Circle, look back and point the finger at me, but don't overdo it . . . OK?' His pale face lit a warmer glow of yellow once more. Off he went, pirouetted halfway across and said out loud, 'You win . . . I was wrong to grab the urn . . . I could have hurt myself.' I could have split my sides laughing. He had a wicked sense of humour but I always felt 'treat someone decently and you fear nothing'.

Getting back to the night he cut an artery and what lay ahead: that's all I needed, another bloodbath. I arrived down at his cell and bollocked him. 'I thought me and you had a deal,' I barked, 'that you wouldn't cut yourself, that if you felt pressure you'd send for me, we'd talk and I, the soft gobshite, would give you a few fags and you'd play the game but no . . . you had to fucking cut yourself and fuck up our nights, you gobshite!' I was almost pleading with Anthony because he had let me down. Of course I was feeling heat from another source; my every decision was being examined and this happening so close to the last bust-up made me look like I was a soft touch.

Ant looked at me almost tearfully. 'Jeez, Mr C . . . I didn't know it was you that was on, I thought it was ACO Bloggs . . . if I knew it was you I wouldn't have cut myself.' He was telling the truth: I had swapped with another ACO but the roster sheet didn't reflect the change. Either way I was the one with the crock of crud on my doorstep now. This would be by the book. Handcuffs on, no shit, team picked, van parked out front and down to hospital. Clear instructions: 'Handcuff this bollox to the bed if needs be' were my parting words. I had enough.

Next morning at handover I told the CO of the night's fallout, its highs but mainly lows. As I gathered my civvy jumper and was about to leave I added, in order to lick ass, that I had told the staff to handcuff the prisoner to the bed if necessary. Sledge shoved over the door and, in the presence of other staff who were collecting keys etc., let me have it. 'You did, did you? Makes a big change from the other night when you sent a prisoner out without handcuffs,' he spat, almost frothing from the mouth. I dropped my jumper on the table and replied 'How dare you? I had that prisoner handcuffed, I did it myself and he was handcuffed going from here . . . who told you that shit?'

Once more he surged. 'Listen, John – the prisoner made a toerag of you that night, led you around like a donkey and you buckled.' There was a sneer of disgust on his face as he spat the words along with the dreaded 'John'. My head spun: I knew the prisoner was handcuffed going out; didn't I risk my job by refusing to let him out earlier and sending away an ambulance, what more could I do? Sledge grabbed the clipboard with the daily roster on it and headed out to address the morning crew. I trudged the walk of shame: every one of the staff had heard the tirade. Head bowed, I couldn't wait to get away. Now I was being lied about. How much more of this could I endure?

Driving home that morning was a nightmare. Normally I took in the early morning summer sunshine, looking forward to getting up after a rest and going for a run or doing the weekly shopping and seeing 'normal people'. As I drove along, my head was running through the night's events again. The word 'toerag' went round my head time and time again. I could hear it and all its connotations. Worse, the staff had heard it.

I was jolted from my reverie by the screech of brakes. It was pure instinct: belting along at pace, I drove up behind a tractor and trailer. They were crawling, I was speeding, the trailer was high, and had I not instinctively jammed the brakes on, I would have been decapitated.

This had to be stopped. So angry was I that I decided I would sleep a few hours and return to the jail to have it out. I must have been totally exhausted, because it was nearly 3 p.m. when I awoke. No harm, next day would do. The following day I was on evening duty, the 1 to 10 p.m. shift. I arrived in at 12 p.m. and asked to speak to a senior manager. He nearly shit himself when I outlined what happened the morning before and the ongoing abuse I was subjected to. His concern, though, wasn't for me: it was confronting my tormentor and he himself being dragged into it. 'Put it on paper,' he advised, adding, 'You know what the CO is like . . .' I certainly did know what Sledge was like. I was on the receiving end of dog's abuse, uncalled for and unfair for ages. All I wanted was a sit-down discussion to get to the bottom of it. Reluctantly he agreed to do it after lunch.

On my way over to the ACOs' office to cover for dinner, who passed me but one of the crew who took out the prisoner whom I handcuffed and who supposedly made a 'toerag' out of me. 'Hey buddy, didn't we send yer man out in cuffs the other night . . . Sledge accused me yesterday morning of sending him out without handcuffs . . .?' As I was saying the words my voice trailed off. My colleague's face screwed itself into a ball of misery, going red and then white. 'Eh, John . . . we took the cuffs off him in the ambulance, we didn't want him kicking off in the ambulance.' I couldn't believe it: all I had gone through, all we had gone through and those two had decided once out of my sight to take the cuffs off! Nice guys indeed. 'You fucking destroyed me, boys . . . fucking destroyed me ye did . . . thanks very fucking much . . .' and I walked away shaking my head. Sledge and the staff breaking for lunch passed me by and I felt as if Sledge was aware of exactly what really happened but was content to leave me to stew in my own shit.

Now I was between a rock and a hard place. Proceed against Sledge and the facts were that he was correct: the handcuffs *were* taken off the prisoner, but in the ambulance as I continued in charge of the jail. In doing that, I would have to drop the two officers in the shit and accuse them of disobeying a direct order and a fundamental warder's tenet: keep the cuffs on until the prisoner is dealt with. I was furious. I was also beaten. I had Hobson's choice: nearing 2 p.m. I espied the senior manager coming through and rang his office. The conversation was short and to the point: 'I have no complaint to make.' The sigh of relief was audible down the phone. I was fucked.

Moving into dark November, life was awful. Once more I ran into Sledge. He was after a certain officer for some reason. On that particular evening Sledge should have finished at 5 p.m. The officer concerned was late turning up for evening duty. I knew that he and Sledge were at war. However, this officer adopted a different approach from my supine 'lie down and let him kick me in the arse' approach. He fought Sledge at every turn. This infuriated Sledge, and to make matters worse for me, this was the officer who had taken the cuffs off the prisoner in the ambulance. I actually hadn't a lot of sympathy for him, but I had a bellyful of my own misery to contend with.

I was in charge of recreation in the hall. The internal phone rang. It was Sledge. He had an infuriating habit of trying to put on a different voice at times. But I knew it was him. Basically he informed me that I was to question this officer as to why he was late and take action if I was unhappy with his ability to function in his job. I knew what that meant. I trudged down to the locker room. No matter what decision I made, I was going to wind up like Michael Collins signing the Treaty: I was signing my own death warrant.

I spoke to the officer concerned. I had motive to shaft him and pay him back for shafting me earlier with the handcuffs, but all my life as an ACO, I believed in the Corinthian and sporting approach: give a man a chance. His message to me was simple: stay out of the fight between him and Sledge. The reason why he was late was that he was taking advice of a different nature regarding his treatment. I smelled no drink off him, there were no slurred words, therefore all I could do was send him to his post and dock his time lost. Before he walked out he said, 'Don't get involved doing Sledge's dirty work.' I replied that any decision I made was mine and mine only. Little did he know what awaited me.

Off to the recreation hall he went, and I wondered where Sledge was and how I was going to break the bad news to him. As I exited the locker room – the old prefab in the Cage area – suddenly Sledge sprang from a doorway. He was in civvies, wearing a warm woolly hat pulled down over his forehead, his anorak collar up to his ears. A soft glowing light shone over the side gate entrance and something deep within me told me to get to it before something bad happened to me. As I focused on the soft yellow glowing light over the door, Sledge said one word: 'Well?' I told it straight. The officer was sober, correct and fit for duty . . . in my opinion. I spoke to him and saw no need for concern. I would dock the time off him.

Sledge nearly exploded. He moved right into my space, I could smell his scent and I felt like this was a horror movie. 'I knew it!' he sneered. 'I knew it . . . indeed I was told it by others – you're fucking yellow, John – you are a yellow coward – no fucking backbone – others said that about you too.' I didn't believe that others had said it, because one thing I wasn't was yellow in doing my job, and everyone knew that. Others may have pandered to his suggestions about me, but that was a different scenario. A strange thing happened: I was now in the place beyond fear. I burst out laughing at him – OK, it was nervous laughter but it was the laugh of a man who never ever in his wildest dreams believed this could happen to him.

He went to grab the collar of my greatcoat but I put up my hand instinctively. Now I was about to be milled by a colleague: Jesus Christ. Then a big shadow filled the soft-lit doorway where safety and freedom beckoned. It was a fellow ACO who was my friend. I don't know whether he guessed what was going on, whether he needed to go to the toilet, but I was never as glad to see him in all my life. As he walked towards us in the narrow alleyway, he asked out loud, 'What's wrong here, guys?' Seeing my chance, I sped past Sledge and headed for the doorway. 'I fucked up again . . . well, according to Sledge I fucked up again.' He stepped aside to let me through but blocked the path of Sledge. We never spoke about that episode. But he saved my job that evening. Maybe he saved more than that?

What more could possibly go wrong? Well, there were a few more scenes left in this nightmare. Moving towards late November of that year, our domestic life was blighted by the serious illness of my mother-in-law. My wife was making long trips for the right reasons and still keeping her job going. Life was a grey blur. I was due my long weekend off from work: Thursday, Friday, Saturday and Sunday. I was recalled for duty on the Sunday. That was a nuisance, but who would I complain to?

My mother-in-law's health wavered from severe to critical and back. After spending the guts of the week with her we decided as a family to return on the Saturday night because I was at work Sunday morning. The journey back was quiet: the kids were asleep in the car and my wife was lost in familial thoughts; I was dreading the next day in hell. Coming near the house, our car hit a patch of black ice and skidded. A big drain lay to the right: it was a near thing. Once we were inside and the kids settled, I gathered up the scattered post from inside the hall door. One envelope was very familiar: the brown one with the window that held my cheque.

But who had sent it to the house? Our pay cheques

always came to Arbour Hill general office, where we collected them. On the front of the brown envelope were scrawled the words 'Ring prison soonest!' The hand-writing was familiar: that of another ACO who had also been given a hard time by Sledge but whose place in the firing line I seemed to have taken. I rang the jail and was told I was not required for Sunday. The guy who told me was also the beneficiary and he was suitably apologetic, saying it was Sledge's decision. Well, it was the wrong decision but had I the heart, the balls and the guts to fight it? Had I known the shift detail was changed, we could have stayed with my mother-in-law.

Around midnight we got a call. My mother-in-law had deteriorated. My wife struck off; I remained with the children. A few hours later the phone rang. The news was grim: the lady had passed away and my wife had not got there in time. Sledge had now messed around innocent people, people who weren't part of our 'feud'. I was never more angry with him than then. Next morning I rang the jail and told them I would not be in because of the loss. I didn't look for leave even though I was entitled to it. I feared abuse and humiliation. Instead I took a week's sick leave and backdated it to cover the rest days off as well. This had to end, but how?

At last a new year dawned: 1993 came in and I hoped for a more peaceful year. Sledge gave me a wide berth. He was a sly fox. He knew that he had messed up over the recall and the situation that emanated from it, the funeral. Throughout all of this, going back to 1991, I tried to be a dad, an ACO, a runner, a student, a friend and ally to my colleagues and family. But by Christ it was a slog through muck much of the time. When I recall my fortieth birthday celebration I can see us sitting at the table and the candles lit. Everybody was laughing and joking, but all I thought about was work.

Sean Courtney was a high-profile prisoner with us. An army chap, he had unaccountably murdered a woman who asked for directions. The media took a massive interest in Courtney. It was the start of their affair with 'exotic' crime. In jail parlance, Courtney was solid gold. Mannerly, self-contained, looked for nothing and threw himself into his sentence, head down. In the outside world he was a killer, evil. That's what the warder has got to separate in his mind. The crime committed outside is separated from the criminal in your charge. If you cannot balance that, go sell ice cream.

Guys were good to me at work. Often they gave me a lift home. One night a guy who was clever and, I often thought, wasted in the prison service gave me a lift. On the way he stopped for petrol. Up to that juncture our conversation was banal: jail bullshit. Back in the car, he gave it to me between the two eyes and without warning, in a calm, almost mesmeric voice: 'John, why are you allowing yourself to be abused and tortured like that?' I answered, 'Don't know what you're talking about . . . nobody is abusing me.' Calmly, he laid my last two years out in front of me. 'All the guys see it. They're upset but you just put up with it . . . when are you going to shout "Stop"?'

That was my rock-bottom moment. Like a dirty secret, I had wanted Sledge's bullying to remain a thing between the two of us, a thing that was private and unseen by the rest of the staff. I had failed. I knew Big Jim knew, I knew a few shit-stirrers in my own rank knew, but I was flattened to hear it confirmed that it was a jail-wide issue. We parked in the dark outside my house and spoke for two hours. I was drained at the end of it, but a spark had caught. He told me that another officer who was being bullied seriously had thought about bringing a shotgun to work and shooting Sledge. I burst out laughing; he looked at me and said, 'I'm serious.' Before he left he said one more thing: 'We will help you, but you've got to help yourself too.' I wiped away the tears from my eyes as I headed to the sanctuary of the warm light outside my front door.

That few months of calm and the fact that I had handled the escorts for Courtney's trial had restored my confidence somewhat. The conversation with my colleague had given me a glimmer of hope. A Monday in early March began as routine. Our panel was off Tuesday and Wednesday. I was detailed off both days, and one of my colleagues was recalled on the Wednesday. I was happy – I didn't like overtime. It was a cheap way of running a jail into the ground and wearing you down. That night at home the phone rang. My wife answered it; it was for me and it was the jail.

We had got a new ACO, a solid lad. Big Jim had taken an uncertified sick day (USL) the next day. As I was up for a recall next, he was letting me know I was on duty. I needed the recall like a hole in the head. I explained to him truthfully how the Hill ran. The ACO would tell Sledge in the morning that Big Jim had taken a USL. Sledge would then ring me and I would be in for around

10 a.m. That way I could help get the kids ready for school, get an extra hour in bed and live a little. Most other jails ran it in such a way that whoever was up for a recall was automatically called in. Sledge, however, was something of a control freak and wanted that power to himself. The new man thanked me and said that that was a strange way of doing things. I laughed.

Next morning the phone remained silent. At 9 a.m. I rang and asked to be put through to our tea room, where we had our meal breaks. An ACO answered. 'Am I on today?' I asked. A silence, a throat being cleared, and, 'Well, John, such and such an ACO has been brought in . . . eh . . . ah . . . it's nothing to do with me . . . Sledge brought on the Wednesday man.'

'Sound,' I replied. Once more I was reassured that it had nothing to do with him . . . heaven forbid that any of my colleagues would plant a boot on my prostrate body as Sledge stood over it. 'I know,' I lied.

'Hmmm', I thought as I replaced the receiver. Sledge had made his first blunder with me. I went for a long run. I turned myself into Sledge (and no one knew him better than I did, from our days as 'friends' to nowadays as foes). He would have relished shafting me. His train of thought ran thus: Big Jim and I were deep friends. We had been together since joining up, almost. Funnily enough, even though we confided in each other, I could never bring up Sledge's treatment even though Jim did, only for me to brush it away. Bullying does that to you. Back to Sledge's mind: 'Ah yes, Big Jim went down to give Cuffe a handy recall. Well, I'll show them . . . ha ha ha. Bring on the Wednesday guy, and that puts the two of them in the box.'

I knew Sledge was afraid of Jim, so really it was me who was being shafted.

Later in the day Sledge would have gone for his run. He would have rehashed his actions as he galloped. Then something clicked: a little dark cloud came across his horizon. He wasn't entitled to shaft Cuffe like that. 'What if Cuffe complains that he has been done out of overtime . . . can't have the governor hearing that, and me running the jail,' he would have figured. Passing the Wellington Monument, he would have the solution: recall Cuffe on Wednesday and put off the other guy, make up some cock-and-bull story that it would have taken Cuffe too long to get in and he needed an ACO from nearby: sorted. A smile and a kick of speed as he rushed back for a bite to eat.

The problem was that Cuffe was also out running and figuring. In fairness, Sledge was scrupulous about apportioning overtime. This was a huge departure for him. I knew he hated certain officers, but never once did he let his thoughts interfere with fair play in the monetary stakes. When I got home I took the phone off the hook. The jail would not be able to contact me. I had warned my good pal from two miles away never to come to my house with a message from Sledge or the jail after the episode where I was forced to go to work and leave my kids behind with a babysitter on *my* day off.

Next morning, the Wednesday, I was up at seven and took the phone off the hook again. My wife went to work. Without being told, I knew I was recalled on the Wednesday to make up for the hasty decision on the Tuesday. But the beauty was simple: no one actually told me and, as I had already rung the jail on the Tuesday morning enquiring about overtime, only to be told my services weren't needed, I was ahead of the posse: home and hosed. I went for a long run around the time Sledge would have gone for a run. I once more put myself into his mindset. Confusion and doubt: no smiles, no sudden spurts of power running. This time it was going to be different.

Thursday morning I decided to die on the battlefield or something to that effect. A colleague met me, gleefully announcing, 'Wait until Sledge sees you. You're in the shit.' I took in his cocky countenance. He was the guy who was bleating about it having 'nothing to do with him'. Squaring up to him, inching into his space, I replied, 'The only one in the shit this day is Sledge.' And no sooner had I uttered those John Wayne words than who appeared but the devil. Sledge came from behind the grey stairway. For some reason still unknown to me, he opened with, 'Will you deal with Mr Cuffe or will I?' The guy he said this to was the same rank as myself. 'No one will deal with it,' I said, loud enough for a few officers and prisoners to turn around.

Sledge was a survivor and, being an atypical bully, the last thing he wanted was a public confrontation. 'I'll see you in my office after breakfast!' he said. I walked past him. 'No you won't: I'll see you in the office now!' and I kept walking. I went towards the Circle gate, the officer who opened making sure he had no eye contact with either Sledge or me. Sledge had to run to keep up with me. He jangled the keys to his office, all the time trying to regain composure. He then sat at his desk. 'Sit down,' he barked. 'No, I won't fucking well sit down. I want to see the governor this morning: make that nine o'clock!' He was ashen-faced.

'Sit down, John' – only this time it had gone from a bark to a plea. He was fiddling with a piece of wire that had been confiscated from a prisoner. For some reason I had a pair of pliers in my hand. 'I won't sit down – you took away twelve hours of overtime belonging to me. You did it because you thought Big Jim was setting me up. I didn't want the fucking overtime – I never spoke to Big Jim about it. I told the night ACO that you – only YOU! – could decide who fucking well came and went here.' He was rattled.

'You don't understand . . . ' he whinged.

'Oh, I understand all right – you have given me hell for no reason for almost two years. I never did anything to you . . . I looked up to you, for fuck's sake. I admired you – I fucking well hate you now; my wife missed her mother's death over you, you bastard. Does that make you feel good? I sent that fucking arse-licking prisoner out in handcuffs and it's well you knew it – the boys took them off but you rode me. The other night I was asked by powerful people in this jail to write an account of your bullying of me so as they could lodge it with others in the Department of Justice.'

His reply was textbook: 'Did you do it?'

I laughed, a laugh of liberation and rage: 'No, I didn't do it. Can you tell me why you are torturing me . . . why are you trying to humiliate me?'

He was beaten, but not dead. Again he asked me to sit down. Again I told him to fuck off. Imagine that: two men telling each other to fuck off. How had I reached this low? 'You don't understand . . . I . . . eh . . .' – he tried to continue but got tongue-tied. In truth, I myself was weary and just wanted to get out of the room and back to a normal life. We let the air in the room fill the space between us. A clock ticked. He looked up at me, his face pale. 'Do you want to see the governor?' I was wasting my time seeing any governor: you don't beat City Hall, and if it came to the choice between Cuffe and Sledge, the former wouldn't win. Anyway, I felt great: I had said more than I ever felt I could say. I felt cleansed, almost pure. I felt sorry for Sledge, rooted to his chair as the clock ticked and the piece of wire halted the flow of blood to his fingers. Belatedly I dropped the pliers and shook my head. 'No – no need to see anyone – I've said what I had to.' He was relieved. 'There's nights going on Saturday – I'll give them to you – it'll make up for the day you lost.' He stuck out his hand. We shook. 'Will you go for a run today at lunchtime?' I nodded and walked out.

The rest of the day was a blur. Staff sidled up to me, a quick shake of the hands, a wink, an 'about time' type of thing. I was just glad to sail into calmer waters. It was an awful journey. Tim Field, an expert on bullying, wrote: 'Bullying consists of the least competent, most aggressive employee projecting their incompetence on the least aggressive, most competent employee, and winning.' A pretty accurate summary, I would say.

8

Clear Water

I have come to regard the law courts not as a cathedral but rather as a casino.

Richard Ingrams (editor of *Private Eye*, b. 1937)

The courts are the ultimate theatres, roulette wheels dispensing justice, often determined by a quirk of fate, a flaw in a law or a well-paid brief. Justice, though 'blind' and supposedly equitable, often is anything but. People unaccustomed to the courts turn up expecting their tormentors to get their just desserts, only to find that their own character is in question, their own past raked up and cast at them, while their aggressor watches them squirm and is not required to testify.

Most courts are mundane and boring. As a young man I loved them. In time I saw them for what they were: lotteries and money-making machines full of life's discarded. Justice was like a giant pig: it suckled a multitude. Free legal aid is essentially a lifetime guarantee to the criminal fraternity that no matter what, the state will insure them fully against any retribution or consequence.

We make the laws, you break them, but we will pay for your defence: it's madness when you think about it. It will never change. The legal fraternity are plugged into a golden tap and any attempt to remove it would be batted clean out of the ground with cries of 'War on the poor who cannot afford a defence!' Go on out of that, you hypocrites!

Of course the criminal justice system put bread on my table, slates on my roof, as it did for the Gardaí, the solicitors, the army, the court clerks, the translators, the note takers, the expert witnesses, the judges, the tipstaffs, the security companies, the pubs around courthouses, the Probation Service . . . need I go on? I shouldn't throw too many stones from within the glasshouse. Still, as time went on in the job, my disenchantment focused more on the legal system than those locked up within it.

The old and often decrepit courtrooms, those august and grey theatres scattered across the land, are the arenas where great and trivial cases are acted out. Going into 1993 with some clear water starting to flow between me and the darkness of '91 and '92, I could resume my career as a warder. The courts often were oases of calm for me, places where others felt the heat of the moment but for greater stakes: their very freedom or reputation. The judges, bewigged, often bejowled and Dickensian in gait and features, with black flowing gowns, humped over and clearing their paths through the throngs, broke the tedium of jail time for me.

The barristers, equally coiffured in grey wigs, with plump bellies, pinstripe waistcoats and black gowns, revelled in this nineteenth-century stage with its 'If it pleases my lord' and 'But of course, your honour' and its attendant bowing and arse-licking, as genuine as a million-euro note. Not to be outdone, the court clerks, the solicitors, the guards, the expert witnesses all get in on the act of bowing, bending and nodding as they mumble platitudes.

Sitting unobtrusively but with a ringside seat for this charade and showmanship is the humble warder, a square peg in a round hole, unloved by anyone. To the accused he is the great bogeyman, who thieves his liberty if it all goes pear-shaped. To the barrister, the warder is a sign, a signal, a reminder of who takes the prize away, or not, at court's end. The Garda, bottom of the professional pile in court, needs someone below him, and the warder fits that role. The accused is the meat in the sandwich, the raison d'être for all the actors to assemble, to justify their salaries and roles. The warder develops the knack of being seen but not noticed, tiptoeing around everybody almost apologetically.

On one serious appeal, a lengthy sentence reduction was the prize on offer, and I watched as the three-judge appeal court swung into action.

Three tipstaffs walked out on stage and pulled back great green-studded leather-backed wooden chairs for their masters. Each then flustered around with their respective worship's notebooks, only withdrawing when their masters smiled at them the way I indulge my Jack Russell after she wags her tail at me. The court clerk called out the case and the appellant's team bowled first, trying to get in a few early runs. I watched their worships as they reacted to the bowler's words, eyebrows arched or faces like poker players.

It was then the turn of the state to rebut what had been presented. In this particular case the state played what I call a rather weak few strokes, but the appellant's team had done the work for them earlier: they had inadvertently or carelessly recalled a previous unrelated case for our prisoner that was similar to the one they were now appealing. From almost nodding off, my ears pricked up: so too did those of my colleagues and the appellant. The prisoner shifted uneasily in front of us, glancing between his family and the legal team. The three judges noted the shift in tack too.

They left the courtroom to consider what they heard. The prisoner nodded to me to come closer. 'What the fuck is the barrister at?' he demanded. Experience has taught me that at times like this it's best to say nothing, let your eyes convey sympathy and encourage your complainant to continue, to vent. 'He's fucking well trying to get time added on for me, not taken off. What did he bring up that other case for?' he almost implored. My own sentiments exactly. For us the game had changed. We had an unhappy customer who might get time added on, and in Irish courts that would be some feat. At best his original time would stay as it was.

Now was the time for me to talk, to earn my corn. 'Look, don't lose the head now, keep calm, nothing is decided – maybe the judges will cut it a bit. I know your brief didn't play a blinder, but . . .' With that, a cry of 'All stand!' rang across the room.

Early in my career I figured judges were like the rest of us, prone to doing good and stupid things in roughly the same ratio. I decided that their presence didn't merit my rising off my arse, so I perfected a move akin to raising my right cheek an inch from the timber bench. This I did as the three tipstaffs vied to be tipstaff of the day. The middle judge then started to read the judgement. A long story short: no need to vary the original court's decision, in fact there was a case for the sentence to be lengthened, but, all things considered, they would leave things as they were.

Again the three manservants appeared like extras from *Macbeth* and moved back the seats for their masters. This time I was on my feet as they left the courtroom, in order to ensure my prisoner didn't try to choke the brief or chase the judges as they disappeared into the void behind their benches. We quickly handcuffed him and descended the stone steps into a basement area that had a single cell. Down in the belly of the beast, our captive was fuming. 'I don't want that fucker anywhere near me, Mr Cuffe . . . I'll fucking nut him if he comes down here . . . I'm telling you that.' I took the threat on board – it was real. My companion and I spoke to the crushed prisoner, the usual shite as spoken at wakes and funerals: 'Lookit son, it cudda been worse . . . what have you done . . . three years . . . Jesus, you're almost there . . . don't fuck it up now over that prick' stuff.

He didn't buy it. 'Christ, Mr C, I hope you don't count your wages the way you count years. That cunt stitched me and . . . ' With that a black-gowned ghost appeared at the top of the stairs. Grey wig like a scarecrow's head blown sideways, a sheaf of papers under one arm, a handkerchief in the other hand. Behind him was his devil or junior and a black-clad woman, a legal secretary or a witch from the same *Macbeth* scene. They descended the stairs carefully, mincing little footsteps picking out the next step. No wonder our man got shafted: the barrister wore silver-buckled patent black shoes.

Meeting them halfway and stopping the procession, I informed them that their client didn't wish to speak to them at this moment. 'You are telling me that I cannot meet my client?' he asked grandly. My mind went, 'No, you daft-looking dope – I just said your client doesn't want to meet you just now – never said you cannot meet him.' Clearing my throat, I said, 'Your client is extremely angry. I haven't stopped you meeting him; I am duty bound to tell you that he may attack you. We will do all in our power to ensure that does not happen, but it may not be pleasant. It's up to you if you want to proceed.'

Turning around to ensure his entourage was still with him, he snorted, 'Tell him I'll be up on Monday evening.' As he spoke he fumbled in a pocket in the great gown and fetched out twenty smokes. 'Give these to him,' he gestured the package towards me.

'I'll tell your client that you'll be up on Monday evening and you can then give him the twenty smokes yourself.' I turned on my heel and went down the steps. The ghosts in black exited, muttering amongst themselves. 'Sorry about the smokes,' I said to the prisoner. Normally I would accept them, check them out and hand them over. 'You were right: it's the only fuckin' battle we won all day,' said the defeated litigant.

I very rarely hated a prisoner, but in the case of Brendan O'Donnell I will make an exception. You can do your job to the zenith of perfection and professional correctness, but nobody will own your mind. It's what keeps you sane and safe in those great institutions that warehouse prisoners and would try to do the same to the staff. I treated O'Donnell with the professionalism I showed to everyone in my charge for the thirty years I served. On reflection, I think the word 'hate' is the wrong word to use: 'despise' is better. Yes, I despised him. A heavy-set, curly-headed, overweight slob with a drooping moustache: characteristics that exactly matched mine on occasion.

When I over-ate from the stress of events or jail ennui, I was prone to piling the pounds on. O'Donnell in silhouette looked a bit like me at twenty-five. I despised that. I despised his nicotine-stained fingers: he would allow a butt to almost burn itself into his fingertips. I despised his cadging of fags from everybody he encountered. I despised the measured way he walked, fearless and oblivious to the mayhem he caused. I despised the depth of calm that shielded him from us getting a fix on him. He dwelled in a parallel world.

I despised the society that permitted this useless shit to terrorise a community with carnage. I despised his parents, his neighbours, the Gardaí, the social services: anyone who could have headed that fucker off at the pass. What would it have taken? Don't be alarmed or shocked when I state this. A well-placed shoe up his arse every so often would have been the best reminder to the bastard that life didn't owe him, that he wasn't the master and that, like the rest of us, he had to take his place in the queue. O'Donnell was tolerated; his behaviour was tolerated and put down to rural Ireland bullshit of him being 'different' – the same rural Ireland that hid incest, child abuse, sex abuse, corrupt Gardaí, rotten priests and thieving politicians. What made us Irish: ultimately it's what made us bad and mad.

But what I despised about O'Donnell most was his

slaying of three-year-old Liam Riney with a bullet through his little head: his ear, to be precise. Soft fair hair, beautiful curls, open, honest face . . . just like my then three-year-old. The terror that child felt as the car with his mother sped through the Clare countryside can only be imagined. He was forced to walk, trusting his mother who was in double the terror – terror for her child and terror for herself – and all because some useless piece of shit decided to live out a fantasy film raging in his twisted head. Who was shot first? The pleas, the stifled cries, and the final screams to a God somewhere: all the while O'Donnell feeling powerful with a gun in his smelly hands. And the priest, poor Fr Joe Walsh – perhaps a gullible but definitely an honest, charitable and caring man – led to his death by that bastard as well.

Tom Barry, that great republican and freedom fighter, viewed the victims of the Great Famine with a certain disdain. How could they, he asked, allow themselves to starve and be coerced by a handful of landlords and their agents? Would it not have been better to get out, fight and die trying, rather than simply to lie in a ditch or bed and succumb without a fight?

Many years ago two companions and I were out fishing in a currach. I had just come home for the weekend: nice clothes on, totally unsuitable for fishing, a laden wallet in my pocket and an expensive watch on my wrist. I noticed my companions making eyes at each other. Quickly I knew they were going to throw me into the water. Standing up, I said, 'Lads, let me take my wallet out and put it on the seat please and let me take off my watch, I don't want them ruined.' As the watch was placed on the currach's seat I drove forward and took the two of them into the brine with me. We roared laughing, but instead of me meekly being the butt of the joke as the other two laughed, now we could share the water, the joke and the craic. Nobody will take me somewhere against my will.

Locking up at nighttime, I would wander through the landings. As a supervisor I shared what my colleagues did; turning a key and banging a door out was our stock and trade – it wasn't beneath me. A young officer was locking up North Two landing where O'Donnell resided. Always standing in the door like a country man watching his neighbour's cattle, he said little but those beady balls of brown eyes took in everything. 'Bang it out there, bud,' barked the warder. I was impressed: no quarter given, no faux respect, just a 'Bang it out there, bud.' O'Donnell, the chain-smoking triple killer, asked, 'You wouldn't have a fag, sir?' My colleague barked, 'No . . . bang it out, good man!' O'Donnell paused and said, 'I'm talking to the devil now.' His defence was of insanity and hearing voices: men greater than I can attest to the truth of that, yea or nay. The warder paused.

'You're talking to the devil right now?'

'Shit,' I thought, 'I hope he doesn't get into a long-winded discussion with O'Donnell.' We all wanted to go home.

'You're talking to Satan now?' went my man again. O'Donnell nodded. The warder continued: 'Will you ask him if he's got the six numbers for Saturday's Lotto?' I chuckled all the way home that night.

Brendan O'Donnell was the ultimate coward. Big guy

with a gun and a woman, her son and a compliant, gentle priest, but when the reality of long boring nights in Dundrum Asylum kicked in, and when his status was that of another piece of life's detritus – usurped by some other twat wrapped in his killer dream – O'Donnell stockpiled his tablets and checked out of the hotel of life.

I did hundreds of grey days in the courts. Most were uneventful: sad places, really. The biggest lesson is that justice isn't dispensed there. Rules and loopholes are exploited by highly paid men and women. Justice is just a part of the product. It's a casino or lottery often decided upon by the whim of the judge. To me, the Four Courts on a busy day resembled something from the time of Jesus. A marketplace trading in human misery, the great and the mighty, the rich and the poor, the guilty and the innocent, all came under its tall dome. On occasion, we clashed with its arrogance. On other occasions we clashed with the Fourth Estate, who saw it as their duty to preach from the ditch.

Internal intelligence allied to Garda information told us that one of our prisoners, who was facing trial on serious charges, was a live escape risk. We picked a strong team for the case: me, of course (!) and an officer that I chose. No way was I going to court with the lottery of the detail giving me a dud: a guy who had to be babysat himself. Once in the Four Courts, our prisoner demanded to go to the toilet. I had warned him to go when we were back in our reception. Toilets in the Four Courts were dives and dangerous places. A knife hidden under a toilet bowl or in a cistern, somebody waiting in the next cubicle to mug you: one could never be careful enough.

I checked out the three toilet cubicles. I then fed a three-yard length of chain onto the prisoner's wrist and allowed him into the cubicle. I placed my foot in the doorway. He grunted in anger. 'I can't go to the toilet with those chains on and your foot in the door.' Niceties go out the window at a time like that. 'Shite or get off the pot . . . I don't care,' I replied. Sometimes the less said the better.

At the top of a very crowded stairway our man's barrister lurked, files under the arm, glasses on the end of the nose and his entourage around him. He wished to speak to his client. On a morning like that, the entire area was full of people. No office for consultation was available. I nodded to my colleague to pull back a bit, and I did likewise. The barrister then demanded that I remove the handcuffs so he could speak to the client. Normally I seek compromise, but something in his manner and tone set me off that morning. 'Speak to your client here, we have no office available, no secure place to take the handcuffs off. We aren't interested in your conversation.'

He exploded. 'How dare you! I am entitled to speak to my client and you're telling me that I can't?' Actually I had said nothing of the sort. Incidentally, when you train as a prison officer or become an ACO, no one actually tells you what rules apply in courts: no one knows the exact powers you have or don't have. I went for broke. 'No, as I said, speak away to your client: I don't have a place where I can safely take the cuffs off and, like I said, we are not interested in your conversation.' I could have added, 'By the way, you bollox, you are paid a fat fee to visit your client in prison and take instructions up there, but you'd probably prefer swallowing a brandy at that time of the evening instead.' Instead I said, 'The handcuffs remain.'

They spoke briefly: the air was full of tension and my head was going nineteen to the dozen. Where did I stand here? Had I made a call that would hold up? Satisfied that I had, I strode with the others towards the courtroom. Outside the door I instructed my colleague to remove the cuffs. Some judges freak if they see a handcuffed prisoner in court. In the US, prisoners come into court shackled and manacled, wearing an orange boiler suit. Here, we go through the pressed suit, collar and tie bullshit of pretence. 'I will seek a direction from the judge,' the barrister warned me at the door. 'Seek what you like,' I replied, 'I'll have something to say to the judge as well.' Childish shite when I look back.

The case proceeded. My colleague and I exchanged looks and smiled at each other: so far, so good. A week earlier in the Dublin Bridewell District Court a solicitor had spent an hour in the cells for allowing his mobile phone to ring in court. Now a phone rang out in our court: it kept ringing and ringing. Everybody checked their pockets, briefcases and papers. The judge, a gentleman, looked benignly at the ceiling with a faint smile on his lips. I smirked to myself: I hoped it was my barrister. Eventually the judge asked a junior brief to lift his copy of *The Irish Times* and 'be so good as to turn off that infernal phone'. The startled junior fumbled under the papers, jamming his thumb onto every button as the phone refused to shut up. Red face meeting a grey wig, he mumbled, 'Apologies, your worship.' Finally, silence amid a smiling courtroom. The morning tension finally lifted . . . for me at least.

Coming up to lunch break I decided to change tack. Our prisoner had to be fed. My colleague had to be fed. I rarely went for a lunch break, as I always had a fear of something going wrong. As the judge adjourned for lunch I appeared at the barrister's right shoulder. 'You can speak to your client for a few minutes if you wish. We have to source a lunch for him; my colleague and I also have to have our lunch.' An olive branch of sorts, but really more to save myself unnecessary shite back in the jail. Our governor wouldn't be great to back me in a row with the legal world. Most governors would be of the same ilk.

He nodded and briefly spoke to the client. That evening the court broke until the next day. I raised my arse two inches off the hard bench to honour the departing judge. I liked this man; the rest I generally only rose one inch for. I nodded to my old adversary and he came to his client. The courtroom was secure. I covered one door, my colleague the other. Once the conversation with the prisoner ended, the brief approached me.

'Look, sorry about this morning, I got off on the wrong foot: accept my apologies, please.'

'I'm sorry too: I could have handled it better myself,' I replied. No face lost on either side as the courtroom emptied for the evening.

Frank McCann and Sean Courtney were amongst the first prisoners who attracted huge media interest. High-profile murders, seemingly stable backgrounds, and both men had been highly regarded within their communities. The media couldn't get enough of them. In the case of Courtney, a very well-mannered and polite young man, within the precincts of the courthouse his family were approached by a photographer asking them to come outside for a photo. I told him to fuck off and then reported him to one of the ushers. Hounding the innocent families is not on.

McCann's case was put back for a long time because he set fire to himself in the Hill: again a most compliant prisoner, but a case that involved the loss of life of a child and a woman. Prison officers leave the emotion outside the gate when they turn up for duty. Jail is the punishment. The jailer is not the punisher, nor are they society's conscience. To us the question generally is a simple one. Is the prisoner compliant, mannerly and not troublesome? If he ticks those boxes, then he's a 'good prisoner'. Hence someone like McCann would be seen as 'good' within the system but a young man doing six months for larceny and who fought the system would be seen as 'troublesome – a pup'.

Towards the end of McCann's case a dispute arose between the prison staff and his legal team over access during meal breaks. Once more we were in the grey area. My reading of the situation was that the ACO was correct in his decision, but being correct in jail parlance doesn't always mean 'right'. The presiding judge knew the ACO was correct; the legal team likewise. If not, a ruling would have been made against him. What had arisen was a simple issue. Staff decided to play by the rules, take their lunch breaks, feed their prisoner and themselves, and not run an ad hoc system that facilitated the legal system but was never acknowledged.

Word came back to the jail. The governor got on to Sledge, and Sledge sent for me. He ran the scenario past me, awaiting comment. I replied that my ACO colleague was entirely correct: shades of my earlier handcuff issue. Sledge knew this before he asked me. 'Would you go down tomorrow and see what can you do to sort it out? I know we are correct, but . . .' No need for elaboration. Whilst delighted that I was chosen to sort out a problem not of our making, I was cognisant that I wasn't going to let my colleague down either. Once more we were asked to blur the lines.

On arrival in the courtroom I made a beeline for the defence team. I told them that they would have access to their prisoner during lunchtime, as I wasn't going to use the cell beneath the courtroom. It was a dive, and actually having a prisoner like McCann in the body of the courtroom made sense: he wasn't an escape threat. We were a three-man prison-officer team as the case closed, so two of us would remain in court and the other would get food for all of us. The court Garda was present as were others. There would be no problem.

My colleague returned fairly quickly with a burger, chips and coke for McCann, a fish and chips for myself and a bit of grub for himself. We made small talk along the lines of 'Liverpool for the Cup' and other inane bullshit. McCann joined in. The court Garda read his paper and poured tea from his flask; some of the various legal eagles sat around, eyes closed. Halfway down the courtroom sat journalists with earphones plugged in. Their eyes were also closed. The previous Sunday on duty in the jail I had read the *News of the World* magazine. On the back of it was an advertisement for a simple listening device along the lines of 'Plug me in and hear the most secret conversations', festooned with a scantily clad lady being listened to by a nearby man suitably plugged in.

Some of the journalists with their earphone gadgets: were they listening to us? My paranoia regarding the outside world was elevated. As we spoke I suddenly said, 'See those bolloxes sitting behind us halfway down with their eyes closed eyes and earphones in? Maybe they are listening to every word we are saying.' My partners thought I was going mad.

That time whilst the jury is out is akin to a high-stakes game of poker. The legal teams, the accused, the victim and/or their families all await the result. As the jury is ushered in, the air is charged with emotion as the room is sucked bone dry of moisture. 'Has the jury reached a verdict?' the court clerk asks. The foreman stands and says 'Yes.' At that stage we swing into action. We tell the prisoner to stand up, we are on full alert, and anything can happen: emotions are at the extreme. Sometimes a shaking hand gives away the feeling of strain; other times it's the crease on the suit trousers that wobbles as the legs shake.

In the case of Frank McCann, the verdict was 'guilty'. He sat down. We watched but gave him breathing space. The courtroom quickly emptied. Outside came a roar from the Garda team that put him away. It was guttural and it was understandable. The print press quickly left to file their story. Soon the only people in the courtroom were ourselves, our prisoner and a handful of his legal team. This was the wake from the prisoner's perspective. The funeral would be the closing of the cell door that night as the knowledge of a life sentence kicked in. There are no winners. The dead won't come back: the pain is but momentarily eased for those left behind, a glimmer of victory tinged with sadness.

I went outside to radio the prison van to collect us as soon as possible. Some of the victim's family were in the grand hall of the Four Courts, clinging to the site of the verdict. It's a painful sight: decent people who would never normally cross a courtroom door, now standing around almost unsure what to do. The trial, the denial, the laying out of the facts kept them going. Now it was over: no longer would they be at the centre of that world. The Gardaí move on to another case; for them it's a sort of wake too. Hopefully they feel some form of justice. Inside the courtroom we sat again: by now it was just us, our prisoner and the court Garda.

A call from the prison told me the van would be a little late. My colleague heard the radio message and nodded. The Garda in the courtroom wanted to go home; I saw it in his face and body but he wouldn't come near us to ask. Possibly he saw himself as superior to us: fuck him then, let him stew. I walked out again into the grand hall. The family knot was still there. They rightly wanted to see the killer of their girl and child walk past them, let him hear them, let him feel their anger, their loss. I understand that. Inside, the Garda finally cracked and came over. 'Will ye take him to the Bridewell until yer transport comes?' he keened.

'No,' I curtly replied. 'Too dangerous to move him until my van comes.'

A radio call: the van was outside. We got up from the gloomy courtroom and made our way out, handcuffs secured and McCann between us. Suddenly the little knot of family pushed defiantly towards us. The anger was palpable. I could taste it. One of them said out loud, 'Frank, we will wait for you no matter how long, we will get you.' I felt for the man who said it. It would be a long wait indeed. Here they had a microsecond for one last drive, one satisfying attempted punch or lunge, one last chance to scream and kick. Decent folk that they were, they didn't. That didn't make them any less angry; it didn't make them weak. No, it merely accentuated their tragic loss. Naturally we would have protected our charge, but we would have understood. Life just ain't fair.

Sledge ran a tight ship. All courts were covered, all escorts ran on an overtime basis; however, if a court case or quick hospital trip arose that could be covered over a short time, Sledge deployed an ACO and officer to run the escort. We were happy with that: generally a trip to morning court, plead, beg and bully for the warrant, and back in time for the lunch or lunchtime run in the Park. So when Sledge deployed me to take a new and young prisoner down for a new court date, it was with confidence that he said we would meet for a run at lunchtime. Down we went, into a virtually empty courtroom. Easy-peasy, I thought. What can go wrong here?

The judge entered; the defendant's barrister and solicitor stood up. So too did the state's legal team. The Gardaí, two of them, took notes, a new date was set, up stood the judge, I didn't even move my arse, and out through the back door he went, followed by his tipstaff. Up I went to the only other person in the courtroom, the court clerk. 'Can I have a warrant for my prisoner, please?' I asked. This was routine: a scrawl on a piece of paper and we would be free to go. The court clerk – a grey-haired,

red-nosed, elderly-looking man who seemed to have a slight scent of whiskey on his breath – didn't even look at me as he gathered his papers. 'Too busy . . . going with the judge to another court . . . meet me at lunchtime.' Before I could ask where we would meet, he was gone out the door behind the judge's bench. I was livid. Now I had a prisoner and an officer until lunchtime at least. I had brought no money for food for either the prisoner or myself. I wasn't supposed to be going to court in the first place.

The officer had a fiver. We took the prisoner down to the cells and placed him in an empty one. The Mountjoy staff came to my rescue. They fed both the prisoner and myself. Once my colleague returned I went in search of the court clerk, into this courtroom, into that courtroom, into this office, into that office. Did I find him? Did I fuck.

Lunchtime came and went. I now had a prisoner illegally held without warrant. Knowing what I know today, I would have rung the prison and told the governor to come down and relieve me as I wasn't permitted to illegally detain the young man I had in custody. The warrant holding him had expired at 10.30 that morning; it was now 3 p.m. and I hadn't a fresh warrant. We were in breach of the law, and if the young man was smart enough he would have demanded a habeas corpus. Three o'clock turned into four, and four turned into five. Now I was panicking: no warrant, and no court clerk.

Then up the steps from the Tilted Wig (a pub we nicknamed The Wilted Tit) side of the courts complex came my man. My father – who, when he was on the drink, was not a nice man – always gave the game away when one of the curls on his head fell over an eyebrow, almost as if the drink loosened the hair. That was a sign to watch out: trouble was close at hand. The sight of this bollox, the court clerk, with a looping forelock over an eyebrow, brought back bad memories to me. 'Hey, you!' I called out. He paused, not having a clue who I was. 'Remember me – the warder you refused to sign the warrant for this morning? Can I have it now or will I release the prisoner?'

He tucked the offending lock back up, only for it to fall down again. For a second I was looking back at my well-boozed father. 'I need a warrant!' I spat through gritted teeth. In an effort to pull a sheet of paper from a thick sheaf, he dropped most of it on the ground. Good manners dictated I would help pick it up. He looked glazed, fumbling for a biro, staring at me and trying to avoid stepping on the heap of paper on the ground. He scrawled his name across the bottom of a warrant. 'Print your name under that scrawl,' I demanded. 'Why?' he asked. 'Because my governor will want to know why I was detained so long in court today, seeing as the case finished at 10.45 a.m., so I need to tell him who held me up.' In truth my governor couldn't give a monkey's and, perhaps knowing this, he replied, 'Tell your governor to contact the court office if he has a problem,' and promptly left.

We got back to the jail at lock-up time: almost 8 p.m. A wasted day, a disgraceful day where it was driven home to me how far down the pecking order we stood. Still, we got two hours' overtime, two dinner allowances and two tea allowances, so we weren't entirely defeated.

A few days later a trial that involved multiple incest allegations was due for setting a date. Once more we trundled down. The sitting judge, a man who ran an effective courtroom, didn't mince his words. This case, he told the assembled crowd, would turn stomachs and would not be easy for those involved. He ordered counselling to be made available for the stenographers, the court clerks, the legal teams, the jury and the state witnesses. Interestingly, he omitted the warders: the men and women who lived cheek-by-jowl with such people 24/7. I despaired. We were a forgotten service, a secret service, and only we could save ourselves.

Around 1996 I was tipping along grand: no ambitions to advance in the job. Governors didn't seem to rule the system and the rosters for COs were crap, so 'better the devil you know' kind of thing. Running was consuming my life and I was well advanced in my Open University studies despite the Department of Justice's best efforts at fucking it up. While I was out running one Saturday with Sledge, he informed me that he was taking the Sunday off. His normal deputy wasn't available to act up as CO, so he would ask the newly arrived ACO to stand in. I hadn't the slightest problem with that. Sledge asked me to keep an eye on him, see that he didn't make a balls of it, and on we ran. I did think that it was rather daft: I was to keep an eye on a guy who was essentially keeping an eye on me – on us all. The CO was the front-line commander in any jail. Staff feared and respected a CO more than a governor.

The next day was uneventful. The acting CO collected the Sunday papers, went to the governor's and general office area and probably read them. We went about running the jail. In fairness to Sledge, the machine was well oiled to run without a hitch. Around 11 a.m. an officer came to me looking for a few hours off in the afternoon to do a run. I told him to see ACO Blah, who was the CO. He looked at me slightly bemused, but off he went. We had two lads who played a bit of rugby and they came to me looking for the afternoon off. Once more I referred them to ACO Blah. Once more they looked funnily at me.

Every job has its old soldiers, guys who can either make your life a misery or make it handy, never having gone for any promotion but also able to put a few sticks in any supervisor who gets too uppity. The trick was to manage them. Cut the slack where slack was needed, but call in those favours when needed too. So I wasn't too surprised when a veteran arrived on my patch. 'Ah, Mr Cuffe, what the fuck is Sledge up to? Three ACOs with sixty years' plus experience between them and he puts a guy with a year in charge of ye all and us too.' He was fishing and I wasn't biting – at first. 'Fuck off, you shit-stirrer,' I told him good-humouredly.

As I went for my lunchtime run, I admit my mind did wander. What was Sledge up to anyway? I didn't see any malice in his actions: he didn't see the conse-quences, nor did any of us want the gig. However, fatally, he never asked us, thus giving us the opportunity to refuse. At tea time, 4.45 p.m., ACO Blah arrived to supervise the feeding. 'Jesus, that was the handiest day I ever put in,' he said as he dumped the recently read heap of Sunday papers on our desk. He then lit one of Sledge's fags that he kept for his cleaners and touts. 'See ye tomorrow,' he said breezily as he left for the evening with not a care in the world. We were eejits and I was now annoyed.

As luck would have it, on the notice board was an advert for a new COs' competition. I went over to the general office, printed off the forms, filled them out and waited until Sledge came in the next day. 'Everything go all right yesterday?' he asked. He knew well it did: he had rats who kept him informed. Indeed, at times I wondered if he wasn't supernatural, almost as if he could spirit himself into the place. I handed him the application forms. 'What's this for?' he asked. He knew well from a cursory glance. 'Out of courtesy I am showing them to you first so you can give them to the governor.' Sledge tossed them back at me and said 'Give them to him yourself,' and then walked out. He knew that he had goofed and was annoyed. I felt a little surge of pride.

Days later, while collecting my pay cheque, I met Sledge and his then deputy, a man who even then was more than capable of being a governor but who was disillusioned with the system at the time. 'This man is stepping down for a while; seeing as you are interested in going for promotion, you can act up – I'm taking three weeks' holidays next week and you're in charge.' My ACO colleague, the acting CO, was delighted to shed the mantle: he smiled gleefully. What had I let myself in for? Sledge wore big boots; it would take a big man to step into them.

I have to say the place ran like clockwork. Sledge covered every base, every eventuality and gave me the belief that I was well able for the gig. The staff, fair play, didn't act the bollox and we worked as a team. In a way I was a relief for the staff, from Sledge and his ways, but we all knew that it was his methods that made the jail the best in the country. So we kept to the script and every big decision I made was on the premise of 'What would Sledge do here?' In time I grew into it – almost enjoyed it. In fairness, the troops made it easy. If a thistle needed grasping then I grasped it. If an arm over the shoulder was needed, I provided the arm. I was never too proud to seek advice, knowing well that the decision was going to be mine in the final analysis anyway.

Moving into 1997, I was chasing a quadruple. I was going to be interviewed for CO, I was completing my degree, I was selected for training as a hostage negotiator, and I was about to run my eighth marathon. All would converge around October of that year. I topped the interview selection for hostage negotiator. It was an area that really interested me. I flew my finals in the OU degree: Hons in the bag. The marathon was on course, 100 miles a week. I was actually the first to be interviewed for CO. I felt that I had nicked a top-ten spot. I didn't know the interviewers, nor was I happy that I was first, but I always backed myself strongly in those things.

In Beladd, the prison officers' new training centre in Portlaoise, we were put through our paces for the hostage negotiation course. It was mentally challenging and intense. Every scenario was covered and you were stripped to the bone by the intensity of them. Then out came the CO results. Four or five guys who I personally had put through their paces in the Hill were now ACOs in the Joy and also on the hostage negotiating course. All of them made the panel of thirty. I didn't. I was shocked to the bone. I knew I wasn't a failure; I knew I was a good CO. I knew I had the respect of the staff, but how in the name of Christ had I not even scraped in at number twenty-nine or thirty? This was devastating. The irony was that I wasn't going to accept the rank: I just wanted to make the list. I wanted to see that I had the smarts and the balls for it. Now I was denied that. Not one for my bucket list.

It impacted on the hostage negotiation course, and whilst I made a high placing on the final test, the instructors asked how come I dipped at a certain point. I referenced the CO results and panel. They understood. I got a phone call from Sledge wanting to know what overtime to submit me for in Beladd. To tell the truth, I didn't care about overtime that day. Sledge rang though for a different reason: it was about the CO results, even though he wouldn't admit that. I told him my feelings, my thoughts and asked to be relieved of the post. I didn't want the staff or myself to be embarrassed by a busted flush. Sledge didn't mince his words. 'You're my deputy – that's that. I'm off three days next week; you're back in the saddle . . . I'll leave a note for you.' As pep talks go it was poor, but from Sledge it was possibly the best he could do. It brought a smile to my scorched head as I put the phone down.

Funnily enough, on my return I was treated almost as a hero. The staff saw the system as inherently corrupt. Only the pets got promoted, they said: the yes men. Better, they blamed our own governor for not promoting me, and they all told me that I had their respect. 'Glad you didn't get it, buddy,' one of them said. 'Good guys are hard to get: we didn't want you leaving us.' Never did losing feel better.

After completing my degree, I decided to do a master's degree. Trinity College was offering a master's in drug abuse and alcohol. When I rang to enquire about the course, a rather snooty man suggested that it might be beyond me: more suited to governors and senior Department officials. His tone made me more determined to apply for it.

I applied through our governor. The paperwork was submitted via Beladd, and on to the Department for a decision. Time went by, the closing date passed and I had got no word. I blamed our boss for not sending on my application. He rightly was annoyed; he had sent it on with a strong recommendation as to my suitability. I then focused on Beladd, 'Not us, boss' was their reply. They shovelled it up to Justice. There the trail went cold. I did have the name of the official in Justice the application went to, though. I submitted a FOI application clearly asking for the chain of letters regarding my master's application to Trinity to be forwarded to me.

A month later a fat brown envelope landed at Arbour Hill for me. A covering letter signed by the guy who had received my Trinity application informed me of the contents. It was a mixed bag of information, some of it applicable to prisoners' files, some of it applicable to pay sections, but absolutely nothing about the request to Trinity. The guy who assessed my application must have had difficulty in finding my Trinity half sheet, initialled and noted by our governor and the Beladd training boss. I was exhausted and allowed the system to beat me . . . for now. I took the file home and shoved it in a drawer under my bed. In time I would resurrect it.

The murder of Veronica Guerin shook the nation. Her

exposés in the *Sunday Independent* were compelling reading. Two things stood out: her ability to nail a story was excellent, and she seemed to be ahead of the Gardaí. This was dangerous: either she knew more than the Gardaí or they were using her. That she was blown away on a sunny June afternoon returning from a trivial court case was horrific. The failure of the state to deal with big criminals had created a vacuum into which Guerin stepped. Her articles were required reading as they stripped away the allure and anonymity of the criminal barons. She paid the ultimate price.

Now the state went into overdrive. Arbour Hill, a backwater jail that housed sex offenders, suddenly got three new prisoners. Initially it was all hush-hush, but hush-hush tends not to work in jails. They were Charlie Bowden, Russell Warren and John Dunne. The East Wing ground floor had three cells cleared out for them. Pretty quickly we knew that they were supergrasses or 'Specials'; years later, reading accounts of those men and how they spent their jail time was an eye-opener. The suggestion was they did 'cushy time'. The Gardaí had got three valuable assets and figured that putting them in the Hill would ensure their safety, compliance and a 'soft time'. Well, their safety was ensured, their value was a matter for the court to evaluate, but a 'soft time' they did not have.

Sledge smelled a rat and possibly figured out that those three, especially Bowden, were common thieves who would hang their own mothers to get off. If the guards thought those guys were going to have a jail life of cigars, champagne and broads then they were gravely mistaken. I have to say in my thirty years of service I never saw guys do such hard time. Each was confined to his cell for most of the day and all night. They got out into a converted three-man cell where they were locked in for recreation and their own protection. Gym was accessed for an hour when all the other prisoners were locked up. Visits were especially watched because, bluntly, we didn't trust anyone involved with them.

Bowden gave an impression of intelligence. His army record as a bullying corporal who was dismissed for assaulting a recruit should be enough to tell you of his intellect. Russell Warren – most times I called him Warren Russell – was a nervous, frail-looking fellow, deep, and he certainly had an intellect but wisely kept a low profile. John Dunne struck me as a guy who simply fell into the wrong company at the wrong time. He barely registered with us.

Sledge kept his own counsel regarding those guys. Once he got a tip that Bowden had a phone in his cell. This shocked us: we had watched them like hawks, so how did he manage to get a mobile? You are as strong as your weakest link. To me the weakest link was the Gardaí. We tore the cell asunder. Bowden looked at us with the pity of a man who reserved it for incompetents. Then Sledge spotted him looking at a boom-box radio he had for the gym. As fast as lightning Sledge picked it up, burst it open, and buried behind the speakers was the phone. 'Fuck you, Charlie . . . you're not in the army now or with the guards,' spat Sledge. I was impressed.

The Gardaí loved Bowden. At first they regarded us as clowns. They didn't want us on the escorts with him or the two other rats. They made representations to the governor for us to be dropped from the security teams to court: 'too dangerous' was their reasoning. I had to remind the governor that once a prisoner was sent forward for trial, they were in our custody. I also told him that the only way we could guarantee the Specials' security was to be with them at all times. I certainly didn't trust the Gardaí. On escort to Green Street courthouse they would arrive at the jail, sirens blaring, helicopter in the sky, roads blocked and enough weaponry to start a small war.

Initially I loved the drama: police motorbikes forcing old ladies to pull over as the Garda escort van drove the wrong way down the street. Bee-baw, bee-baw . . . real cops-and-robbers stuff. Then one day we arrived at Green Street, got out of the van with Bowden, and as I looked up, I saw a group of workmen on a building near us, fixing the roof. 'Who are they?' I asked the cop in charge. He started roaring to get out of the yard. On the way back to the jail I realised that my colleague and I were the only two gobshites without bulletproof vests. That told us everything we already knew.

Just as quickly as they arrived, Bowden and his buddies disappeared into oblivion once more, having done their deeds and deals. Veronica Guerin is dead, but not for a moment do I believe that the guy fingered for her death did it. There was a lot of bluster and bullshit, mutual applause, around that affair. At the end of the day only one person did real time for her murder. And to me, it was just another spin of the roulette wheel.

9

Break on Through to the Other Side

The future's uncertain and the end is always near.

JIM MORRISON (1943 – 1971)

The *Sun* newspaper (they call it the *Scum* in Liverpool) once had a writer called Ronan O'Reilly. In April 2005 or around that time, Ronan had a bad day so he took it out on the Irish prison officers. In a vicious diatribe, he told a shocked nation that we were wannabe Gardaí, not clever enough to have made the grade, and that hired bouncers on any nightclub door in Dublin would do a better job.

Even through my thick skin, Ronan had poked a place I didn't think could be hurt. Not for me, but for my kids. Can you imagine what they would think if one of their friends quoted the sick piece back to them? Anyway, as fate would have it, the following day's editorial distanced the *Sun* from Ronan's hate piece: a first, I am told.

What would a bouncer on a Dublin nightclub door do, Ronan, if he was a mere couple of feet from death at any given moment? No, not personal attack – that definitely comes with the bouncer's job – but death unannounced, death by one's own hand, death by a fellow inmate's hand, or death some time later after leaving jail? In times of pain, pressure and panic I didn't reach for the bible or scripture. I hummed, silently of course, the lyrics of Jim Morrison, Creedence, Van the Man, Rory Gallagher, Bob Dylan or Neil Young. Occasionally the words of Leonard Cohen hit the spot, and a few times Kurt Cobain was handy.

'The future's uncertain and the end is always near' wrote the great Jim Morrison of The Doors. And indeed it is. A jail may hum along peacefully, all going well on the surface, and then, out of the blue, death strikes. They say that suicide rates are high in prison. I disagree. In fact I'm astonished that they are not much higher. Take a town with a population of between 15,000 and 20,000. What would the average suicide rate be in that town? Now take a town of similar dimensions but with the population transient, drawn from the dregs of life, from what's deemed criminal . . . what should be the acceptable median of death by suicide?

Suicide, during my career, came stealthily and never to those for whom you'd have expected it. Prisons by their nature have a percentage of moaners, cutters and cry-for-helpers. In time a pattern forms. Those who cut, cut only deep enough to draw attention to themselves, to release an inner tension with the flow of blood. Apart from cutting the wrists and arms, they also slash their legs on occasion: rarely the neck or vital arteries.

In essence they become a nuisance. They use up huge amounts of goodwill and drain staff resources with trips to hospitals. Also in time they fade down the worry list:

you know and they know that they ain't gonna die. In time some, if not most, give up that game. One or two keep it going to the last: arms and legs with scar tissue like an ancient rhino who was out in the sun too long. Let's look at the ones who tweak the system for whatever reason, but don't intend on dying. Here are a few examples.

It's night-time, normally around 11 p.m. The officer arrives down to the ACOs' office. 'Sorry to bother you, boss . . . tried to put him off but he wants to see the ACO.' Now this 'wants to see the ACO' comes with a caveat. You are being tested by the prisoner and, initially at least, by your own staff. Being too tough only gets you so far; being too soft means the staff dread being on watch with you. You go for the middle ground, you become yourself: sounds easy but believe me, it takes time and practice. Let's assume I have passed the staff test. I grab a master key and we trek up the landing.

One such night as I trudged, long night still ahead, poor sleep earlier, I ran my antagonist through my brain. Mentally taking out his file, I saw him as a shitty coward, a pup who, if mammy had slapped his arse at three or four, wouldn't now be trying to take me on. A security man ran him out of a shopping centre once. Our guest found out where he lived and, with an accomplice, turned up one night and raped the security man's wife. My bottom line was already in place as I swung the door open. No deal. No dice.

The tired fluorescent cell light spilled past me, the smell of sweat and glue (non-addictive) filled the air. His comrade was assembling something with matches, a boat or plane. My man sat back, chair tilted onto a pipe that carried heat, legs on the bunk bed. I glared at the pal, and then looked at the requester. 'You wanted to see an ACO – you have a problem?' No, not Clint Eastwood or Mr Wayne, just a tired and pissed-off John Cuffe.

'Eh . . . What 'ospital is on bleedin' call thanite?'

We both knew what he was at. This was the first card in a game: a threat of cutting or swallowing something so I would have to send him out.

Filling the door frame I replied, 'Not a clue, not my problem: I won't be going out with you.' A pair of queens to his pair of tens.

'I heard it was B-Mount . . .' he countered.

I took it up wrong: 'Peamount? That's for people with TB and diseases . . . you got a disease?'

The feet came down from the bunk and his mate laughed. 'Fuckin' B-Mount [Beaumount], not bleedin' Pee-mount . . . right?'

Silence. It's heading to make or break time. 'Is that it?' I ask. The prisoners look at each other again.

'Can I have a mug of tea and a slice of bread?' he asks. I oblige. Night saved for the giving of two mugs of tea and four slices of bread. The intent was there; the will was there, but so was mine. This time I won: I didn't always, though.

We had a lifer, a bully who cut and severed every inch of his visible body. All my talk tended to fail with him. He swallowed batteries, forks, knives, toothbrushes, cleaning liquid. He slashed himself in front of us, once sticking a fork into his belly. All the talk in the world couldn't deter him once his demon roared. However, he knew as well as we did that he'd no more kill himself than Santa would. Another stuck his finger into a bandsaw in the carpenters' shop. I took him, his finger and the escort to the Mater. The Mater shrugged their shoulders and told us to hump him to St James's Hospital. Would they give us an ambulance? No. Finally a taxi came and we arrived at James's. The taxi man asked who was paying; I referred him back to the Mater. The surgical team took the finger from me. The prisoner told them he didn't want it sewn back on. The standoff continued, with the surgeon pleading, the prisoner playing hardball, and both ignoring the two officers in the room.

The surgeon walked out and finally decided to bring us into the game. He spoke to me as if I was the guy's parent. I told him if he didn't want the finger back on, then he didn't want the finger back on. The surgeon asked me to talk to him. I did, kept it short and to the point: we weren't friends, not even in the common-ground area within which prisoners and staff agree. Coldly I told him the consequences, adding that my relief was arriving in ten minutes and that the rest of the staff hadn't an opinion either way. It was make-your-mind-up time. He nodded and whispered 'Yes'. I spoke to the surgeon, my relief arrived and I returned to base: nothing personal, all in a day's work.

You want to hear of something closer to death? Night duty once more, 3 a.m. approx. A young officer comes to the gate of my office. 'Hey John,' he whispers, cognisant that a jail sleeps. I come to the gate. 'I'm not happy about Bloggs – he's . . .' No need for any more. The officer is a good kid, doesn't act the bollox, good with prisoners, always on time and never moans if asked to do a job: if his 'gut' says it ain't right, then it ain't right. We climb the steel stairs, two steps at a time. Down East Two, walking firmly: never run unless someone is being attacked, then sprint.

Peeking through the spy hole, I pause. This prisoner is bollock naked, he's standing on a pile of books, he has a belt around his neck and that belt is fastened to the bars of the window. Twist the key too fast and hard, and he walks into the next world. Take too long and he still walks to the other side. Gently and firmly, strongly but silently I feel the lock come back; I push the door in gently: only one of us can enter the cell at a time because the door is too narrow for any more. I need to lock on his eyes. 'Hey man – you OK?' I ask as I take the first step forward. He doesn't answer but mercifully he looks back at me, and then glances at the window. I step closer again, almost like a cat. Behind me is my young colleague, equally silent and stealthy.

Now I am within jumping distance. 'Jesus, man, you have the shit scared out of me – come down, for Christ's sake,' I say . . . truthfully. My colleague talks now; his voice is soothing and sensible. 'Hey, we'll have a cup of tea, man – I'll help you down – there's a good lad – let me lift that belt from your neck.' I needed his calm voice. Death was an instant away: all the questions, all the whys, the why nots, the who did this and the who did that, who checked him last, all the blame game and getting-off-the-hook shite. My colleague's intuition saved a life. No extra dosh in the pay docket come Thursday. No letter of merit, no medal, no 'A young prison officer saved a man's life last night' in the news. Nothing but the grateful thanks of his supervisor and hopefully the man he kept alive.

Why did this chap decide to act like this seven years into a twelve-year sentence? Would he do it again? Did a devil visit his cell, did his victim call out in his sleep, and was time heavy? We never got the answers. He spent the night in the padded cell; I gave him tea and toast. Our talk was minimal and all we hoped for was that the trust would come back: us trusting him not to do that again, him trusting himself not to do it again. Life went on and he survived. Had not my man checked him at 3 a.m., would I have been ringing an ambulance and the governor at 3.15 reporting a death? *C'est la vie*, folks.

Closer than that? It was St Stephen's night and I was out on the grounds doing a final external check. It was starry dark, the kind of night Oscar Wilde wrote about in *The Ballad of Reading Gaol.* It was past midnight and the jail was settled. Christmas is a maudlin time in jails. I am not a great lover of it: too many Christmases with a father who got sentimental and sloppy from the drink, recalling a past and folk who meant nothing to me, but messing up Santa's gifts. It was easy for me to work within the belly of the beast on a Christmas night, really easy; it's as if I was wrestling my own demons from Christmases past and here was the site for that battle. I welcomed the challenge of Christmas night in jail: do your damnedest, demons, and I will meet you head on. I would lose nobody on those nights.

The medic – our nurse, a walking saint and wonderful lady – dispensed the medicine. We took solace from each other and the night team. This was a good night team, in to do a job, not to recover from alcohol or over-eating. In the segregated area for Special Observation and suicidal prisoners, only one gave us concern. The nurse, a great reader of the mind, gave this guy a lot of attention. I did too. We took him out of his cell; gave him tea, toast, a few fags and a chat. We were in no rush: the night was long, we had the time and the medicine was issued; he was our last. He opened up to the nurse; I listened. He spoke about how his father abused him, abused his mother and took the few bob he earned.

He went on: his employer worked the shit out of him, but our prisoner was happy to work, to get away from home, to earn that few bob and salt away a bit of it before others took it. It was a hard tale, not garnished in the telling, just plain potatoes, salt, milk and fish, like my dear old mom's Friday dinner. I was slightly concerned, but we cannot own anyone. 'Look, if you come under pressure, ring the bell, this lad here will sort you out – I'll come down myself – you're not going to do anything daft now, are you?' My nurse nodded her head: it was time to go. Walking away, we all agreed we were ahead.

Out in the cold black night, my radio licked into life. I was already running as the message came through – 'AÇO Cuffe to Seg, bring keys . . .' – urgent, but not panic. One of my colleagues had grabbed the keys and was there ahead of me. The nurse was on her knees, working frantically; sweat started to show on the back of the blue shirt of one of the officers. An oxygen bottle was being opened. A ligature – the top of his underpants, knotted hard – had worked its way deep into the neck and throat area. His face resembled a crushed blackberry – I didn't recognise it. The nurse looked at me; in her hand was a Hoffman knife, small and shaped like a scimitar, but with a scalpel edge. It's for this very job: cutting ligatures.

She couldn't get her hand inside the ligature to allow

the knife to be inserted. No time to waste, I stuck two fingers inside the ligature thus increasing the pressure: in other words, tightening the noose. We had no choice. His neck area seemed to gurgle. 'Oh fuck,' I thought. I asked the nurse to put the Hoffman behind my fingers and cut like fuck but leave my fingers intact; with one slash the ligature gave way. Quickly the staff put him on his side; the air was connected, then compressions started and after what seemed like a trip to hell, he finally vomited back into life. The doctor had been summoned but the life was secured before his arrival.

No sooner had we sorted that out than word came that we had a severed artery on another wing: a cut at the elbow joint area, deep into the soft skin on the other side. This seemed like child's play after our war zone beforehand. The doctor patched him and he had to go out. Our man in the Seg – the one saved by nurse and staff – was back with us in the land of the living. His blackberry face took on the proportions of a human once more. Up in the staff room I inhaled the smoke from the cigarettes the officers puffed. I, a non-smoker, needed the hit of tobacco. Leaving the premises, the doctor commended the staff. He told me that previously he had only ever seen those blackberry markings of blue and black patches in a post mortem situation. Naturally the next morning's news bulletins didn't tell you about that.

Some months later our man was released, and back into being abused by all and sundry, I assume. I took a phone call late one night in the jail. It was obviously from a bar: glasses and voices in the background. The caller wanted to speak to a very popular ACO.

'Sorry, he's not on duty,' I said.

'Who are you?' the voice asked.

I hate the title 'Mr' – it means nothing, really; a barrier, perhaps. But I replied 'Mr Cuffe'. As it turned out, the caller was the guy the nurse and staff had saved. We made small talk and I told him I was the guy in his cell that night. He then remembered me, and chatted for a while: a human looking for a conversation, and the only people he could talk to were his ex-jailers. 'I'll tell ACO Blah that you were asking for him,' I said, ending the chat. 'You do that, ACO, tell him I said hello . . . he's a good man, had me in Loughan House and treated me sound . . . mind yourselves.' Click and the phone died. A month later word filtered to us that he was found hanging from a tree in a wood. Lonesome to the last, fucked by life, used and then abused and dumped. He took charge of the only thing he owned: his own life. He checked out and cashed his chips in a dark wood on an equally dark night.

I have alluded to gut instinct before. It's always correct: perhaps not at the very moment it gnaws your insides, but it's a portent of what's ahead. You must master it, not let it master you. The balance is delicate. If you keep telling staff that you have a 'bad feeling' and nothing happens, you become the boy who cried wolf and, to the troops, a worrier and a guy best not to be caught working with too often.

Once more we were in the Seg area; the nurse was a different one but also had empathy and a feel for the surroundings. We were at our last port of call: a prisoner in the Seg for his own protection. He had been depressed and out of sorts. We opened up, the light spilled out into the corridor and he turned down the hip-hop music he'd been listening to. 'How's it going?' I asked loudly. He turned off the radio and came to the door. The nurse gave him his medication; he swallowed it with a drink of water from the tumbler she gave him. Looking me in the eye, he replied, 'Never felt better, bud.' We were both operating one gear up: I started it with a 'How's it going?' and he met me head on. It's a subtle world in jail: we were talking as if we knew each other for a long time but tonight was the first night we met and spoke. Each takes something from the other's conversation. The nurse watched and listened; so did the officer in charge of the area.

He asked for a smoke. We brought him out into the lobby. You cannot smoke in those cells; smoke triggers a sprinkler system and floods the cell. As he puffed I watched him and he me. All low key, all friendly. But a silent conversation was taking place between us: the eyes and edges of the mouths transmitted it. It went like this. Him: 'I know you have me rumbled, so tonight I ain't gonna do a thing . . . I smell your fretting.' A long drag on his fag; I swallowed a sip from a coffee mug the class officer had handed us. Me (silently): 'Look, I know you feel like doing something big tonight – I'm not going to let it happen – hang tough – better days will come – I've been there too . . . don't laugh – I have.'

No one heard us converse, but we did. No one heard a word. He finished the fag, thanked us, took the cup of tea and three slices of jammed toast back into the cell. 'Goodnight,' I said. 'If you need anything ring the bell, if you want a fag or tea – not a problem – don't do anything you don't have to,' I said, breaking cover and leaving it ambiguous enough. He turned up the music, loud enough for it to go chukka-chukka-chukka but low enough to be mannerly. 'I'm fine – honest – thanks for the tea and fags – I'll call if I want a smoke . . . goodnight.' We, the staff, looked at each other as the grey door was gently shut and mastered. 'Keep a good eye,' I said to the class man as we departed. He nodded. Perhaps he had heard our silent conversation.

Three days later I was recovering from my night tours at home. The radio carried the bad news. A prisoner had been found dead in his cell. I knew the rest. Our man had checked out, attached a ligature to the bottom of the sink, and dragged himself into the next world. Was I sad? Not really: we weren't friends; we didn't know each other. What did I feel? Truth be told, relief that it didn't happen on my watch. I felt bad for the ACO and team it happened to. I did feel a loss, though: what if we had spoken out loud, or was it all – this silent conversation – a figment in my mind? I feel that something out there alerts us to each other. The trick is how to convert underground connectors and make them useful. This guy could have checked out on my night. I spooked him to defer it: that's all I could do. He was in the departure lounge, just awaiting the flight.

Sledge had the sixth sense of a seventh son. The fucker, I believed, possessed three or four eyes. He read a prisoner like a book. We were having our tea one evening when suddenly he stood up and asked me to accompany him to a cell. We got a key and I opened the door. 'All right?' said Sledge. The prisoner, startled, replied by nodding his head as a morsel of food was swallowed in an awkward gulp.

'Come out onto the landing,' Sledge invited (an offer that couldn't be refused). I was lost as to what exactly was going on. Had the prisoner got drugs in? Highly unlikely. They spoke for a few moments and Sledge said, 'I'm worried about you,' calling the prisoner by his first name. 'You're going to the pad until the doctor sees you tomorrow.'

Meekly the prisoner trudged between us to the strip cell. We took his clothes, gave him a non-tear blanket and a plastic cup of tea. He seemed slightly lost. The medic spoke to him, and then we left. As we went back up to finish our tea, Sledge said, 'I've a bad feeling about him . . . something in my belly . . . better be safe,' and that was it. We finished our tea, life went on and a year or more passed. Then one night Sledge remained late (normally a chief finished at five in the Hill). I was in charge of feeding the jail and Circle area for last supper. I barked out 'East One and Two!' and both of those landings skipped down for their tea, bun, jam and bread. You keep a weather eye at times like that: watch out for heads slumped, guys too giddy, a row over someone bumping into someone else at the tea canteen.

The night was boringly simple. Sledge arrived over to me and we parked our arses on the Circle radiator beneath the stairwell, where we had a perfect view of the descending inmates and their brown trays. A few of the inmates joked with Sledge: small banter. He enjoyed that; there was a humane side within him as well as demons. As the North Wing came down, Sledge's persona picked up like a Jack Russell that spotted an Alsatian. He went silent, stepped forward a foot from me and his eyes locked on someone or something. An inmate was heading back up the stairs with a tray of buns and tea. He was the one Sledge was interested in.

Sledge beckoned him over to us at the radiator. 'All OK?' said Sledge, placing his right hand on the edge of the tray. This was an old trick of his. The tray was no longer a weapon to be flung, and if you wanted to go, you had to drop the tray . . . not to be recommended. They chatted away: Sledge wanted me to hear, but I was also focused on the feeding. We were all tired and needed to get home or, in the case of the prisoner, back to his cell. Finally Sledge let the tray go and the prisoner actually smiled at him; he got a kick out of Sledge holding the tray. Up the stairs he went, giving us both a smile and a look.

Sledge looked ahead as we fed the West side and simply said, 'Something's not right . . . I can't put my finger on it . . . I'm gonna put him in the pad for the night.' I was not on the same wavelength at all, and I prided myself on picking up a vibe: not here, this guy was the epitome of boring normality. However, Sledge had top-class form and I wasn't going to argue because he was normally right. It was the same guy Sledge had put in the pad more than a year earlier for the same gut feeling. I told Sledge I would remain back with him and we'd transfer the prisoner when the jail was locked and the day staff gone home. He appreciated that.

We had got a new chaplain and, generally speaking, we always had a great relationship with the chaplains. They do a thankless and great job. We don't meddle in their area; they leave us to ours. On occasion we might have a difference, but it's always for the right reasons and always resolvable. Only once did I ever have a row with a chaplain. We had a prisoner kick off: this was a violent row, and it took four of us to restrain and pad him. Inside the pad he was berserk, kicking the door, threatening all and sundry. He resembled a caged lion with a toothache. My philosophy was simple: once they were behind doors, we were safe, they were safe and we had control. Out in the open in a jail you can lose control, and this makes the job squeaky-bum at times. He hammered the door, he roared blue murder and I'm sure all of Stoneybatter across to Guinness heard him. I didn't care: he was dangerous and I was concerned for our safety. Roaring and shouting was a price I was happy to deal with. The then chaplain approached me and asked to be taken down to him. I refused, simply on the grounds of safety for all concerned. Chaplains have special rights and responsibilities. It's in our interests to give them unimpeded and unfettered access within a jail. Not on this occasion, though.

I told the chaplain that when the prisoner cooled down, I would permit access. The chaplain replied, 'You know that I have the rank of an assistant governor and I'm allowed to see the prisoners any time I wish.' The former was a new one for me. I was the man in charge of prison operations at that moment, and someone telling me that he held a pay rank equivalent to an assistant governor was starting to seriously piss me off. In fact most prison officers regard the rank of assistant governor as similar to the guy who holds the flag for a marching brass band at a football match: if they were any good they would be blowing the trumpet or even banging a drum. The chaplain, without realising it, had insulted me. We got over our contretemps; he never mentioned that rank again and I never reminded him.

This new chaplain, we got the feeling, was weighing us up. He had a particular thing about the padded cell. As it happened, so had we. Putting somebody into the pad was a big step with severe consequences for all concerned. Something goes wrong and you could wind up in the Coroner's Court, the Circuit Court, fighting for your job, justifying your decisions. I am aware that other jails on occasion had a more flexible approach to the use of a pad; an argument or verbals with an officer could result in a trip there. In the Hill we didn't do that. The pad was for the protection of a prisoner or the housing of a violent attacker until a ruling was made regarding the next step. However, this chaplain, like all chaplains, was to be informed of anybody put in the pad. We complied; it was the way we always did it. Our policy once a prisoner was padded was to fill in the Pad Book: details of the causes, times, staff present, etc. We then filled in a form that went to Justice and the governor. The doctor and chaplain were informed immediately.

As luck would have it, the chaplain was on site that night. Sledge crossed into his office and told him of his intentions. When he came out, Sledge beckoned me over. 'The chaplain wants to talk to the prisoner . . . I'll let him . . . go off for a cup of tea.' A half hour later Sledge dropped into the radio room. 'Thanks for staying back. The chaplain has spoken to him – says he's ok – had a bad visit, but not to worry . . . head on – thanks – you going for a run tomorrow?' I nodded and headed for the gate; Sledge followed. 'I'd have been happier to pad him, but the chaplain seems happy that all is OK . . . strange the feeling you get at times – did you get it?' I shook my head, adding, 'Not tonight, but then I'm fucked from being in the Circle all day – my head is cooked.'

The next morning as I approached the main gate reporting for duty, I espied knots of officers chatting and then moving on. The departing night staff were telling a tale. It was simple. The prisoner Sledge had spoken to the night before had hanged himself at around 2.30 a.m. He had been checked a few minutes earlier, but the staff were too late. The jail was like a morgue for the rest of the day. My eyes met Sledge's at the breakfast table. A whole conversation took place with those interlocking eyes. He and we saw out the rest of the day. Prisoners are spooked and scared, so too are staff: count me in. Loss of life isn't in the deal. Later, out running, away from the jail and prying eyes, we vented and blew away the tension.

Sledge didn't blame the priest; I didn't blame the priest. We blamed ourselves. We should have gone with the initial feeling. It was Sledge's gut, but then when is a system run on gut? Was it scientific, was it qualitative or quantitative? Gut belongs to neither: gut belongs to you. How many people has your 'gut instinct' saved? How many incidents were averted, courses of life changed by your instincts? The truth is you don't know. Coming near the end of the run we stopped blaming ourselves. There was no point: we didn't control the game; we were merely participants with limited inputs. Death, when it arrives, is rapid. You cannot reset the default system; you cannot take it back. It's forever.

One day a young prisoner arrived across from his workplace to collect something from his cell. He had never come to our notice before, good, bad or indifferent. He was in a treble cell on the East. Those cells used to be the class officer's office. The shortage of space saw them converted into three-person cells and the officer evicted, piling his requirements in a storage locker. The Lord giveth, the Lord taketh and the officer offers it all up. The class officer opened the cell door, sprang the lock, told the young man not to be long and took a walk around his landing.

The walk encompassed eighty paces. On his return – mere moments – the officer inserted his key to spring back the lock. He glanced in, and horror. The young man was hanging from the window, dead as a doornail. A shout down into the Circle: 'Ring an ambulance! Get the medic!' I was covering the control and communications area. I got on the blower: 'Ambulance urgently to Arbour Hill prison – we may have a fatality!' The shout down had been ice cold, with a hint of desperation and finality. I walked out into the Circle. The place was frantic, and all action was on the East Two area.

I admitted the ambulance crew. They raced up the stairs, oxygen in hand. Too late, and we knew it. They walked down and shook their heads. Some time passed as the medic and ambulance personnel did what they do. Then a bit of commotion, the barred gate blocking entrance to the communication and control centre swung open, and a body bag passed my open door on a trolley. I stood up and crossed myself. I didn't know what else to do. I sat down and took over the numbers book. I discharged the dead boy and after his name I wrote in bold 'RIP'. We now had twenty-seven prisoners on the East Block and 126 prisoners in the jail.

It was sudden and shocking. Later we were told via the grapevine that this young lad missed his mother. He had asked other prisoners if he died would he get to see his mother, who had passed away years earlier. Some prisoners convinced him that the possibility existed. I hope his mam was waiting for him. No warning, but we pick the pieces up and keep on going.

Another example. It's a weekday morning. It's around 8.20 a.m. and the doctor is in attendance. He arrives promptly at eight every day and is gone around nine. Basically he deals with trivial requests and prisoners just wanting to hear a different voice. The prisoners eat their recently collected breakfast behind their cell doors. The officers eat theirs out in the mess or staff canteen. Each block is covered by a single officer who answers any bells from the cells and locks up the prisoners returning from the doctor's parade: easy-peasy. What could possibly go wrong?

A cell call bell goes on East Two. The officer walks up, sees it's about halfway down; its glowing red light shows him where to go. The voice inside shouts out, 'Give this paper down to cell four please' as it's fed out under the cell door. The officer stoops to pick it up and check if any cannabis is wedged inside it, then drops it as he flicks it ahead of him with his feet on the shiny landing floor. I've done it myself many times. At cell four he bangs the door with his open hand and flicks the paper under. 'Nice one,' comes a voice from the cell within.

Now he is back outside the buzzing red-light door. Quickly he turns the key; a man is hanging from the window. Shout into the radio, 'Doctor to East Two, assistance to East Two now!' It's already too late. The doctor works away, the sweat seeping out through his jacket; an ambulance has been summoned. Forlornly he looks up at us . . . gone. 'Why?' is the question. The theory is this. The prisoner wanted to go to Dundrum, where he assumed he had a better chance of escaping. We had him down as an escape threat. Feigning a suicide attempt whilst the doctor was on site surely would add to his chances of getting up there.

If you want to kill yourself, why come down for a breakfast: why not kill yourself during the dark and long night? Why set the bell off? After all, you wish to die: why bother letting someone know? They will find you at the 9 a.m. unlock for work anyway. We can only surmise. I would never have had this guy down as a suicide risk: I had him down as bad news and trouble. A few nights before that, he had asked to be trebled up with two like-minded prisoners who were very disruptive. I refused. The duo were in a double cell; the space wasn't there but, most important, the combination was deadly. Each of those three had pushed the system to the limit. The evening of the suicide was the evening I had the jug of boiling water laced with sugar thrown at me. The prisoner who flung it by implication blamed me. My conscience was clear. We all have choices: don't mess with darkness.

Death outside prison also affects those within. The loss of a loved one is compounded by the feeling of helplessness and captivity. The guilt trip kicks in, the regrets, the feeling of being doubly imprisoned and the embarrassment of going out, possibly in handcuffs: grief of almost a double loss. A prisoner who was a model inmate but had a rap sheet that stank, twice locked up for rape, had a brother stabbed to death down south. Sledge sent for me: would I go on the escort? Handcuffs on at all times, the trip would be to the funeral home and it basically was an in-and-out job. No problem: could I pick my own man? 'Already picked for you,' replied Sledge. 'It's Rocky . . . your pal.' I laughed. I would have gone to the gates of hell with the Rock; we did indeed travel that far at times. Rocky had a way with prisoners that was unique; put simply, they just walked ahead of him and, dare I say, loved him. Soft of voice, warm of demeanour, he had a brain that was as sharp as an axe. The biggest thug in the place would be converted into a model citizen by Rocky in a short time. If Rock failed then the prisoner didn't last with us, and that would be rare.

We headed off into the winter night. The rain hammered down. In the car were the prisoner, the Rock, myself, the driver (an officer) and the chaplain. The funeral home was actually a converted garage with the coffin on a table, or that's how it appeared to me. We moved closer to the open casket, lit by a flickering fluorescent light. The priest said a few prayers and retreated politely. I retreated too; the driver sat at the door and Rock, though hand-cuffed, tried manfully to bundle himself into oblivion. The prisoner then nodded and we all sat back.

The door swung open and in came the father with a few mates. He had drink taken; my sixth sense kicked in. He stared at the son in handcuffs, then at the handcuffs and then at us. 'Take those cuffs off, in the name of God.' He was angry, he was beaten and this was the final ignominy. The handcuffed son stood up, bringing Rocky up with him. 'Dad, it's fine – I have a deal with those men

– they are sound . . . leave the handcuffs alone.' The father hugged him and, standing back, pulled his frame to the full and addressed me. 'It's awful, sir, isn't it? One son in the box and one son in the cuffs.' I answered the only appropriate way I could. 'I am so sorry for you and your loss – it's awful indeed.'

The clock ticked on the wall and the wind drove in the garage door, wetting the floor behind us. The father started to get cross again: this could now get messy. Rocky looked at the driver and winked; the driver disappeared out the door. Rock then whispered to the padre to say a decade of the rosary. He beckoned me over and muttered, 'When the Glory starts we are out the door.' The padre started: 'Our Father, Who art in Heaven . . .' and on it went. 'Glory be to the Father . . .': as he said those words we were at the car door. The father followed us out and dragged a twenty pound note from his pocket; he pressed it into the son's hands. The handcuffed lad gave it to me. 'Dad, those men, Rocky and Mr C – they'll take care of that and me. There are no problems – honest.' They hugged again. 'Can I give him some fags?' the dad asked. I took them, gave a quick glance inside the pack and handed them to the son.

We drove back mainly in silence. Rocky tried to get a conversation going, but we were all lost in our thoughts. The rain now came in bucketfuls, the sky lit with lightning and black clouds swept across the moon. Packy, our driver, had chosen a different route back and only he seemed to know where we were going. The lightning lit the inner car up at times as pale faces stared ahead into the blinding rain. The dad's words rang in my head: 'It's awful, sir, isn't it? One son in the box and one son in the cuffs.'

10

Goodbye to the Hill

And I realized that there's a big difference between deciding to leave and knowing where to go.

ROBYN SCHNEIDER (b. 1986)

There comes a point in your career where you're so far into it that getting out is no longer an option. That ship has sailed. Kids, marriage, your pension, debts, mortgage all rule out any escape route you might fancifully look at. You dig in and plough on. If you survive to the retirement date then you've won that battle.

We bobbled along. Marathons came and went as frequently as my weight went up and down. From barely able to run two miles to magically upping that to a hundred miles a week, such was the life I lived. Meanwhile prisoners came and prisoners went, most uncontroversial and nondescript. Then Dean Lyons arrived, and a first look would tell you that the boy hadn't the strength or badness in him to rip open a rice pudding, much less two old ladies in sheltered accommodation not far from us. Two women had been gruesomely slashed to death near Grangegorman

Psychiatric Hospital and Lyons was placed in the frame for it.

Like the Gardaí who haunted Sledge when we had the Specials who were implicated in the Guerin murder, now different Gardaí flocked onto a new telegraph wire: Lyons became their interest. He had to: they nailed him for two horrific murders. If I ran a mile with Sledge over the ten years, I ran thousands. Staff figured us tight: a schizophrenic relationship, perhaps. As I've mentioned, most runs Sledge and I never talked. When we did, Sledge set the agenda and it was mainly harmless bullshit. He offered no confidences, nor did you penetrate that thick skin of his.

However, he figured correctly that Dean Lyons no more murdered those ladies than Old Mother Hubbard did. He was curious about the amount of Garda attention he was getting over Lyons, but he never went too deep into it. He did prophesy that Lyons would be freed. He was correct.

Towards the end of November '98 a thief tried to break into the chaplain's car in the prison car park. The cameras picked him up and a group of us, four I think, arrived out to stop him. At first he told us he had permission to be at the priest's car. Sledge told me to get the chaplain, and as I moved, the thief pulled out a syringe and lunged at us. Now the game changed. Initially I hoped he would run off: attempted robbery of a car and all the shite, the lies, the denials would be a waste of time for us. 'Run away, you fucker,' I silently thought.

When the syringe came out, he was going nowhere. We formed a circle around him and his eyes danced from one of us to the next. By now we were on the main road and the home-going traffic was trying to drive around us in the dark. I had him lined up to be flattened when Sledge, a fearless man, ran past me and at him, sending the thief and his syringe into the air. The syringe landed in a storm drain inside the compound at Collins Barracks, but we had the thief on the ground. The Gardaí from the Bridewell came and arrested him. Subsequently we gave them statements and a video of the entire escapade. The would-be thief was out on a ten-year suspended sentence. At the minimum the ten years would automatically kick in . . . or so we thought.

About five months later I came across a paragraph in the *Irish Independent*. It was about our man: the judge told him that the existing sentence was not going to be activated, that no new sentence was going to be handed down, that the judge wanted the Probation Service and welfare to engage with him. I spat fire. We weren't summoned as witnesses; the case as presented or defended by his legal team made us look like Keystone Cops: a joke. At that moment I simply threw in one of the towels from the job. Fuck them and the Gardaí, if that's the way they want to play it . . . fine.

Sledge had gone for promotion. He had done this before and had been successful, but this time I felt he would move if he got it. Call it 'gut'. He did and he did. Part of me leapt for joy that he was leaving: he was a cloud always on my horizon, from pitch black to just a few wisps in the end, but it was always there. On the other hand he ran a brilliant jail, the best I ever worked in. My oh my, a rock and a hard place. Would I trade his oppressive-at-times presence, even though we now got on well, and a well-run jail, for freedom and peace of mind? There was really no contest: I wanted Sledge out.

Thursday was always arraignment day, when the courts were in full swing. This meant simply that the prisoners we had on remand were brought before the Circuit Court and new trial dates or remand dates were set. That particular Thursday I was in charge of the court escort, which entailed eight prisoners accompanied by eight officers. A bit of planning worked a treat. Match officers to their clients in temperament and type. Then collect a bale of files and warrants from the general office; get the prisoners through reception for dressing and searching. Finally pack us all into the jail van and away we go.

As we waited for the main gate to swing open, Sledge appeared in the gatehouse doorway. He was in good form, with a big smile on face. He saw us in the waiting van and suddenly he started pointing to his head and lifting his hat up and down. 'What the fuck is he up to?' I asked the driver. The driver, solid as a brick, sharp as a tack and a great friend of mine, replied, 'I think he's pointing to you and your hat.' The gate swung open and the cargo of human freight was eased out into the April sunlight. 'I don't have a hat,' I replied. A knowing smile from the driver. 'Ah, that explains that then,' and he shifted up a gear and into the traffic.

We should wear hats to courts, but I hated them. They got in the way. There was always the danger of leaving it behind and if a row broke out, you lost vital seconds trying to find a place for it or, worse, you looked an idiot as it was knocked off your head. I solved all those problems over the years by not bringing a hat at all unless I was sure a verdict would be delivered, because the press would snap you coming out and the jail would see the photograph. That particular Thursday the courtroom was packed like a sardine can. Black-gowned, bewigged, sweet-aftershave-scented lawyers, Gardaí who nodded to them for friendship and recognition perhaps, witnesses, and court clerks.

Of course the warder and his manacled prisoner had to be there: they spoiled what would be a great day but, like the queen bee needed the drones, the courts needed the prisoners. Notebooks out, expensive pens in hands. I myself always had an expensive pen; I loved writing and I loved fine fountain pens and biros. There was no room to move, the proceedings went at pace and I listened to the low voice of the court clerk and the lower voice of his eminence and worship. I felt like screaming, 'Speak up! I can't hear you!' but I knew my place. On this day the eight files were in my hand, biro poised to note the dates. My troops and their charges were wedged within the room. My senior officer nodded to me and led them out of the courtroom to the basement. Sex offenders could not be mixed with the others, so we held them cuffed in the basement corridor rather than in the cells.

I scribbled out the eight names, but it was almost impossible to get to the court clerk, such was the crowding around him when the judge finished. I gave a Garda sergeant near me the list and asked him to pass it to the court clerk. 'He would be annoyed if he heard that,' replied the Garda. Confused and as if we were having two different conversations, I asked the Garda, 'Annoyed? Annoyed about what?' The Garda whispered, 'They are known as Court Registrars,' as he gave me a look of pity.

I grabbed back the list and pushed my way to the head of the queue. I had the most important clients in that room that day: eight remanded convicts who were now held in a place not suitable. I had eight staff putting themselves in danger keeping those prisoners safe from those who would assault them, and we were debating niceties and titles in a dusty courtroom.

The clerk peered over his glasses at me. 'I need eight warrants for those listed prisoners, they are sex offenders from Arbour Hill, I have nowhere suitable to detain them safely, I need those warrants to get them back to Mountjoy first and then Arbour Hill.' I had served straight down the middle of his tennis court; now it was up to him. He grunted, 'Come back in ten minutes.' Ten minutes later I had the required paperwork. I collected my warrants, called our van, got in and out of the Joy, and back to the Hill in time for lunch and my long run in the Park. Remember that chain of events because pretty soon it would all change.

Sledge had accepted his promotion and an era was drawing to a close. You know my mixed emotions at this stage. The jail, too, went into a pre-mourning, pre-jubilant phase: giddy yet sad, free yet trapped. Sledge's persona reflected by addled thought processes. It was a Tuesday and I was recalled to take charge of a District Court appearance.

I was in good form because if the case ended early I would be home for lunch and to collect my kids from school. Never ever underestimate the sacrifices prison staff endured over the years – not seeing their family, savage and compulsory overtime, threats, shit managers, bigger shit Department of Justice mandarins – and yet they turned out great kids and great families. I went over to the General Office to collect the warrant and riding instructions: was he held on any other warrants, what security level was he, did I need any other info?

I then made a beeline for my partner for the day; we would take the prisoner to reception and would search him together. No way was I ever going to be surprised by a prisoner suddenly producing a weapon in court and attacking us. As I exited the General Office door, Big Jim, one of my best buddies, walked in. He was down for a Circuit Court trip and he was also due on that day anyway. 'Oh: you're going to the Circuit,' he nonchalantly informed me. We had spent our careers together, did many things together, and battled on the football field. He was a confidant and I was likewise to him, but we both had a flaw: we could get giddy at times, lose the run a little. We both were aware of this.

'Oh yeah . . . and who decided that?' I asked.

'I did,' he said.

Now Big Jim was confident, bordering on cocky at times, but this was pushing it. We had a few issues here. I was recalled as a plain-clothes District Court supervisor, I was senior to him, and I was also the acting chief. The other issue was that Sledge was the real boss and he was the man who called those shots. So 'I did' wasn't going to wash. I went to Sledge's office: common sense and clever thinking were being lost during my angry walk. Sledge looked up from his desk, not expecting a war: he actually smiled.

'Big Jim tells me that I'm going to the Circuit and he's doing the District,' I said. Sledge's face changed and he turned a defensive angle on his swivel chair. His default under verbal onslaught was to say little.

'Yes,' he replied. 'Is there a problem?'

I hit the roof: flashbacks erupted. I tried to calm down. 'The problem is simple – I was detailed by you for the District. I'm in plain clothes, I have no uniform and I don't like being told by an ACO junior to me what to do.'

Sledge rose. 'Big Jim needed to be back before one . . .'

I cut him off there. 'I couldn't give a fuck – I've a life too. Who's the boss here? Who's the chief – you or Big Jim?'

He went whiter: big mistake but I didn't give a fuck, my old default had kicked in and I wasn't going back there, afraid and lonely again. Stalemate, then another eruption. 'By the way, mister,' he sneered, 'don't ever go to court again without your uniform hat – I saw you last Thursday at the gate.'

I had him now. 'I'm glad you brought that up – never ever gesture to me like a demented monkey like you did that day – speak English, I understand it.' He came from behind the table. I pulled myself up higher. 'You weren't so fucking cocky below in the Circuit Civil Court a few years ago.' It came out of my mouth before I could stop it. The spoken word cannot be taken back. He placed his arse on the edge of the desk.

'Go on,' he dared.

It boiled down to this. We had a prisoner who violently attacked a quiet lad. We couldn't prove it, but the word was that he did it. Sledge brought him into an office in the Circle area, laid down the law and questioned him. The prisoner shouted back and tried to come over the table towards Sledge, but was met by the man himself coming in to defend himself. We intervened and removed the prisoner back to his cell. We all had done our duty properly, including Sledge. Months later we were summoned to the Civil Court where this prisoner was suing the state for an alleged assault. He alleged Sledge had attacked him. He hadn't.

Sledge had called me into his office when the summons came: I was down as present that day, hence I was a witness. I asked Sledge what he thought. He tossed the summons to me with the words, 'I don't know what he's talking about – I have no recollection of anything like that.' I was flummoxed.

'But something happened – he tried to attack you. We used as much force as necessary to remove him. Open and shut – not a problem for us?' I said.

Sledge picked at his nails with long pliers. 'Well, I have no recollection of any of this.' He looked over at me. 'You do as you want to do,' he said as he got up.

On court day the state's solicitor informed about fifteen of us witnesses that only the CO and ACO Cuffe would be required for evidence. I had turned up in uniform with a plain-clothes jacket. For some reason Sledge turned up in civvies: a white trench coat buttoned to the collar. He looked ridiculous. The prisoner, the alleged victim, represented himself and tore lumps out of Sledge. We were shocked: a man who had the jail at his beck and call, a man we all feared, was now reduced to a muttering monosyllabic idiot on the stand. It was all 'you did this' and Sledge replying 'I have no recollection of any of those events.' Maybe he didn't.

I had watched the judge and he was perplexed at Sledge's defence. The judge seemed a nice man. I was called. The prisoner questioned me as a witness to the events. I refused to engage him with my eyes. Instead I looked directly at the judge. I started to outline the truthful facts; the judge relaxed in the chair. 'Thank you, Mr Cuffe . . . at last some common sense . . . go on.' I went through every angle, the rights of the prisoner, our duties of care, our right to use force where and when necessary. The judge thanked me, threw out the case and we actually raced out of the courtroom. I found the entire experience mortifying.

Sledge hugged me outside the courtroom and clasped my hands. 'Thanks – thanks – thanks,' he kept repeating.

Now I had hit a sore and he was annoyed. First I had implied that Big Jim ran the show, and then I had reminded him of a particularly embarrassing day. He brought his face into mine. 'That was then and this is now,' he sneered. Not to be outdone, I retorted, 'Eaten bread is soon forgotten.' As it was my official day off I went for broke. 'I'm going home: get someone else for the District.' I then stormed out.

Word got to Big Jim, and he headed me off at the gate, 'Do the District – don't go home.' I relented and did the court, but the taste was shite. Now the last few days of Sledge were oppressive once more, and Big Jim and I had a strained relationship, even though we both knew it would pass. My running diary reflects it better.

21/4/99: Cross tempered run with self over the pig Sledge.

22/4/99: Stressful day dealing with evil, God is good and we have been this way before.

23/4/99: Aftershocks of yesterday, rotten feeling.

The ACOs had a night out for Sledge before he left. I wasn't going to go, but Big Jim told me it was the right thing to do: be seen to go and close off the past. I went, I found it staid and sober: to me the good humour was forced and Sledge out of uniform was half the man he was in it. I tried to pretend and managed to get through the night. It was a relief to go home. I'd say that Sledge felt the same. He wasn't a social butterfly, yet his loss to the Hill would be enormous, and my feelings and opinions of him had to acknowledge that. My last running log entry regarding him is 7/5/99: 'Sledge's last day in the Hill, God bless the past.' I'd like to think that was a sign of my forgiveness.

My end game was now in motion, except I wasn't yet aware of it. Two new chiefs came and went. Both nice men, but they weren't Sledge. Sure, the place relaxed, but too much so. I was free from him, but part of me hankered for him too. Now the union – which he had dealt with superbly even though he wasn't a member – started to flex its muscles. The new men had different ideas. We just didn't buy into them entirely. What took Sledge ten years to assemble was now falling away on a weekly basis; I as much as anyone else was to blame. Sledge drove the ship and made it easy for us; now that we had to steer the same ship, we looked at everyone except ourselves.

It's the little things that fuck you. An elderly prisoner had died sitting on the toilet. Jack the ACO, a legend and character, was in charge that night. The prison was required to go to the Coroner's Court; Jack and his crew had to appear. The governor asked me to represent the jail:

he was too busy, the new CO wasn't familiar and blah de blah. I wouldn't have to speak, he assured me. I never had a problem with speaking, but it didn't suit me to go: once more I had promised the kids a treat after I collected them from school that day, but I was told the court would be over early and would I please do it. I relented. Down we went; the case was open and shut.

Once it was over I radioed for transport to take us back. Two of the lads were after a night duty tour and were wrecked; the rest of us just wanted to go home. Jack took us into Busáras for a coffee. I was doing big running miles so I had water. No sign of the van: out I went again. The van wouldn't be down until 2 p.m.; the driver was now covering the landings during lunch hour. 'Fuck that' was the collective response. With traffic, the van wouldn't be down until 2.30 p.m. and back at 3 p.m.. I had told my children that I'd be outside the school at that time. We didn't have mobile phones, and four little ones would be expecting me.

When we got back, I raced in the gate and clocked my card at 2.55 p.m.. I drove like a man possessed the ten miles into Meath and met the kids on the back road, already halfway home. I had let them down. Next day at work the then CO kept on about the governor not being impressed. Eventually it dawned on me that I was the unimpresser. I went over to the governor and spoke to him. 'Ah, there was a guy from the Department there and he said it finished at twelve and ye got back later and you didn't tell me the result and I felt foolish' was the gist of the conversation from him to me. What do you do at a time like that?

I could have said perhaps yourself or the assistant governer should have gone down. What result did you expect after an old man died naturally on the toilet? Instead I said, 'My apologies, you are correct . . . I should have gone over to your office and given the result to you.' He waved that away – 'Arrah forget it' – and we left it at that, hanging eternally.

As the senior officer in charge of the group who attended that Coroner's Court, it fell to me to submit the travelling and subsistence claim. All we could claim for was a lunch each and an hour's overtime during lunchtime. A few days later some of the crew came to me. 'Hey John, they won't pay the lunch hour and sub.' I was puzzled.

It appeared that groupthink figured out that we deliberately decided to milk a lunch hour with its subsistence and overtime. The facts were different. We had no choice but to remain at the coroner's. The jail wouldn't release the driver: what exactly could we do? What were we expected to do? Work for nothing and live on fresh air? But the detail refused to sanction the paperwork. I spoke to a senior manager. 'Ah, John, you know yourself, ha ha ha ha.' Actually I didn't know, but by poking him I found out that they thought we manipulated that hour for payment purposes. I was livid: four kids from five to ten on the dangerous back road and I'd risk their lives for a measly hour and a lunch allowance? The staff, myself included, were eventually paid after we got the union involved, but another slice from my iceberg slid into the water.

The new chief and the chief after him suffered because they weren't Sledge. No one could replicate Sledge: he was a one-off. I offered to give up the acting chief position. That was refused: no one else wanted it, and the brass knew that. I came to hate the job: the old regime was straightforward, for better or worse – and generally it was for better, despite my early years of shit treatment. We were now operating to a different beat, a march out of sequence. Sundays with Sledge were days when we drew our breath, allowing the jail to recover at a nice easy pace. Nothing moved out of the jail. The gym was opened for the prisoners. The staff walked the yard and chatted and relaxed. In the radio room, if all was well, you got the chance to read a paper. Now Sundays became days we hated: every so often some prisoner was going on an escorted outing. I assume this was Departmental regime change. The problem from our side of the fence was simple: the wrong prisoners were getting out, troublesome ones.

One who had earlier tried to bite the leg of a colleague of mine was now wandering out on escort, visiting his mother's grave. He took the staff on such a tour that they seriously wondered if she had died at all. Another, a serial cutter and a twenty-carat thug, got outings to his sister's house for a few hours. A third had been convicted of kidnapping and assault. He somehow managed to get out to see his mother, even though he was a short time into a fourteen-year sentence. If this was the Department's version of rehabilitation, it was only a matter of time before it came back to bite them. One thing was certain: under Sledge those three had as much hope of getting an escorted Sunday outing as I had of playing for Man United. The staff were getting giddy, they were spooked with this Sunday stuff and our grip was slowly being prised from the jail. We all shared the blame. Soon we would be back in the mid-1980s if something didn't happen. This gnawed at me. I got restless. Two events threw everything into sharp relief for me even though they were twelve months apart.

I had been chief for a particular day and 5 p.m. beckoned. The sun was high in the sky and the jail was fine. As I headed towards the radio room to do a final check before I left, the East One class officer approached me. 'Boss, I got one in the strip cell; he's after shitting all over the place down there.' The evening ACO emerged from the office; he was in charge for the evening and added that the smell was so bad that he wouldn't be going down to check on the prisoner. I decided to leave that for a moment.

Down we went and I asked the class officer to open the cell. The hot weather had amplified the warm smell of faeces. 'What's the problem?' I asked. I got no reply, only a big stupid smile. We weren't dealing with a deep intellectual here, but we were dealing with a guy who had the cunning of a street fighter. Bollock naked he stood, moving like a boxer on canvas, right foot up but toes keeping touch with the ground, similarly with the left foot: almost a rhythm. He was moulding or squeezing what looked like a sponge ball in his hands.

I was a trained hostage negotiator, and the training had mainly confirmed to me what I already knew and was actually good at. One of the key components of any negotiation or indeed conversation is to know when to shut up. I was talking but the recipient wasn't listening: I might as well have been talking to the light over his head. He then grabbed the initiative. He wiped his hands on the 'sponge ball' and then smeared both hands across his face, looking like a solider under camouflage. The 'sponge ball' was a ball of excrement. The smell was awful.

I ordered the door locked. The officer then told me that the prisoner claimed to have a blade up his arse. (That didn't surprise me. I once had to search a prisoner in a cell who had a portion of a broken blade behind his glass eye. He plucked out the eye and handed me the Sellotaped piece of blade.) We figured he was bluffing on that one, but the possibility was that we would have to search him or send him out to hospital.

The ACO was beside me and I told him that I didn't care about the smell; the prisoner was to be checked every twenty minutes. I told the officer the same. The officer, a reliable warhorse, I told to go for a shower at 7 p.m., dump his uniform and I'd sanction a new one from the stores, likewise for any of the staff who dealt with the prisoner. As I pondered my next move, the evening staff were returning from tea break, including one of the older ACOs – a Mountjoy veteran and a character. Characters are part of the jail jigsaw; I wouldn't have operated like him, nor he me, but I appreciated his style. 'A problem, Chief?' he went. (The 'Chief' part was a private joke: I had tried to lump the role on to him a few weeks earlier.)

I outlined the events. He laughed. Mountjoy staff are the best; they have to deal with everything, thus nothing fazes them. Our main problem was to get them to lower their body temperature to Arbour Hill levels when they transferred in. A falling cup would elicit a sprint, looking for action: to us it was a cup that fell by accident. 'Tell you what, boss . . . give me twenty fags for our man . . . I'll talk to him . . . and while you're at it, get twenty for me.' Each chief had an allocation of fags and tobacco, which he dispensed to cleaners and trustees who did jail work. I had access to that loot, and twenty fags here and an ounce there often smoothed the day's running. I handed over the fags. The ACO looked at me: he read my mind. 'Go home, Chief . . . there's no more for you to do. I'll sort it.'

As I drove up to my house the kids raced out. I had earlier dumped my own gear and boiled myself to near death with a shower at the jail. 'Daddy, daddy, daddy . . . what did you do today?' asked the youngest. Another asked whether I shot any of the bad guys: wildly imaginative kids, mine. I assured one and all that the bad guys were going to bed early that sunny night because some of them were bold. They screamed with delight. 'Good man, Daddy.' How do you tell your kids that you stood two feet from a man playing handball with a lump of shit: in fact how do you tell anyone that?

I sat in the garden with a coffee as the kids played. The phone rang and my wife came out. 'The jail – they want to speak to you.' In I went, hoping they hadn't had to search him or send him out. A voice went, 'Hello, Mr Cuffe. Relax and enjoy the sun – problem sorted, and the prisoner said sorry for the shite but thanks for the fags. He's cleaning the pad now as we speak and before you say – no, I won't let him out. Have a good evening and that'll cost you another twenty smokes tomorrow – for me. Ha ha ha.' The line went dead and I laughed: unorthodox, but it worked. Twenty fags tomorrow were guaranteed, but something profound hit me. What were we at, who were we, why did we do this, were people aware of what we had to do? Where in the manual – if you had a manual – would you locate how to deal with a prisoner holding a shite ball? Would you look it up in the index?

The next profound moment came with Larry Murphy. I had seen a hundred Larry Murphys and heard worse tales than his gruesome acts. He had kidnapped a woman, stripped her naked, raped her and dumped her trussed-up body into the boot of his car then drove to the foot of the Wicklow mountains at 6 a.m. Her god was awake: some hunters, also out early, chanced upon the scene and saved her. Murphy now became a suspect for many missing women in a radius of sixty miles from his home. The press had him as the top exotic from the sexual perversion rogues' gallery.

I was in charge of the Circle the second day Larry was in the jail. For the governor's parade, the prisoners are lined up along the wall in that area and one by one they go in looking for an extra visit, phone call, day out, legal form, complaint. You name it: perhaps just a chat to break the monotony. The chief sits with him and the request and prisoner's name are noted in a big brute of a book. That book is then passed out to the Circle ACO and he brings everyone up to speed with the requests and orders. Larry neared me. He was a small, slight, fair-haired lad. Nothing about him stood out. Pale as a bag of flour, plain as a cup of milk – no horns, twisted eyes, deformed ears, buck teeth, smelly armpits – just a common-or-garden human that you would say 'excuse me' to in the queue for the bus or the bar.

For the first time, that scared me. It might have been

my missus in that boot, or my eldest girl. Where was my anger, where was my hatred towards him? It wasn't there. Previously I had locked up guys who molested children and yet I was able to talk to them, discuss football, the Open University, the crossword. Now I questioned myself. Were our feelings numbed so much over the years that we really saw those guys as 'normal'? Once they were obedient and conformed to jail, did that satisfy us, or should we be looking deeper? What was our role?

A few years earlier, Malcolm MacArthur had been sent to the Mater for a procedure. MacArthur was notorious in the media. He killed two innocent people without remorse, then got locked up on the basis of a single charge with the other held on account. Donal Dunne, the unfortunate victim of the latter crime, was rendered baggage by a brutal criminal justice system that fails to take the victims' feelings to heart. The biggest aura that surrounded MacArthur was his alleged connection with the elite of Irish political life. Not everyone gets to kip on the Attorney General's sofa. Malcolm was arrested in that gentleman's house.

MacArthur came across in the media photos as a dandy, a man of letters and academia with a twisted mind. In truth he was a most compliant prisoner who possessed nothing notable on the educational front; he seemed to loiter around the print shop making tea and cleaning the floor. His cell bordered on the filthy. And he kept to himself. The deepest conversation – indeed the only conversation – we ever had concerned tomatoes and the curative affect they have on your prostate.

The Mater put Malcolm into a public ward on the Eccles Street side. Up the steps and into the first ward, and there was the infamous man. Soon enough the media would be lurking for him, as would every crackpot in the city. The staff called back and informed us of the set-up. The chief sent me down to see what could be done. I met the charge nurse and explained our predicament. She nodded in agreement and told me that she would have him moved upstairs to a small room away from that area. I thanked her and added, 'Malcolm's all right . . . he won't give ye an ounce of bother.' She literally winced as the last word came out and gave me a look that bordered on incredulous pity. Malcolm had murdered her colleague: my big mouth, my jail jargon, my little understanding of the victim and indeed the perpetrator horrified her.

The above highlights how we view our inmates and how we treat them. Put another way, it's an indication of our professionalism that we can separate the criminal from the crime and treat them with the humanity that's required to run the system. However, somewhere in all of that we lose a portion of ourselves. During the Larry Murphy time, my mind was whirring nineteen to the dozen. I was questioning myself all the time: our normality, our attitude. I was almost becoming suspicious of outsiders' shows of affection to my kids due to the deluge of priests, teachers and professionals that came through our doors over various sex abuse scandals. Brendan Smyth had uncorked something deep within us all and that genie would not be easy to put back in the bottle.

My mind was made up. I would go, but to where? This story is essentially a story of my life in a jail. I will refrain from dragging my family into it too much, but I did convince myself and them that a move to the west would be a good thing. We bought a huge site: a dream between two woods. Arbour Hill was now coming to the end. My head was hell-bent across the Shannon. An escape on escort on a Sunday whilst I was thankfully off convinced me that I made the correct decision. The place was untangling and I hadn't the fight for another ten years of rebuilding, and what we endured from 1985 until Sledge settled around 1993. I had to get out, find a new start.

My ACO colleagues marked my departure with not as much as 'bye-bye Johnny'. I wasn't too surprised . . . I had grown apart from guys those last few months. I wasn't the best at attending functions myself, so you get what you put in. The staff, those on the frontline, my troops, brought me down to the local pub on the Thursday; they made a beautiful presentation trophy of two footballers competing for a dropping ball. They felt that I was a supervisor who always gave a guy a break, a sporting chance. I was humbled. Rocky, my mate, told a pile of lies about me as a great guy. Deep down I was delighted; a bit of flattery does us no harm. I spoke from the heart at the end. Without the troops, I couldn't have survived this far. It was the truth. The staff had to go back to work; in fact, I ran them out. I traipsed behind them to collect my car in the Hill. While I was passing through one of the myriad corridors in the officers' staff quarters to get to the back car park, who popped out of the shadows but Sledge. He grasped my hand. 'Good luck down there,' he said (I was going to work in Castlerea). It was kind of awkward at first. Neither of us knew what to say, although both thought the same things.

Quickly, he grabbed his running bag; he was now top

chief in another jail and needed to head off. 'You're not used to committals and warrants . . . you'll get used to them. Watch out for the guards, they're full of bullshit when they try and slip you a dodgy and out-of-date one . . . it's normally buried down in the middle, you take your time and read them carefully. Those cunts would hang their mothers and you're not their mother.' Great advice, as it would turn out. With that, Sledge slipped back into the shadows, out another door and out of my life.

11

Tipping Point

How do men act on a sinking ship? Do they hold each other? Do they pass around the whisky? Do they cry?

SEBASTIAN JUNGER (b. 1954)

Where were you when JFK was assassinated? I'll tell you where I was: safely tucked up in bed on a cold November night in 1963 as a full moon lit up my beautiful bay. I was reading the *Victor* comic when my father came in and turned on the radio downstairs. The dial went from station to station, whirring atmospherics of noise as different languages babbled away. I knew something bad had happened, as the house went silent apart from the radio. As I sat on the top step in my pyjamas with my *Victor* still in hand, one word kept coming across: 'Kennedy'. Eventually my father found AFN and we heard the sad news: 'John F. Kennedy was shot today in Dallas, Texas.' Something bad entered our world, a page was turned in history and I was privy to it.

Mid-October 2003, around 5 p.m. on a beautiful, sunny, late-autumn day. The trees in our woods were heavenly. I was preparing a meal for the children on the cooking island in the middle of our dream kitchen. The two oldest were in secondary school, and travelled by bus; the two youngest were in primary. I had switched to permanent nights in order to be around. The back door to the kitchen swung open and as it did I glanced at the clock. Its time froze for me forever. One look at my son's face told me all I needed to know. He was in shock, his beautiful young face a mask of pain, of 'Why, why me?' He had been attacked on the school bus, by at least nine: the numbers went as high as twelve as the youngsters involved ratted out the others.

'Attack me, abuse me, assail me, but leave my kids alone' would be the mantra of most good parents. I hugged him amid deep gulps of air and sobs from his racking body. Slowly he told me about the assault. It was a cowardly attack from behind, his head forced down as blows rained on his head and body whilst he strove to keep the belt on his trousers intact as one of the youths tried to open it. It was fierce, it was brutal and it was demeaning. In another incident at the end of sixth class in primary school, a thug had left a rusty nail on his seat that stuck into his back in the classroom. We knew who was behind all of this . . . the problem was we couldn't prove it. It was all over jealousy: don't ask me what type of jealousy, let's describe it as rural Ireland's hateful attitude that if you seem to be doing better than me, who slaved in this hole all my life, then I'll visit all types of hell on you and your family. Think *The Field* and the 'Bird' scenario.

He couldn't eat. I tried to reassure him. I cursed myself aloud and then silently for bringing my children to this hell. The little boy that I held as he breathed his first breaths was assaulted on a bus by animals and I couldn't do a thing about it. Part of me wanted to get a baseball bat that was in my shed and go down to the house of the person I believed was behind it, and batter the entire family of inbred bastards. Instead, after giving him a cup of tea and leaving him safe in the love of his sibling, I went for a short walk before the rest of the family arrived home. As I walked my mind drifted back to when I was about ten. In my village the Atlantic Ocean laps our shore. When we played football we were always careful to ensure that the ball didn't land in the sea: if the wind was offshore then your ball was gone forever. You can guess that we lost balls on a regular basis: they were precious and hard to get. I had a brown plastic ball and I dribbled it ahead of me down the village. We had a match but I noticed that some of the boys, the older ones, were trying to kick it into the sea: the wind was onshore, which meant that it blew back in. I got a helpless feeling.

The ruse, of course, was to steal my ball and get rid of those the ringleader referred to derisively as 'sprats' (I tower him by about a foot nowadays). The ball drifted in to a spot near the pier and disappeared. A few days later I went down again to where we played. They were playing with a ball: I can still see it; it had been painted a bad shade of dark brown but unquestionably it was my ball. I asked for a game and got it. When the ball landed at my feet I picked it up and raced for home. Near the post office a lad of about sixteen, a hard chaw who was on holidays in the area but had all the other kids in thrall, stopped me. He tried to take the ball off me. I resisted and suddenly he met me with a ferocious blow to the nose. Blood was everywhere. I lost the rag, dropped the ball and tried to kick him. He then visited upon me what would today be termed GBH. He battered the shit out of me, kicked me all over the road.

I could feel the pain once more as the assault on my boy reopened a chapter I had forgotten about. The physical pain I dealt with, to a point, but the mental pain stayed forever. How could lads whom I played with since I could walk allow this fella do this to me? It was utter humiliation. We lived in an old barracks and coastguard station; there was a washhouse to the rear. I went in there to clean myself up, tidy my torn jumper and wash my bloodied nose. I took deep breaths and headed for our house, vowing to say nothing. As I neared the door I heard the sound of the harmonica as my father played it. All within was for now serene. My mother saw me through the window, raced out and dragged me outside. 'Don't tell your father,' she implored.

I did tell him. The music ceased and my father put on his coat and headed down the village. He met the near-six-foot thug who milled me, and dropped him with an uppercut. Fair dinkum, one might say: you batter a kid, I batter a kid, and all is even-steven. However, with my father there was always a quid pro quo. Instead of viewing what he did as perhaps not the way to do business but as sending a message out, he wallowed in guilt for about a month, in which he became dependent on the whiskey bottle to blot out the entire episode. As I walked alone from school, two miles on the road, and the other kids raced ahead – the 'sprats' guy organised a boycott of me –

I was left to rue many things: one was the battering, another was the horrible tension in our home, my father's solace in the bottle and having no one to talk to. I blamed myself for the whole thing. I was separated from the pack, not wanted. It was a lesson I took through life, and I vowed never to become too close to any group ever again.

Having gone over that scenario, I didn't want the same outcome for my lad. He didn't want us to do anything about it, pleading that we would make it worse: he was right, of course. We took the course of speaking to the parents of those involved: all polite embarrassment and part-denial until their offspring admitted their parts and gave us another name. That night we had called on nine homes: we were beaten, broken and heartbroken. The school, the school bus, the Gardaí . . . all the agencies involved were useless. I went to the Gardaí in order that it be noted but no further action taken for that moment. If this ever happens to you, don't go there. They couldn't give a toss. The school almost made us feel as if it was our own fault. They were pathetic, and certainly in my years as a supervisor I would hate for a second to think I left either a member of staff or a prisoner as disempowered as that school left us.

The upshot was hell. The boy was ostracised on the bus for the rest of the year: a school year that didn't end until May. He was termed a 'rat' by thugs who battered him as other lads in the school were told not to play with him or associate with him. For me, I was having an out-of-body experience. Every day seemed deep blue: yes, really, the atmosphere took on that hue in my world. I watched the boy's face, my family's faces, and I cursed myself for ever moving. I blamed this . . . I raged at that . . .

I slowly went insane. My wife was the glue that held us together. The staff in Castlerea kept what was left of my sanity intact. They were magnificent and supportive.

Around April 2004 a car passed the kids on the road; the thug whom we deemed to be behind the attack lowered the window and gave them verbal abuse, telling them to go back to the slums they came from. That was it. We were beaten. I have left out a book-full of abuse and hell: we had enough. We put the house up for sale and I looked for a transfer back to Arbour Hill, where there was a vacancy for an ACO. Work was supportive. The senior chief took my transfer and processed it, saying all the right things. I wanted us back for the summer so we could resettle, almost pretend that we never moved, plug in to our old, idyllic life – some chance.

A perfect storm was coming together for me. For years the press had a field day about prison warders' overtime. If it wasn't our overtime, it was our sick records. So let me give you a quick lesson on both those hot topics. The truth, not Irish Prison Service and Department of Justice spin.

Overtime was introduced and abused by the Department of Justice because they didn't want to recruit the correct number of staff needed to run their dysfunctional jails. Staff were *compelled* to work overtime. Families lost sight of their fathers and, in some cases, mothers because of this compulsory overtime. Under the old system, after working twelve consecutive days you had Thursday and Friday of one week put back to back with Saturday and Sunday of the next in order to give you a break before you headed off into a ten-day tour of duty. Did you get all four days off? You might be lucky to get one of them.

'Sick' was a particular bugbear. Under the system brought in around 1988, officers worked a fourteen-day cycle. That cycle had eighty hours built into it. In week one you worked five eleven-hour shifts; in week two you worked two eleven- or twelve-hour shifts and were off five days . . . supposedly, and overtime permitting. If you had a bad flu or your body was creaking from overwork and you went to the doctor in week two and got a week's sick certificate, the Prison Service marked you for seven days sick, even though technically you weren't liable for work on five of those days, nor were you paid. This practice inflated the sick records and gave an erroneous impression to the public. The Prison Service and Justice regarded officers as cannon fodder to be worked until they dropped. You don't believe me? They forced officers to opt out of the European Work Time schedule. You had the crazy situation where potentially a lorry driver who exceeded his driving hours could be locked up by an officer who had completed a twenty-four-hour shift: not an unusual shift in jails, let me inform you.

Michael McDowell was now Justice Minister: a man who once wrote an article that left me in no doubt about his feelings towards prison staff. He wouldn't have rated us, but the feeling was mutual as far as I was concerned. Justice and Prison Service staff are, in the main, grazers. They graze harmlessly most of the time, but when an attack dog makes demands of them, a few of the grazers go for the throat. Ireland was going through a giddy Celtic Tiger time: in Bertie Ahern's words, the boom was getting 'boomier'; Charlie McCreevy was dispensing with largesse special savings schemes and we were all partying . . . according to the Lenihan dynasty, anyway. Someone needed a trimming, and the focus came on the Prison Service.

McDowell saw the figures: paying out massive overtime to him was crazy. The problem, though, was created by his Department. You were compelled to do overtime: that's what they wanted. The public smelled blood; writers couldn't get their heads around the fact that a knuckle-dragging, ignorant warder, to them at least, could earn eighty grand a year. What they never factored in was that the guy who earned that had possibly little or no contact with his wife and children, and more than likely relaxed with a few beers in the pub after coming out of work bleary-eyed and bolloxed. His social skills centred around 'dirt birds', shite management and whether his native county might ever win the All-Ireland. A big belly finished off the stereotype. And half his overtime went in tax.

Most warders, myself included, tried manfully to mix family life with work, always vowing that their kids would never ever work in a jail. We were presented with a document, after much huffing and puffing regarding the blight of overtime. Overtime would go and be replaced with a thing known as 'annualised hours'. Each officer would contract to work 365 extra hours per year: this would be built into your pay. A limited number of hours were available on a seniority basis. Hello there: this was still overtime, but under a different name. We were still expected to work long hours but we wouldn't call it overtime: it was now part of our duty. This was worse than the old system.

Under the old system around 33 per cent of the staff

made themselves available to work unlimited overtime; 33 per cent wished to work only moderate overtime. The remaining 33 per cent did no overtime. Now the second-tier guys – the 33 per cent moderates – were scooped into the system along with a chunk of the third-tier guys. It was disastrous, but at least the public were assured that overtime was abolished in the prisons. Pure optics, and naturally we rejected it. Indeed, the experts who put the process together stated that most prison officers would be seriously discommoded.

Back to the drawing board, with the press playing its part now – editorials in *The Irish Times* and *Irish Independent* lambasted us as greedy. Ronan O'Reilly wrote a particularly nasty piece in the *Sun*, as I have mentioned; that paper's editor the next day had to disassociate himself from his own writer.

My transfer seemed to be dragging around this time, so I made enquiries. The answers I was getting weren't adding up. Also we noticed that Castlerea was getting visits from Garda personnel and the army: men armed with clipboards and biros wandering around taking notes. We of course knew that this was all part of putting us under pressure. The Gardaí would do as they were told. The army would do as they are told.

One morning after a night shift I decided that instead of going home I would do the weekly shop in Athlone. I went to the ATM and as I took out my card, I noticed two butty little skinheads hovering around near me, definitely giving me an eye. 'How unusual,' I thought, 'two would-be robbers up this early . . . they are keen.' I placed the car keys between the fingers of my right hand: if they came for my cash, they would get a fist of keys in the face. But no, as I moved away from the ATM they approached in a friendly manner. 'Hello . . . we will be up to your place soon,' the first fella said. What amazed me was how coherent they were for junkies or would-be robbers. 'Your place' clearly meant Castlerea; they knew I was a warder because I had a civvy jumper over my uniform shirt and trousers.

I still kept the keys poised, just in case. The second guy piped up: 'Yeah, we're looking forward to it . . . we were up there last week.'

'How long will ye be with us for, lads?' I asked. The reply flattened me.

'Well, that depends on your lads: how long will ye be on strike for?'

They were soldiers, not gougers or junkies who wanted to rob me! I burst out laughing; they joined in although we were laughing about different things. 'There'll be no strike, lads – rest assured – we won't be going outside the gate.' And off I went, still laughing about my encounter with my would-be replacements.

Jail life continued, humdrum. We had five-a-side matches in the mud. My biggest regret was that I was a guy who prided himself on fitness, but for my six years in Castlerea I was never fit: I was always coming back from an injury, a pull, a strain, a dose of the flu. Never in my entire life did I get such a run of injuries. My football prowess was simple. I had an engine that tracked from box to box; I wore my opponent down to my level through sheer grit. I possessed a wicked shot and once I decided to mark you, well that was that. Now I was reduced to standing in goals: my metatarsal was broken but I never got it fixed. I had other pain to contend with.

Around May 2004 I enquired about my transfer once more. I had an unblemished record, never a moment late in my career, yet there seemed to be a glitch with my transfer. My entire family, house and future, to put it bluntly, depended on moving. McDowell and the Prison Service or Justice – different sides of the same coin to me – started to up the ante. They closed down Spike Island after spending millions upgrading it. They transferred the staff to Limerick and Cork . . . just like that. They then closed down the Curragh. That was always on the cards: the army didn't like us being on 'their' patch so they got back their jail, in much better condition than the dump we inherited from them. Shanganagh with its thirty acres of a youth facility was shut down as well.

My transfer was to become the mustard after the meat of this dispute. All transfers were embargoed. No one would take responsibility for that decision; well, no one would tell me whose idea it was. The biggest thugs in the job – the biggest winos and wife-batterers – were facilitated with transfers over the years, and here I was in hell and caught up in a row not of my making. The governor blamed the Prison Service, the Prison Service blamed the governor, and the union twisted and shrugged and gave out about them all: 'You know yourself, John . . . that's the shit we have to put up with over the years.' Actually I didn't: how could my transfer impact on the greater scope of the Prison Service? If not for me, then why not for my family?

The machine – that big brute that grinds on – eventually beats you. No straight answers, the clock ticking and time passing. The summer was high and we decided to give it one more shot. We took the house off the market; I withdrew my transfer. Bitter experience in 1991 made me do this. When I looked to transfer from Spike in late 1985 I wrote that I wished to be transferred to Shanganagh Castle or any prison in the Dublin area. I got Arbour Hill. Sledge came to me in '91 and told me I was moving to Shanganagh. I nearly died of shock: I hadn't looked for it. Apparently the Department was looking over and updating their transfer requests and my name came up for Shanganagh. Back then, Sledge had his knife in me, and it suited him to move me. I had to write a statement that I didn't want Shanganagh or any prison in the Dublin area. That ensured that I wouldn't get a transfer when I no longer wanted one: they had beaten me.

Funny, isn't it? I was transferred to Shanganagh Castle in 1978 even though I hadn't actually looked for a move. I wrote out the transfer in the Training Unit office and it went through in hours. I was transferred to Spike within a week of requesting it, and to the Hill in '85 within a fortnight of requesting it. And you wonder why I ooze with hate for the Prison Service and how they treated me and my family?

One night around 2 a.m. a staff member came to my office. A quiet but steely lad, he shut out the great big steel door, sat down and came straight to the point. In hushed tones he told me that he and his colleagues were very aware of what I and my family had gone through. He looked around and then added that I was to give one name, or indeed two or more if needed. They would then sort out the troublemakers: all secret, all quiet, but they would leave a message and calling card.

I was flabbergasted. Never in a million years would I have this lad down for *that*! Back in the early 1980s, as I have mentioned, a group of ex-prisoners called themselves the Prisoners' Revenge Group: the PRG. They seriously assaulted some members of staff – as usual, it was the good guys who got the hiding – and they burned down the house of another. A strong rumour circulated but was never substantiated that a group of warders went under-cover themselves and wreaked wicked revenge on that group. Coincidentally or otherwise, the PRG died a death. Now I had a man in my office offering to do a number for me: he wasn't joking and it wasn't bravado.

I stood up, went to the window and looked across at the railway bridge across on the Ballyhaunis road; I wiped away a tear. The thought that my own colleagues, my friends, were prepared to do this for my family moved me. I clasped his hand and motioned him towards the door. 'Thank you . . . thank you . . . you have no idea how much that means to me, really. But this is my fight, my problem and you lot are not getting dragged into it.' We embraced and he slid back into the landings and semi-darkness. Wow – that shook me. I had friends, friends who cared, and until the day I die I'll not forget that gesture.

By autumn 2004 things were back to 'normal' at home. The bullying got worse. No one could help us but ourselves. This time I held firm on a transfer. We would sell the house first, no matter how long it took. We had various auctioneers but none could shift it, so we took down the signs and decided what will be will be. Life would decide our next move. The following June, out of the blue, a knock came to our door. A couple had heard in a local pub that our house had been for sale the previous autumn: would we still be interested in selling? We sold the house to them at a fair price and I never once looked back at it. It had become my Hotel California.

We rented in Athlone, and the first thing I noticed was the warmth and friendliness of the people there. I was so traumatised that at first I was suspicious of them. The kids had by now put a band of steel around their inner minds, and my wife and I regarded this as a positive move. Inside I crucified myself for moving in the first place. Also, the sad news came through that Sledge had passed away. I missed the man I thought I knew; I didn't miss the man who gave me hell. I didn't make the funeral. He wouldn't have expected it, but a day doesn't go by when I don't think about him, the positives as well the negatives. In the overall scheme he was like me; he also fought demons and darkness.

Out running that November, I passed through a dark wood. Thunder erupted and a deluge poured down. I kept running – I love the rain whilst running – but the wood took on an almost evil darkness. The flashes of blue lightning started to unnerve me and as I ran the back of my mind made me cautious not to take a direct hit from one of those bright yellow or blue lightning strikes. At the brow of a hill I paused, still under the canopy of the wood but by now in almost total darkness save the flashes of lightning. I looked up and let out an unmerciful roar: *Why the fuck us?* I cursed the people I thought were behind it, and for a second the air filled with the pungent scent of evil. I made my way across the path and back to my car as the rain came down; darkness claimed the rest of the day, occasionally lit by lightning. I was having a breakdown.

That month the deal for the new house back east fell through. I was simply crushed. I just lay down and begged my mother to come and take me away. My doctor understood and put me off duty . . . long term. I visited a psychiatrist and went through everything with him. I was diagnosed as suffering from post-traumatic stress (PTS). I was to be off work for nearly a year. With less than two years left, I wanted to be pensioned out on medical grounds. Once more the machine went into action. I did all the running, submitted certs, visited doctors, visited psychologists. The Prison Service, my employer, sat tight. Not once did the Chief Medical Officer look to see me, despite my requesting to see them. I looked for a meeting with the Prison Service – nothing doing. Every time I rang, I got no further than some biro jockey who blocked me at the gates.

Did I feel guilty for being out sick? Hmmm . . . I felt shit that my employer of twenty-eight years left me to dangle, left me to my own devices. I was truly burned out, but I figured that with compulsory overtime I must have worked in excess of three years extra at that stage. Whilst I gave over 800 days to the Department in overtime – yes, I calculated it – they stole my precious time off with my family, my wife and my kids.

As Mr Gogarty and Mr Bailey journeyed to the home of Ray Burke, an erstwhile minister of mine in Justice, with two envelopes stuffed with thousands of pounds, Gogarty asked whether they would get a receipt. Bailey taciturnly replied 'Will we fuck!' Did I feel guilty about letting the Prison Service down by being out sick? Look at Mr Bailey's words for my reply. By the way, Mr Burke, former minister, eventually spent time in the Hill for corruption.

The Prison Service sent me to an appointment with a clinical occupational psychiatrist. He seemed fair and understanding. He gave me the distinct impression that I would not be going back to work in a jail, ever, but maybe my ears deceived me that day. I had nothing to hide from him: I told him the truth. However, when his report got to the Prison Service they interpreted it differently and his suggestions were ignored. This left me to make the next move, and in order to focus my mind they sent me a letter saying my pay was to be stopped. We were now coming up to Christmas, I was almost twenty-nine years in the job and they were stopping my wages. I rang the Prison Service but as usual didn't get beyond the front desk. I wanted to see the Chief Medical Officer. I wanted to see the Director General. I wanted to speak to someone who could make a decision.

'How can you do this to me coming up to Christmas? How can you stop my wages? Where do I stand?' I asked.

Silence at the other end, and then, 'Well, you can make an application to the Medical Officer to pay you a pension rate wage.'

'Are you fucking serious?' I thought to myself: the same Medical Officer who deems me unsuitable for retirement. I explained that to the voice at the other end. I added that I would get no money for Christmas. The answer was sublime: 'You'll be able to get it back when the MO makes a ruling.'

I croaked, 'But that might not be until January and that's also the MO's decision . . . isn't it?' This guy at the end of the phone might have had a big title but he was a messenger with no power, and very little empathy. I hung up . . . devastated.

Sitting in my bedroom with the phone lying on the

bed, I was goosed. No room to move, not sure what would happen when the wages were stopped, I was in limbo; I might actually lose my job. Mild hysteria entered the brain: Christmas coming, no money from the job, my children, my wife – the shame of it all. I lay back on the bed and for the first time in my life, my brain died. I hadn't an iota, not a smidgen. This was one bad dream. Then the phone rang again.

'Who the fuck can that be?' I asked myself. At the other end was Jesus Christ, my saviour. My mother must have intervened for me. 'How's it going, friend?' went the calm, almost melodious voice. I paused and replied, 'Not well, my friend . . . I'm fucked.' The voice went on: 'John Cuffe, fucked? That's not the John Cuffe I know . . .' I laughed, possibly for the first time in weeks; a grain of praise suddenly lifted me. 'Do you want to come back to work?' went the voice. I answered in the affirmative but expressed worry about certain aspects of how to go about it. The voice spoke; I listened and nodded. Before the call ended the voice told me to visit my doctor and get a cert allowing me back to work, then promised to ring me back in ten minutes once he confirmed a thing or two.

Ten minutes later the phone rang again. 'Now, sir, what day do you wish to return on?' went the voice. I asked what way the shift and unit cycles were going. My unit was on night shift on Christmas night, and I was rostered for that night. Assuming I was coming back, the voice added – no need to come back until the New Year. 'Fuck it, I'll come back Christmas Day,' I exclaimed down the line. The voice saved my sanity and possibly my life. No inquests, no million questions, nothing but the height of respect and a willingness to help one fucked-up soul who had fallen on hard times. The voice wasn't of course Jesus Christ, although both had beards. The voice was my chief in Castlerea Prison, Liam Reilly . . . truly a great man.

In retrospect, when the bullying started I should have taken the advice given to the great jazz and rock drummer Ginger Baker. It's easy to see where the tortured and mad genius who played with Cream and Eric Clapton, among many others, got his eccentricity and talent from. Ginger's father had the unforgettable name of Frederick Louvain Formidable Baker; he was a lance corporal when he was killed in the Second World War. He left a letter for Ginger, to be opened when the boy was sixteen. 'God gave you two fists, use them to hammer home your safety,' went the advice.

I had refused my boy permission to do just that. Luckily, towards the end of our stay I went back on that and he took full retribution on a smart alec who saw him as a soft touch from the early escapades. 'Had you allowed me do that from day one, Dad, maybe I might have ended all of that shit earlier,' he said. He was right, but I wanted him to do the right thing. Doing the 'right' thing isn't always doing the correct thing. On reflection and if it happened today, I would simply go to the shed, take out a hurley or baseball bat, and call to the houses of those pups and teach them or their parents a lesson they would never forget.

My family had settled back: Jesus Christ in the form of Mr Reilly had intervened. I was ready to re-mount the horse for the last furlong home. I was going to survive.

12

Knocking on Heaven's Door

Mama, take this badge off of me
I can't use it anymore
It's getting dark, too dark to see
I feel like I'm knockin' on heaven's door.

BOB DYLAN (b. 1941)

Christmas Day 2006 was surreal. We sat around the table and celebrated our first Christmas back 'home' after a five-year trip to hell. Everyone around that table had paid a price of sorts: some more than others. Some had to grow up faster than we ever envisaged; I silently gave a moment's reflection on the hellish trip I had taken this family on. But as I sipped a glass of wine, one thing was evident. We had survived: broken, battered, damaged and just about still believing in Santa, but still together and with a bright future.

We ate turkey, pulled crackers and wore funny hats. The difference between me and the rest of the family was stark; I was wearing the blue shirt and dark blue trousers of my uniform, topped off with a civvy jumper. My first

Christmas meal back 'home' was cut short by my return to duty that night. No matter: we were in a better place. Kisses and hugs and off I struck.

As I drove I stuck on a CD: my entire life has been played out to a background musical track constantly running in my head. From my formative years as a Creedence Clearwater Revival fanatic, through The Doors (no pun unintended!), Grand Funk Railroad, Canned Heat, CSN&Y, Grateful Dead, Dylan, The Band, Dave Matthews, Neil Young, Cohen, Clapton, Moving Hearts, the Eagles, Rory Gallagher and countless others, music defined and made me. I couldn't play a note, but by Christ I could dream.

The motorway was empty as I headed off for the night duty. Coming to the M4 toll I was surprised when I saw the barriers down. No exception or Christmas goodwill from that franchise: they take your €2.90 Christmas Day like any other day. The cashier handed me back my change and wished me a happy Christmas. As the Christmas lights from the houses across the fields from the motorway accompanied me on this journey, my mind turned to other guys who had taken time out from the job. Burned out, tired, sick, heads melted . . . they needed time to regroup, recover. I was now one of them.

What would staff think? Was there a stigma, a sense of not being able for the pressure in the minds of those whom you left behind? Were you damaged goods? Funnily enough, I came across a few Lord Lucans in my day: 'Lord Lucan' was the term we used for guys like that. Lucan, a man of Erris and Castlebar ancestry, did a runner and disappeared after allegedly battering the family nanny to death. He had cash flow and marital issues. The jailer has a funny and often wicked sense of humour: as the missing and absent long-termers returned we compared them to Lord Lucan, finally coming home to face the music; some after six months, a few after a year, one after two years and one after four years. I was now in that company.

The warder also has a great capacity to forgive and forget, to give a sucker a break and not to judge the colleague too harshly lest they themselves fall into that nettle bed some day. They tend to turn adverse circumstances into fun, so that the message gets across: 'We are aware you went through hard times, controversial times, but hey, we all gotta live under this big roof, so let's get on with it' kind of thing.

I edged the car up the long avenue towards the prison. Castlerea has a screen of those horrible Norwegian pine trees that have decimated and hidden the beautiful west of Ireland. I actually recall as a kid looking out the window of my father's bus on the journey to Ballina in the late 1950s and seeing the saplings being set around Corrick and Crossmolina. As I aged they grew into monsters, blocking out sight and light. Like something from a horror movie, the jail is set amid those beasts: appropriate possibly for the mindset of 'official Ireland', hiding its shunned.

The car park gate eased open electronically. I was expected. My stomach lurched and tightened for the first time. I crossed the car park. The gate closed behind me. I was acutely aware that the guys in the control room could see me: 'Oh fuck – what are they thinking?' went my mind. The small gate at the main entrance swung open. Gerry, the gate man – who looked like a cousin of the late Omar Sharif

– stuck out a hand of welcome and said 'Ah, the good Mr Cuffe. Welcome on board, sir. You were missed . . . all quiet in the jail, you'll have a handy night.' My initial fear started to dissolve. I know when someone is faking it; I read behind eyes and watch facial features. Gerry the Gate was an open book: I was missed and I was welcome.

The inner gate swung open. 'Ah, the hard . . . good to have you back, sir,' went a voice (the use of 'sir' by warders is a token of warmth, not of subservience). The day shift – those who came on in the dark that Christmas morning from 7 a.m. onwards – were now filtering home at 8 p.m, back into the Christmas dark and a chance to spend a little time with loved ones. 'Happy Christmas to our Garda Síochána out there who do stellar work at this time of the year; also to the army lads and the navy, not forgetting our fire service and ambulance men . . . oh wait, Sinead just texted in to say thanks to the Air Corps and the taxi drivers' goes the radio every year . . . to hell with the warders, they don't register.

Do you want to know how petty Justice Ministers can get? Michael Noonan and Michael McDowell are the only two Ministers who didn't wish us a happy Christmas during the festive season. Or if they did, unlike other ministerial greetings, their missives didn't get pinned on our notice boards. Oh I know they couldn't give a toss, but some flunky types up, 'the Minister is aware of the sacrifice prison officers make at this time of the year, away from their families etc. . . .' The governor sticks it on the staff notice board and we all silently say, 'Fuck off, you bollox.' However, we also note when it's not put up, and that happens during industrial relations stress.

The voices in the dark called out. 'Hey, Cuffe . . . what the fuck happened to Mayo last September against Kerry?' Another went, 'Don't mind him . . . I think you're still a fine thing!' That had to be Angie, a brilliant warder along with Mary. They kept us on our toes with craic and banter, but God help anyone who crossed them. Female prison officers in male jails were one of the successes in the job over the years. Despite initial scepticism from the men on the floor, the ladies more than proved themselves adequate. Funnily enough, in my opinion it was the prisoners who led the way here. They immediately took to the female warders, seeing no difference in who wore the uniform. Also, most, though not all, of the girls had humanity and maternal instincts that transmitted around the institution, along with a sharp professionalism.

I came to the corridor that led to the main block. A keypad with four digits barred me from the final hurdle. For the first time on my return to the jail, I faltered. My mind went blank: I forgot the code number. Nada . . . zilch . . . white noise . . . the head ceased to function. We were still permitted to have a mobile phone at work, so I rang the block. 'Hey, John Cuffe here. I forgot the number for the keypad . . . sorry.' The calm voice of my chief and saviour Liam answered. 'What aftershave did you use as a young man, Mr Cuffe?' came the reply. I laughed as I keyed in 4-7-11. (Don't try it today: it changes every fortnight and mobile phones are long barred from jails.)

Once in the ACOs' office, still with the high ceilings, still with the garish fluorescent lights, it felt as if I had never gone away. The lads were there: PL, Johnny B, Martin and Brendan. Good wishes and no condemnation from them all. 'Mr C,' said PL, 'all is quiet in the jail for you . . . you have a top team on tonight.' Fair play to them: no withering looks, nothing unsaid. Johnny B gave me a good-natured shoulder and I gave one back: kids in a park, we were. The staff drifted off to what was left of Christmas. Heads appeared in the doorway 'Welcome back, kid . . . Welcome back, head . . . Welcome back, you Mayo bollox . . . Welcome back, you boyo . . .' I was back and accepted.

The night crew was a team from heaven: Mary G, the night nurse, a walking saint; Mary M; Mel; Joe; Cillian . . . this was an A1 team – no beer buffaloes amid this crew. The two Marys hugged me. We settled into the night and I familiarised myself with the place. I followed Mary G around as she dispensed the medicine with a kind word here and there. As the prisoners swallowed the medicine they caught sight of my face. 'Haven't seen you in a long time, ACO,' said most. We had tea and toast as the jail settled down for the night. Not a word of my absence came up. Not a hint hung in the air.

The staff slipped away to their night posts and I dimmed the main overhead lights in the office. I turned on my computer and hit my login code. The Prison Service still got my name wrong. Jesus Christ but a year's worth of circulars hit my screen. It took me half an hour to delete them. I went for a walk and chatted to the troops for a while. I then went to the toilet where a large mirror stood. The reflection showed a man attired in a navy blue jumper with epaulettes and a gold stripe . . . it was me; I was somebody again.

Around 3 a.m. I walked quietly down onto the ground

floor of the block. I listened to the jail as it breathed: a creaking bed here, a snore there. Occasionally I heard the click of a light switch as the night crew tiptoed around checking their flock. Standing in the belly of that beast I looked up at the sky lights. The moon shone as the clouds raced by. I had a good feeling: no one was going to be lost on this night as they slept with their dreams of Christmases gone by, tinged with happiness and pain perhaps, of dear ones, loved ones or ones who gave pain now consigned to the dream world.

I found Christmas a heavy time. I can still smell the packages, the Christmas tree, the cheap talc, the perfume, the toys, the excitement, Mass, the cycle home as the day came up in Blacksod a half century earlier.

I recall the Christmas dinner, the stilted conversation and then my father's strange, keening laughter. Only it wasn't laughter; it was a crying for something from his past, all loosened thanks to Johnnie Walker and spilt across our family, a mawkish nostalgia for something he probably never had in the first place . . . I hated Christmas. Tonight I was where I was in control to a point: I was performing something useful. I wasn't destroying someone else's Christmas. I climbed the steel stairs; I walked down the different landings, past each door with its name cards, its occupants sleeping, and respite for all for a while. The staff came to my office around 6 a.m. to report all correct. They had done a thorough check. No booby traps as you drove home after being relieved. The drive back east was relaxing; the motorway opened ahead from Athlone, I had broken through, come back, got up on the saddle once more. No more night duty apart from my own rostered nights.

Back at work, the chief called me into his office. Closing the door, he beckoned me to a chair. 'Sit down, Mr Cuffe. It's good to have you back; you were missed . . .' I waited for the 'but', but it never came. He outlined how long I had to serve before hanging up my stripes, how I could take my leave and how the entire jail was behind me 100 per cent. The message was no looking back: focus ahead. He would be there for me but he didn't envisage me needing him: on the contrary, I would be of use to him.

My God, what a way to treat a human after some of the shite I had taken over the years. I walked from his office seven feet six inches tall. That lunchtime we went and had a five-a-side match. I was liberated.

The weeks tipped along. Persistent overcrowding was our enemy; space was always at a premium. The numbers rose from 190 when I arrived to 250 without a single new cell being built. The ACO duties ran along numbers one to four. ACO 1 was in charge of the Prison Block, 2 in charge of the control area, 3 in charge of the Houses and 4 in charge of committals and discharges. Number 1 was the busiest and the other lads, where practical, would give a dig out. We worked as a team, as indeed did the officers we worked alongside.

My turn to be Number 1 came and the roster was to last a month. It was what I needed: in at the deep end, and get on with it. Castlerea survived on the basis of two principles. The first was that staff were prepared to work any hours, dig each other out, support each other and not crib. The second was that the majority of the prisoners were compliant and just wanted to do their time as peacefully as possible. There were a significant number of malcontents and troublemakers, drug abusers and pure riff-raff who wanted to break the system; luckily the staff were well able for that group.

Every day as Number 1 was akin to the miracle of loaves and fishes. Space was gone and staff were at a premium; you simply hadn't enough staff and you had too many prisoners. In addition Harristown Courthouse was attached to the outer wall of the jail, depleting our numbers of staff further. Factor in the troops you need to run a jail: cooking staff, workshop facilitators, discipline troops to man exercise and recreation halls as well as visiting area; throw in the PE officer, the detail staff, the censor, the tuck-shop guy, the escorts to various courthouses in the west, the escorts to hospital, staff out on leave, staff out sick . . . you were always short.

You juggled on a daily basis, trusting your instinct, following your gut and crossing your fingers. We had two large store rooms; we called them 'the Sheds' and used to throw mattresses on the floor and house our overnight intake there. The Sheds broke every health and safety rule, from fire regulations to providing basic water and toiletry comforts. One door led into those 'rooms', with a slit for observation. One particular night I had ten in one room and seven in the next. For exercise and work unlock, you took huge chances. You were required under our own internal rules to have a certain number of staff on the landings to support the class officer and clear those landings; however, you were also supposed to have a certain number of officers awaiting the arrival of those prisoners in the visiting boxes, exercise yards, workshops, gym, etc.

You never had the required number: no one's fault except the Prison Service's. They didn't give us the required manpower. Could it blow up in your face? Of course. One afternoon after I cleared the landings and staffed the yard by the skin of my teeth, a prisoner who was spooked by another – the wrong one, as it transpired – turned back on him and slashed him with a blade. The staff flew into action, preventing a follow-up. On questioning, the prisoner told us he was warned that the Travellers were out to get him; it turned out that he was seriously mistaken. Lives were on the line.

In addition to the normal population you had 'protection prisoners' who wanted or needed close supervision and twenty-three-hour lock-up in the Seg because they had been threatened by others or thought they were vulnerable to attack. At that stage we had up to twenty in this category. The above slashing incident was a case in point. The problem then was that some of the ones locked up were also at war with each other. By law we are obliged to give them all an hour's fresh-air exercise. Another problem arose when they got visits. The second exercise yard was small but wasn't always suitable, depending on the mix: you had to keep a tight check so no prisoner looked for a habeas corpus for not getting his legal rights.

Back then, anyone could walk right up to the wall of the jail in Castlerea. Despite a modern CCTV monitoring system, people arrived up and chucked contraband over the wall. Staff intervened and regularly intercepted drugs, drink and mobile phones tossed in this way. I was passing the yard one morning when a plastic bottle was chucked in. Two of the staff entered the yard; I joined them and we struggled to get the offending liquid. The prisoners chucked it from one to the other as they swigged it down. They then threw it into the toilet area. Never did I feel more useless and pathetic than when they laughed at us. It was all recorded on camera. We brought the Gardaí up and retrieved the bottle, but what was in it? Strychnine, booze, diluted drugs . . . we never found out. Never task people to do a job without providing them with the necessary tools. Make your infrastructure person-proof. Can you imagine strolling up to a Super Max jail in the USA and tossing in drugs and phones?

Nearing Easter I was on nights. In the Seg we had a prisoner who had been in our custody from the Donegal courts, a young man who stood about six foot two, well built and full of chat. He was a loyalist and there was a threat on him, seemingly from his own ilk. He was in the Seg primarily for his own protection on account of his background, but he was also prone to fits. As we went around with the night meds we opened his door. The stench of sweat drifted out as the nurse handed him his medicine. She chatted to him; I stayed out of it. She had a rapport with him; I didn't, I hardly knew him. 'I think you're training too hard. Rest now, there's a good lad . . . you don't want to over-exert yourself.' The nurse whispered to me that she was afraid he would bring on a fit with all the press-ups he was doing in the cell.

An hour later we got a call over the radio for medical assistance to the Seg. The nurse sprinted ahead of me with her kit bag; I carried the oxygen bottle. The staff were attending to the Loyalist kid already. He had had a massive fit and was throwing himself all over the floor. Apparently you should let the person wear themselves out in a safe environment if they have a fit. This was impossible because the design of the cells included heating pipes along the walls. He was hopping his head of the wall and pipes with the convulsions. Two staff were now lying on top of him restraining him as the nurse knelt and dealt with him. Another member of staff ensured his air passages were clear.

I raced up the stairs. The nurse told me he had to go out as soon as possible. Number 2 ACO had rung for an ambulance. I then had to ring the mobile number of a Prison Service official in Dublin, seeking permission from someone I never saw, never met, for a discharge order. Common sense dictated I should ring my governor or chief, but when was common sense used in jails? Back down to the cell with permission obtained I went, like a little school boy. Entering the cell, I observed one of the officers – a giant who played rugby – under pressure; his light blue shirt had turned dark blue with sweat. I took over and I was put to the pin of my collar to keep the lad on the ground and safe.

Now I was sweating. Someone said, 'John, I think that guy needs an armed escort before he goes out – he's under threat from the loyalists – cover yourself. Who knows?' He was correct; I had forgotten all about that. To make matters worse, we already had a prisoner – a patient in Roscommon hospital – with an armed escort. Now I was about to drive the sergeant in the local station mad. I was looking for something I couldn't get, but if I didn't do it and something went wrong . . . The sergeant correctly told me that his only armed policeman was already productively engaged minding one of my prisoners in the county hospital. By now we had stabilised the prisoner and one of the officers asked, 'What you gonna do, John?' No matter what I did it could be wrong but I asked the lads if they were prepared to travel in the ambulance: I couldn't get an armed escort but they could avail of the one already there. They nodded. I told them I would accept full responsibility for everything.

After the ambulance departed I was down three officers. Previous to this, officers would come in to you on nights if you had an emergency, but now that annualised hours were in place and the shit was worked out of them, most saw themselves as unavailable for ad hoc escorts. They were correct. The nurse and I checked the prisoners during the rest of the night and the other staff doubled up on their duties. At about 5 a.m. a tap sounded on the window of the Shed where ten prisoners were sleeping on the floor. I got a key and opened it up.

'Can I go to the toilet?' asked the well-dressed middle-aged man. I nodded down to the toilets near the door. He came back with a plastic bottle of water. 'Officer, I'm afraid in there – there's an alcoholic and he keeps looking at me from his mattress.' I apologised for the predicament he was in. I assured him that I would be outside his door until 7 a.m. or until my relief arrived. Nothing would happen. I locked the door behind him; the morning spring sun was shining through the jail by now and I wondered if those who espouse penal custody would actually spend a night in a jail and see the conditions that staff and offenders share. A man wanted to piss, get a drink of water and sleep safely. We could not even guarantee that.

The next morning one of the senior managers passed me in the car park. I filled him in on the night's events. 'Did you get the armed escort?' he asked. 'Eh, no . . . I tried . . . but was told that the only armed Garda was already in Roscommon minding another of our flock.' He wasn't impressed: by the way, neither was I. 'What would you have done if you were in my position last night?' I asked. A harrumph, and then, 'Well, if I had no armed escort I wouldn't send him out.' I walked on and threw back, 'So you'd let a guy die on the floor because of no armed escort?' He called after me: 'Yes.' I shouted back, 'Well my retirement days aren't gonna see me pencilled in for the High Court or coroner's.'

I was moving towards the end game. Driving down in the mornings I took in the beauty of this nation. Outside Kilbeggan stands a trio of antennae or aerials on a little hillock. On Easter morning I pulled up and looked at their beauty. They resembled Calvary with its three crosses. The weeks slipped by. Big Burley, my soccer captain and confidant – a staunch Mayo man – was assaulted in the visiting box as he stopped a cache of drugs being passed in. He twisted his knee. As usual we were short staffed; I happened to get to him first. I was wandering around outside when the alarm went off. A few evenings later I took back in a group of remand prisoners that we had sent out with the Gardaí that morning. I had overseen their discharge and search. We were ultra-cautious; we didn't want any prisoners handed over by us to produce a knife or gun out on escort with another agency or indeed ourselves. I was very strong on that, having once caught a prisoner in the Hill with a knife taped to the small of his back.

When we discharge remands to the Gardaí we give the Garda in charge an envelope containing any cash, passport and valuables the prisoner might have, lest he get off. I marched the five remands back up the hill towards reception. I held the envelopes in my hand. In reception one of the prisoners was very anxious to take possession of a small wash-bag of toiletries. The red light was screaming to me. 'Ah no . . . you can collect it tomorrow once the reception guy has checked in all your stuff.' Once he was gone, after much moaning and whinging about his soap and toothpaste, we opened the bag. It had a tidy cache of E tablets and other pills. Never trust the prisoner and never trust anyone who takes them out but yourself.

We had a prisoner in the Seg called Snowball, a big lump of a lad who appeared dull but wasn't, with a sparkle in his eye and a smirky smile. He was a serial cutter and no jail wanted him; neither did the Central Mental Hospital, where he actually belonged because he had massive psychiatric problems. Generally speaking he behaved, but when the pressure hit his brain, the bloodletting would occur. I had fair experience of this from the Hill and always figured that each cutter had his own way of operating. Talk to them but, more importantly, listen and observe what's said and how it's said. Snowball and I sparred for a while before we made common ground. Part of my approach was thanks to the nurses. All of them got on great with Snowball.

Around that time local radio had a song blaring called 'The Rose of Castlerea'. Snowball always had it on when we were issuing his night meds. He would walk to the door with an evil, impish grin on his face, narrowed eyes and glance back at the radio. I took it as a challenge, so I started to sing the song as the nurse sorted him; later I upgraded that singing to a short jive with one of the nurses.

> *She may not have been a beauty queen*
> *She might never be a rose*
> *But to me she is the fairest flower*
> *That in the garden grows*
> *Although I'm in Americay*
> *Across the Atlantic sea*
> *Sure I'll always love my Roscommon girl*
> *She's the Rose of Castlerea.*

He liked that: he thought I was mad. I would then ask him what he wanted. 'Ring my mother?' he would say, mainly through his nasal passage. For the price of a two-minute call peace was secured and self-harm averted for the night. I would place the call: 'Hello Mrs Snowball, the jail here . . . do you want to speak to your son?' And she always replied, 'Oh sir, you have an awful job up there. Put him on for a minute . . . I don't have any news for him.' I would hand him the phone; someone made him a cup of tea and a slice of toast. He would hand the phone back to me with 'Say goodnight to my mother.' I would put the phone to the mouth: 'Goodnight, Mrs Snowball, we'll keep him safe.'

Back inside the cell once more, and as I closed the door he would say, 'You're a shite dancer, Mr Cuffe.' I would pretend to open the door again and he would laugh. 'I'm only joking . . .' As the door was finally locked, he would add, 'You're still a shite dancer.' We went off happy, he was happy and the night was safer for us all. He needed a break from us, we all agreed that. He wanted to go to the 'Drum but they hadn't a place for him. He then wanted to go to Limerick for what he termed a 'holiday'. The problem was that Limerick had had him before and he had run amok: they didn't fancy taking him back on 'holiday'. In fact every jail refused us bar one. Cork prison officers fear no one and nothing. Dublin's hardest chaws had been sent down over the years and tamed. They agreed to take Snowball, but Snowie didn't want to go there.

We had stalemate for a few days as we tried to convince him to go voluntarily. Then he went and cut again: not all staff and ACOs were into hand-jiving and singing 'The Rose of Castlerea'. The following Sunday it was decided to send him to Cork, but someone convinced him it was Limerick he was off to. I was chosen to take charge of the escort. I had two choices. One was to tell him we were going to Cork and have him kick off or, worse, wreck the van on the journey south. Two, I could say nothing, keep up the pretence: after all, I wasn't the one who spoofed him. We'd worry about Cork when we got there. I choose the path of least resistance . . . initially, at least.

Big Burley was the driver, Snowball was in the back of the van and off we headed south. As luck would have it, Mayo and Donegal were in that Sunday's National League final. We tuned in the radio to listen as we sped through the countryside. Snowball shouted to me, 'Hey, Mr Cuffe . . . buy me a burger on the way.' Burley and I looked at each other before Burley took the initiative and replied 'Only if you behave.' RTÉ only covered patches of the match; we had horse racing from Doncaster or some other English track, hockey from the north, tennis somewhere else. Mayo was locked in a battle with Donegal. Burley and I were mad Mayo heads then.

Driving through rural Ireland on that sunny spring day recalled the Ireland of Michael O'Hehir, the 1940s and 1950s, the radios on, the men gathered around them, the womenfolk chatting, the kids kicking whatever passed for a ball. Back to the match: the co-commentator, himself a Mayo man, kept referring to the strength of the Donegal bench as the match closed out. We roared in unison at the radio: 'What are you fuckin' on about . . . we have been in two Senior All-Ireland finals, an Under-21, a Minor and a club final in the last two years . . . we should have the strong bench . . . are you mad?' The radio ignored us, Mayo lost by a few points and Snowball laughed in the back. We stopped in Templemore for a toilet break. One of the lads went for the burger and chips. Back in the van Snowball shouted, 'It's taking a long time to get to Limerick.' I shouted back, 'Mr Burley is a shite driver.' Silence: we were heading towards thin ice.

Going up the quays in Cork, Snowball shouted once more. 'Ah for fuck's sake! This is Cork . . . Mr Cuffe, I thought you were an honest man. You're like the rest, a spoofer.' I was genuinely hurt. Cork jail is akin to a packed sardine tin: small, compact and tight, building meeting building like a dog after its tail. It was grossly overcrowded, for years. A reception party was awaiting Snowball. Off he went, but not before giving me a malevolent grin: 'I'll be back next week, Mr Cuffe.' He was: back with a vengeance. One evening he hit an artery and had to go immediately to the hospital. We were short staffed, so an ACO was drafted on the escort. It suited me because a work-through until the next morning was on the cards, which meant I wouldn't be in the jail the following day, even though I would be worn out doing a twenty-four-hour shift.

As expected, Snowball was kept in the hospital overnight. I sent my colleague off to get a bit of grub for himself, but before he left I went down to the hospital shop and bought the *Evening Herald* with its three crosswords, a bottle of Lucozade, a bag of crisps and a bar of fruit-and-nut chocolate. Back with Snowball I took out the long chain and clipped it to the bed: Snowie wasn't going to embarrass me by doing a Lazarus and sprinting up the Athlone Road. I put my feet up on the bottom of his bed. After some small talk, I worked my way through the easy crossword first, occasionally looking at Snowball. Each time I looked, Snowie was looking back at me with that evil grin on his face. Finally he asked: 'ACO . . . do you know why I am doing time?'

Actually I didn't; it never crossed my mind. 'No, Snowball – what are you doing time for?' I replied. His eyes were on fire: whatever meds they had given him weren't making him sleepy, they were stoking his inner soul. 'Ha ha ha,' he went, almost daring me, mocking me. This was near 10 p.m. and I was in no humour for shit. 'What the fuck are you doing time for, Snowie? I'm tired and in no form for any games tonight.' He pulled himself up on the pillow and said, 'I tried to kill a man. Nearly did – stuck him in a bog hole and drowned him. Cops saved him in the end.'

For the second time in my service I felt something evil

cling around my body. The time before that was in the Hill when I had to speak to a prisoner one night about noise coming from above his cell. This guy had stabbed and killed a young man for the crime of looking at him; he never showed remorse and he had a face that was the countenance of the devil. I wasn't interested in negotiating with him that night; I was blunt and to the point. The look on his face and the way he spat his words at me made my skin crawl, and an evil scent filled the air. When we left the cell the accompanying officer said to me, 'That was spooky, John.' It was. We didn't speak about it after. Now that evil scent filled the air again in the hospital ward; my skin crawled and Snowball saw it happen. 'That scared you, Mr Cuffe,' he laughed.

I laughed nervously. 'Scared of what?' I asked, not too convincingly. 'Scared of what you don't know or understand,' he leered, and his eyes closed like the yellow eyes of a tired lizard. I let him keep them shut; occasionally a smile flickered across his mouth and the eyes partially took me in. He had me spooked and knew it. I later found out that he had in fact abducted a youth and tried to drown him in a bog hole: first he dumped the youth's motor bike in the bog hole and then shoved the youth in, keeping him submerged until he thought he was dead. That evening a passing squad car stopped him, unaware of what had happened earlier. After a bit of banter Snowball told the cops what he had done. He was met with disbelief at first, but a cop's intuition led them to drive him to where he said he had done this deed. They arrived to find the youth standing on the top of the bike in the bog hole, barely sucking in air at the surface. Lucky youth: his time wasn't up, but he had encountered the same evil as I scented that night.

My time was drawing to a close. The staff – let's be honest here – carried me to the last: I'd like to think I did my bit, but they were magnificent. Nothing was too much to do; I was privileged to work with such a group of ladies and gentlemen. My duties were routine, with the odd googly spun in my direction, which I always batted away for a six. One evening I was in charge of committals and discharges, and got a radio call to go to the gate for a committal from the Gardaí. There were three Gardaí standing there and a man who was a builder: safety shoes, jeans and sweatshirt covered with the proof of a hard day's graft. Quickly it was very evident that there was no love lost between the Gardaí and the committal. I checked he was physically OK, checked the warrant, wrote out a body receipt for the Gardaí and off they went.

The warrant was a committal document for the non-payment of a bank debt. The Celtic Tiger was starting to unravel, and this was one of the first casualties washed up on our shores at the jail. As we walked, the committal – I won't use the word 'prisoner' here – kept a yard ahead of me. I made small talk, which he ignored. We paused as we waited for an electronic gate to open. Again I tried to engage him; I needed to build some picture of whom we had got, his mental state and mental form. He spat back at me: 'You lot are all the same . . . fucking blue uniforms . . . ye don't give a fuck for people like me who work hard.' The gate swung open and in we went. I held him there for a moment. 'Listen up. I didn't ask you to come here . . . the guards brought you here. We are not guards . . . nothing to do with them; our job is to keep you safe and secure here, so lose the big fucking attitude now.' Suddenly he was a beaten man. We went to reception, where we processed him and gave him a shower. I then took him to see the nurse. I asked him if his family, wife and kids were aware he was with us. He shook his head. The usual cup of tea and slice of toast for those who merited it appeared beside him.

It transpired he had taken a loan out for under €30K. The purpose was to set up his own building business so he wouldn't always have to work for 'the Man': a sentiment I admire in any entrepreneur who has the balls to go for it. I didn't: I stuck to my safe and pensionable job through thick and thin. Suddenly his work dried up and the bank got a committal warrant against him for non-payment of debt. I felt for this man sitting here, covered in sawdust and cement: I was just days from retiring at fifty-five with a bit of a lump sum and a pension. 'Do you want to ring your family?' I asked: there wasn't much more I could offer. He nodded. Before I put the call through he said, 'I asked the guards to take me home as I have a bit of cash I could have given in part payment, but they simply dumped me up here.'

I hated the Gardaí at times. Many had no empathy for anyone; they would willingly walk past us on a strike picket and not feel guilt. Once the call was over and as the man wiped his eyes, I parked my personal emotions. I told him that he would be sleeping on a mattress for the night with ten other men, and would be safe. In the morning he could tell the governor about the cash at home that would be part payment of the debt, and he should be released . . . or at least I felt that's what would happen. I never saw him again. I think about builders, developers and speculators who owed banks billions and millions and plunged this state into chaos. Who decided this human should be jailed for a pittance and those thieves, and those who transferred their assets under their wives' skirts, get away scot-free?

Driving home I was lost in thought. Were we as warders complicit in state tyranny against hard-working people, people who were marginalised, those who got locked up for stealing from Dunnes or Tescos or not having a TV licence? I arrived home that night a lesser man. Welfare thieves were jailed, while white-collar thieves, where prosecuted, were given community service and a pat on the back with almost an apology form the judiciary. Truly we live in awful times.

My last week, and it was my tea break. I headed down to the Grove for a cuppa but left my radio on: I was still Number 4. The radio room and monitoring centre alerted the exercise yard that they had spotted a guy crossing the fields and heading for the wall; he seemed to have something in his hand. I raced out of the Grove and towards the gate. I was going to catch this bollox at the wall. As I ran I was joined by a colleague, ACO Brendan, and we heard the control room say he was about to throw it over the wall.

It turned out to be a package containing phones and cocaine. The package dropped into the arms of an ex-county midfielder warder and the drop was a failure. At the gate was an unmarked Garda car whose sergeant had heard the radio communications and told us to get into the car. We headed up the Roscommon road where we found a young man standing by a gate. 'Get in,' ordered the sergeant. The young man sat beside me in the back of the car: without a doubt he was the mule who did the run, not a bright kid but not a bad kid either. The sergeant turned around and asked him who he was waiting for. 'Friends who drive a Mini car,' replied the young man. 'Do you know them well?' asked the sergeant.

The blood had drained from the young man's face. 'Do you think they will be back for you?' added the sergeant. The young man shook his head. The sergeant then told him he was going to ask one final question, and that the answer better be the truth. The youth confessed that they had met up at a disco, they didn't know each other well, and he agreed to toss the package into the jail. I was happy: that was that, and the sergeant gave me a lesson on how to do things neatly and efficiently. We were dropped back to the jail, the phones and cocaine were in our possession and the young idiot was nabbed. All in all, a good day's work. I would miss that part of it – the rush, the run, the excitement – but not most days we put in, which were like watching paint dry.

On my last morning I drove from the east towards the west. I had longed for this day for so long that it seemed as if it was never going to happen. Now it was almost an anticlimax: I wasn't euphoric, I wasn't ecstatic . . . I was kind of normal. Driving into the jail car park I felt as if I should feel something special, but I didn't. I walked across the tarmac towards the gate and the departing night staff stopped and shook my hand, wished me luck. When I came to the main gate Gerry the Gate gave me a salute. Inside at the inner gate, Mary – tough Mary, warm Mary, Mary who we couldn't do without – said, 'Welcome on your last day, Mr Cuffe.' She hugged me. I was starting to feel different now.

The day was a kind of procession. Liam – my saviour

from the past, my chief – brought me around the jail and then left the others to pass me on. He made me a small presentation in private: I was dumbstruck. Liam had made my coming back so pleasurable and bearable. All the staff had. We took a few photos in the reception: a bit of fun. My head and feet were no longer on the earth; I was in a kind of dream. Kind words here, hugs there, prisoners whom I knew wished me well. Down to the Grove, where Jane had a massive cake with my name on it. Angie arrived, and more hugs. It was great craic, and so warm and loving.

At lunchtime we had a five-a-side match. It was my testimonial, my last game ever. Butty, Eddie G, Burley, Liam, Mel, Cillian, Brendan, Martin, Johnny B, PL, Big Joe, Gerry the Gate – I'm forgetting some – tackles flying in, no quarter asked, definitely none given. Back to the jail to shower: my last game and my last shower here. I folded my Barcelona jersey, placed it in my kit bag and headed for the duty roster. When the detail was read out, chiefs Liam and Aido came to me and asked me to go to the governor's office. I wasn't exactly comfortable with this: the governor and I hadn't much contact and I had been missing from work for a while. I felt a fraud, to tell the truth, going over there. Inside was the entire management of the jail, the union reps, the various heads from trades, gyms, workshops, etc. My tummy gave a lurch but I smiled, and it was a genuine, happy smile. You couldn't but be impressed at such a turn-out.

The governor spoke warmly and kindly about me. No point pretending here; we both embellished our speeches but there was no more war, no more rancour or ill feelings from either of us. I had achieved what I set out to do: I had survived to the end, a bit sloppy towards the finale but with a recovery and face-saving exit. A speech from the governor, a beautiful pen and, believe it or not, my long-service medal at last. The long-service medal is awarded for twenty-one years' service: I got mine on the day I was leaving after thirty years' service. We posed for more photos. Liam told me that my time was now up, and I was excused from duty for the day. I was a free man. I walked to the locker room, collected my gear. Outside the door was a small guard of honour that would accompany me to the gate. I took off my epaulettes and gave them to Big Joe: one of the next generation of ACOs.

Near the gate, one of the lads came from the workshops and gave me a concrete Buddha to take with me. I looked around for the final time; the troops stood and looked at me and shouted, 'Go on . . . get out!' Out through the gate for the last time, Gerry the Gate gave me a salute. Big Peter from Remands was returning and shook my hand: I would miss that gentle giant who did a thankless job in a tight area with little or no resources. I crossed to my car; the gate closed behind me. I opened the boot and placed the Buddha and my kit bag into it. I looked at the sky to see if my mother was watching from the clouds. I could hear the blue sea of Blacksod Bay on that Friday in May 1977, when I left home: the smell of the ocean and salt. Now it was all over in a car park in Castlerea: what a journey!

As I drove down the avenue I didn't look back: my mother always said never look back, for it will only upset you. I pushed in a CD and Guns N' Roses gave me the backing track: 'Knocking on Heaven's Door' blared out. Appropriate, really: warders are the Pat Garretts of the justice system, lawmen but not lawmen, or not what's seen as 'real lawmen' by some. We were and are tolerated.

The staff had booked a night in the local hotel for my wife and me. They were having a farewell party for me. That flattened me, for I wasn't worthy of it. I went up to the hotel room and left my bag on the bed.

I changed into running gear for a run before the wife arrived. I needed to clear the head, savour the moment, smell the survival, and know it was real. My uniform shirt was on the bed. I ripped its pockets and epaulette holders; it had to be rendered useless so no one could use it again. I then pulled the legs of the trousers away. I left the room with a plastic bag containing my torn shirt, trousers, and Doc Marten boots. Outside was a bin and I shoved the lot into it. I ran down towards the riverbank and out into the countryside. I was free.

INSIDE THE MONKEY HOUSE

MY TIME AS AN IRISH PRISON OFFICER

JOHN CUFFE served as a prison officer from 1978 to 2007. Originally from Blacksod Bay in the Mayo Gaeltacht, he now lives in County Meath. He holds postgraduate degrees in crime-related and social issues, and has lectured in Dublin City University. A regular guest in the media as an expert on the criminal psyche and penal system, he has written for *The Irish Times* and appeared on *Morning Ireland*, *The Ray D'Arcy Show* and *The Right Hook*, among others.

Stay up to date with the author at:
@cuffejohn

To Seamus Carney, Padraig Loftus and Padraig Kavanagh: three teachers who gave me a love for language and history. They brightened many grey days.

And to my wife, Kathleen, for her support and belief.